# Turn Of Notable Events

Chronicles of Pivotal Moments That Shaped Our World



J. MOHAPATRA

BlueRose ONE
Stories Matter
NewDelhi • London

BLUEROSE PUBLISHERS
India | U.K.



For permissions requests or inquiries regarding this publication, please contact:

BLUEROSE PUBLISHERS
www.BlueRoseONE.com
info@bluerosepublishers.com
+91 8882 898 898
+4407342408967

ISBN: 978-93-6452-534-3

Cover design: Tahira
Typesetting: Tanya Raj Upadhyay

First Edition: July 2024

*There are no secrets*
*that time does not reveal*

# Dedication

To my loving family, whose unwavering support and encouragement have been the bedrock of my journey; to my mentors, whose wisdom and insights have profoundly shaped my perspective; and to you, my readers, whose curiosity and passion for understanding the world around us make this endeavor truly rewarding. This book is a testament to the collective inspiration and support you have all provided. Thank you for being a part of this journey.

J Mohapatra

# Preface

In embarking on the journey of chronicling the significant events that shape our world, I present to you "Turn of Notable Events," a two-part series that seeks to capture the essence of our times. This compilation reflects a labor of dedication, detailed research, and a profound interest in the events that influence our daily lives and future trajectories.

The world is in a constant state of flux, driven by a multitude of forces including political shifts, economic trends, social transformations, and technological advancements. Understanding these changes is crucial for navigating the complexities of our global landscape. Through this book, I aim to provide readers with a comprehensive overview of these pivotal moments, offering insights that go beyond the headlines.

**Part 1** sets the stage by delving into events that highlight the socio-political and economic currents of recent years. From the nuances of left-wing extremism in India to global biodiversity initiatives, the chapters explore the multifaceted nature of contemporary challenges and achievements. The discussion on landmark events such as COP27 negotiations and the implications of judicial decisions on heinous crimes underscores the intricate interplay between governance, policy, and societal impact.

**Part 2** continues this exploration by examining more recent developments. The rise of ransomware attacks, the evolving landscape of work-from-home practices, and the ongoing battle against the COVID-19 pandemic are just a few of the critical issues covered. Each chapter is designed to provide not only factual recounts but also thoughtful analysis and contextual background, allowing readers to grasp the broader significance of these events.

The compilation includes reflections on a wide array of topics, from the intricacies of India's census operations to the debates surrounding educational cutoffs in prestigious exams like NEET and JEE. By addressing such diverse subjects, this book aims to be a valuable resource for anyone seeking to understand the forces shaping our world today.

Throughout these pages, I have strived to present a balanced view, incorporating multiple perspectives and drawing upon a variety of sources.

The "Relevant Thoughts" interspersed within the text serve to provoke further reflection and connect the reader with the wisdom of various thought leaders and experts.

This book is more than a mere record of events; it is an invitation to engage with the ongoing story of our world. I hope that it will inspire readers to think critically about the issues we face and to consider their role in shaping the future.

I extend my gratitude to everyone who contributed to this work, including those whose ideas and insights have been invaluable. I am especially grateful to my readers, whose curiosity and quest for knowledge make such endeavors worthwhile.

As you turn these pages, may you find both information and inspiration. Welcome to "Turn of Notable Events."

J Mohapatra

# TABLE OF CONTENTS

## Air Quality Crisis In NCR (Dt: 17.11.2021)

- **Supreme Court** had suggestion of 2-day lockdown in National Capital Region (NCR) amid sharp deterioration of air quality. It was a prescription as administrators were seemingly clueless with the crisis.

- Instead of Government commanding expertise in administrative and policy matter, judges, perplexed at slothful governance are tempted to dictate policy.

- But for lakhs earning livelihood outdoors, Pack downs are cruel acts to control air quality. NCR's air crisis is a policy and political failure.

- Despite heavy subsidies on straw management equipment's, formers keep protesting that these remain economically unviable. Yet GOI Punjab and Haryana Governments have fumbled for an alternative policy response.

- Delhi Government's war on vehicles through an odd-even experiment and GOI's belief that electric vehicles will solve air pollution, fail to recognize that burning coal, biomass and farm residue along land desertification contribute to 85% of air pollution.

- Taking 85% causative factor needs political will and policy ideas.

**Relevant Thought:** Judges must be aware of hard constructions and stained interferences; for there is no worse torture than the torture of lows.

**- Francis Bacon**

## Targeting Street Food Vendors (Dt: 18.11.2021)

- Four of Gujrat's urban civic bodies had targeted vendors selling non-veg food on unreasonable and absurd grounds of "smell" and hygiene". It is adding olfactory intolerance to list of intolerances in India.

- The Chairman of Ahmedabad Civic body's town planning committee said, food carts targeted will be those on arterial roads and those near schools or religious places. Civic agency officials attributed the drive to places. Civic agency officials attributed the drive to complaints from some residents.

- But Government of Gujarat clarified that state policy did not intrude on food choices relevant guidelines are followed. Civic officials claimed encroachment as a season.
- In some urban areas of Haryana, local actions have enforced a ban on meat shops during festivals despite there being no state-Level directions on the issue.
- These are dangerous trends for harmonious coexistence food vendors are self-employed vulnerable workforce that was badly hit by Covid pandemic's economic fallout.
- 37.8% of urban households in Gujarat are self-employed as compared to national average of 30.7%. Gujarat's ruling leaders must help in restoring status quo.

**Relevant Thought:** Cooking is a social act. It happens in a context.

**– Abhijit Banerjee**

## Preventing Learning Deficit - ASER (Dt: 19.11.2021)

- ASER (Annual Status of Education Report): 16th Aser data shows government schools are finding favour sudden government school's preferences resulted financial distress of private schools and some were closed. But India needs private schools as they cater to all income classes with a big network.
- Only 27% students have now always access to smart phones for their studies and 47% sometimes. In classes 1 to 3, the figure is 19.9% and 40.8%.
- While 90% students received textbooks, home-learning activities were not communicated to 40% of students in schools who were virtual mode.
- 50% students were logging and devoting to last year's gaps.
- Aser's survey at Karnataka: class 3 government school children who can read only class 1 level textbook were 41% in 2018, but it has

dropped to 24% now. Those in class 3 recognizing double digit number were 78% have dropped to 60%.

- UNESCO reveals 73 weeks of school closure in India against 27% in China. India should do reforming of government schools encouraging more private schools and prevent learning deficits.

**Relevant Thought:** When you have mastered numbers, you will no longer be reading numbers, you read words when reading books. You will be reading meanings.

**– W.E.B. Du Bois**

## GOI's Withdrawal of Farm Reforms (Dt: 20.11.2021)

- GOI's withdrawal of farmers reforms due to protest farmers from Punjab and Haryana was a terrible message for liberal reforms, it needed for mass prosperity. It is the obstructionist opposition politics played by congress on key reforms that they faced such reform reversals which BJP had done when was in opposition.
- A small group of wealthy farmers in 2½ states now have the assurance that the rest of the country will keep subsidizing their economically irrational and environmentally dangerous production practices. A low of MSP will be the icing on this poisonous cake.
- BJP and its governments should learn to never mind for UP and Punjab polls GOI's and BJP should have hold consultations because the rich farmers cosseted for so long period that striking the reforms against them may produce big reactions.
- Farmers reforms message got clouded by including provisions like corporate leasing of farm land – that became a favour to leftwing agitators, who teamed with rich farmers and propagated "big capital players v. humble kisan".
- It is now high stake that future India modern economic power.

**Relevant Thought:** Leaders do not conform; they reform If you conform, you are nurturing mediocrity. If you reform, you are breeding change.

**-Israelmore Ayivor**

## Political Economy of Repealing Farm Laws (Dt: 20.11.2021)

- Farmers reforms have been setback by 2 decades. We can expect more fiscally ruinous sops, loan waivers and freebies. Other reforms may face similar oppositions as farm laws did.
- We can't permanently subsidies a large population based on taxes raised from tiny minority citizens. Min supportive (M.S. Ps) is not going to be viable an not to achieve better. This will only lead to the classic statement, "the rich get richer and the poor get poorer".
- Higher MSPs and more subsidies will misdirect investments in farming. Excess use of fertilizers in water scarce Punjab regions will make land quality poorer. We are heading towards the path of ruin.
- Food prices are already on the rise and any further concessions on MSP will not help. An economy now recovering from Covid is being asked to again bankroll the economy that was not ravaged by pandemic
- It is agriculture. Farm unions managed to get victory in the name of "Annadata-an emotional appeal. But they cannot work against the interests of the Annadata's own Annadata the taxpayer and consumer.

**Relevant Thought:** Voices of the vocal minority always trump the interests of the silent majority. Determined group of vested interests can derail any reform.

**Democracy's Weakness**

## Demands by Farm Unions (Dt: 22.11.2021)

- Samyukta Kisan Morcha (SKM) said that it will continue its protest rallies, including one to Parliament tell the other demands are met.
- Dangerous is the demand for Legal guarantee for MSP (minimum support price) and the call for repeal of the amendments proposed to the electricity law.

- SKM's present demands after repeal of 3 farm laws are unreasonable. There is dire need to reforms MSP and move to a system where farmers respond to price signals in making choices.
- Proposed electricity amendment bill is to address some structural problems and is under discussion between GOI and states, the main stakeholders.
- SKM is bent on preserving status quo mainly defined by free or cheap power. Another demand relates to provisions of a law that addresses stubble burning.
- GOI should now have a red line on unreasonable demands. It needs to hold firm on reforms or it runs the danger of becoming a lame duck government. It is necessary to build consensus for reforms but equally important to stand firm against unreasonableness.

**Relevant Thought:** Voters don't decide issues; they decide who will decide issues.

- **George Will**

## Political War on MSP (Dt: 23.11.2021)

- Dispute between state Telangana and GOI is over the procurement policy for the rabi agricultural season. It encapsulates the political economy in (MSP) driven cereal procurement exercise.
- Telangana and MP are with largest number of beneficiary farmers in the paddy and wheat procurement drives respectively. UP, Odisha and Chhattisgarh are other locations of a significant incremental procurement over last 5 years. Two trends driving it are operational risk in farming increased due to high frequency of extreme climate nudging farmers towards MSP crops to de-risk.
- 2015-16 and 2019-20 Telangana topped performer in rice procurement at 243% and UP with 72.6%. In 2020-21 about 95% of MSP beneficiaries in Telangana were small and marginal farmers. In wheat MP topped in beneficiaries last season followed by UP. 99.1% of MP's marketed surplus of wheat was procured at MSP; 15% higher than Punjab. MP's wheat market is effectively nationalized.

- Economic Reforms are costs are borne upfront and benefits follow Stakeholder buy in requires alignment of their incentives with a policy goal. Reform design has to account for the costs that stakeholders need to bear during the transition.

**Relevant Thought:** Good follow through does not depend on the right intentions It depends on the right incentives.

**- Timothy Ferriss**

## Personal Data Protection Bill (PDP) (Dt: 24.11.2021)

- A recommendation on PDP was finalized by Joint Parliamentary committee on 22.11.2021.
- Most contentions point of PDP is government agencies have been exempted from it. State agencies are among the biggest collectors of personal data and granting them loosely worded exemptions, has attracted dissent notes and qualifies to have extensive debate.
- A Joint committee has clubbed personal data and non-personal data clubbing data should be avoided as non-personal data has business dimensions like protecting commercial data for firms.
- Committee further suggests – an omnibus regulator would deal with both kinds of data may have too much to cope with data captured by electronic hardware should also come under the regulator's purview.
- The regulator can decide if individuals must be alerted to a data breach of any entity collecting their data. Alerts of a breach have to be automatic and conditional to help victims take precautions like change of passwords etc.
- Committee's data definition includes open cons and social media firms which such large quantity of personal data needs to be held to stem cards of publishers.
- Committee suggests a 2-year period before operationalizing the law. This is a complex issue and needs much more debate.

**Relevant Thought:** In the 21st century, data will eclipse both land and machinery as the most important asset, and politics will be a struggle to control the flow of data.

**- Yuval Noah Haravi**

## Covid-Despite Brisk Vaccination (Dt: 25.11.2021)

- Covid has surged in West Europe, the USA, etc., even though 70% of the population is fully vaccinated. India must be very careful as only 30% of the population is fully vaccinated and child immunity Vax, booster shots for 2.5 Cr senior citizens and healthcare workers who received 2nd doses over 6 months are still availed.
- Delhi, Kerala, and Haryana have 90%, 80% and 70% seropositivity respectively in general population. But Kerala has over 5000 daily cases despite 95% single dose adult vaccination. Hence, only speedy universal fall vaccination can mitigate risks.
- NTAGI should recommend the booster dose and requisition support from research bodies under ICMR to pursue studies on vaccine.
- National Expert Group of Vaccine Administration (NEGVAC) must debate merits of rolling out booster doses in private sector for those receiving advice to take 3rd dose. Vaccination in India is entering a complicated stage.

**Relevant Thought:** The MRNA vaccines are really patent at antibody formation; the AstraZeneca vaccine is really good at generating T-cell responses.

**- Helen Parry**

## NFHS and ASER Survey (Dt: 26.11.2021)

- National Family Health Survey (NFHS) confirms that India's TFR (Total Fertility Rate) the average no. of children born per woman has dipped below the replacement level of 2.1. Only 3 states Bihar, UP and Jharkhand have TFRs over 2.1
- ASER Surveys suggest 2006 to 2018 girls (age 11-14) our of school fell to 4.1% from 10.3% Girls (age (15-16) not enrolled in schools dipped to 13.5% from over 20%. Women (age 15-19) pregnant or already mothers declined in this period from 16% to 6.8%.
- Women gaining autonomy 80% have bank accounts from 54% in NFHS (2015-16), 54% have mobile phones against 46% earlier, 77% used hygienic methods during menstruation against 57% earlier.

- Women's Economic Situation: Has not improved. Working women of past 12 months only marginally rose 25.4% from 24.6% earlier.
- Health Insurance coverage has reached merely 41% households.
- Rising Anaemic Women and Children: Since 2015-16, 67% of children under 5 and nearly 60% women under 60 (Global average of 33% anaemic women in reproductive)Intensifies malnutrition.
- Progress: 88% institutional births against 78% earlier signify the healthcare now is accessible. Costly P+11 system is major cause of people slipping into poverty falling TFR implies an ageing population and burden of greater morbidity.

**Relevant Thought:** "Anything that increases the voice of young women tends therefore to reduce the fertility rate".

**- Amartya Sen**

## New Covid 19 Variant B.1.1.529-Omicron (Dt: 27.11.2021)

- The new covid 19 variant B.1.1.529 is in its infancy can batter the society and economy. South African scientist said; this has come to dominate all infections there in less than 2 weeks.
- Three bulwarks are necessary as advance alert
  - ☐ Timely are travel curbs on affected countries.
  - ☐ Strong disease surveillance; which enabled Hong Kong and Israel to identify and isolate travelers carrying the new strain. INSACOG (Indian SARS – Cov-2Genomics Consortium) a consortium of 28 National Laboratories should monitor the genomic by sequencing the +ve samples of all international travelers.
  - ☐ Vaccination should continue.
- GOI had rowed full adult vaccination by the year end but 54% adults are now short of target. If 84 days Covishield gap is cut it may help, Booster doss should also be allowed as these become mandatory from Israel to France now India is to fight it proactively.

**Relevant Thought:** I will not take 'but' for an answer. (Langston Hughes)

## Corporate Ownership of Banks (Dt: 29.11.2021)

- In June 2020 RBI had setup internal committee on issue of bank ownership. RBI announced that it accepted 21 of 33 recommendations of committee Industrial houses to promote banks was not accepted.
- It should be rejected as traditional banking faces existential challenges and regulatory attention will increase. Biggest risk is the inherent conflict of interest when industrial houses are allowed to promote banks.
- Two reasons are (i) Governance failure in Private banks due to lack of independence within the board, the internal defence. (ii) RBI being the external defence, it has unsatisfactory role as banking supervisor.
- India's credit to GDP ratio at 55% is low and necessitates fresh capital. Credit increased from 23.6% to 50.10% of GDP. It is a bad loan problem and credit-GDP ratio inched to 55.45% over the next decade.
- A lose monitory policy prevails for over 2years. It appears to be skill shortage and wrong initiatives in upper echelons of India banking. Also creating a bad bank 5 years after enacting a bankruptcy code is unjustified fin tech and Big Tech have come up as a transformation. Big tech leads to DNA(Data Network Activities Feedback Loop)advantage. Here the risk is emerging regulatory challenge.

**Relevant Thought:** If sound regulation and supervision were only a matter of legislation, India would not have an NPA problem.

**- Raghuram Rajan and Viral Acharya**

## Satellite-based Internet Service (Dt: 30.11.2021)

- **GOI** had cautioned that Star link Internet Services is not licensed to offer satellite-based internet services in India. It is a division of Space X, a private US company,

- 5G is expected to transform connectivity. Overlaying existing 4G networks with non-standalone FG is current technological advance here. Frontier technology is the use of satellites to bypass hurdles associated with terrestrial networks.
- Cost of launching an object into orbit in 1970-2000 was $18500/KG it has fallen to $2700/KG and will go further down.
- Disruption is now coming through LEO (Low Earth Orbit) satellite which is below 10 kgs and orbits the planet many times a day at a distance of 500-1, 500Kms. Traditional and new companies live Big Tech, constellations of LEO are being launched.
- GOI plans to adapt policy to emerging trends. TRAI was asked to recommend a licensing framework for satellite-based connectivity. TRAI made its suggestions that the policy should be agnostic to models, types of satellites or spectrum bonds and it feels existing 2013 telecom policy can be tweaked to remove constraints from tapping new technologies.
- Policies therefore have to account for unforeseeable changes India's success in digital world depends on getting right policy.

**Relevant Thought:** Does thou not understand that there are two distinct forces in us, that of the soul and that of the body, that is a movement and a regulator? - Jules Verne

## GDP Recovery and Economy Uneven (Dt: 01.12.2021)

- India's GDP 8.4% in July-Sep, 2021 is higher than RBI estimate but absolute number presents a mixed picture. GDP for the quarter Rs. 35.73 lakh crore higher by 0.33% than that of 2019-20 corresponding period signals economy is back to Pre-covid level. However, the informal sector has not yet recovered, e.g. Private consumption in Jul-Sep, 2021 is Rs. 19.48 lakh crore, 3.5% lower than pre-covid level in 2019.
- Agriculture, Manufacturing, Mining and Electricity sectors were the bright spots in supply side of economy during July-Sep quarter capital expenditure also is modest. But construction and services,

Trade and Hotels are not back to Pre Covid levels in absolute terms. Contact intensive sectors are still struggling i.e. the informal jobs.

- Another feature of July-Sep. quarter is the high rise of price is captured between real and nominal GDP. Nominal GDP for the quarter grew 17.5% means 9.1% points higher than real GDP. This will generate high tax revenue collections but will be adverse on informal sector. FMCG data July-Sep showed that there was year after year decline in volume sold even though it grew in value terms.
- Therefore recovery of economy is both fragile and uneven. Hence GOI should enforce Vaccination and have more sector-specific fiscal measures as the economy is yet to fully recover.

**Relevant Thought:** The ill-effects of the pandemic are now concentrated to narrow pockets of the economy and monetary policy is much less effective than fiscal policy for providing targeted relief.

- **Jayanth R Varma**

## Vaccine Inequity and Omicron (Dt: 02.12.2021)

- Against the global average of 43% people fully vaccinated the African CDC reports that the continent has just 6.7% of the population fully vaccinated and 9.9% partially. With large unvaccinated pool, a potent mutant strain omicron has emerged from here.
- She US has 110 million unused doses and EU 200 million dosed, even accounting for booster shots. India has 250 million doses with states.
- Only 32% of Indian's population is fully vaccinated Boosters and children's jobs have not started as yet.
- US destroyed 15 million doses between March-Sep 2021.Its trade-curbs on key raw materials had also dented vax production. Hence in many ways US has been the worst offender.
- In Africa a well-planned rollout of vaccines has been impossible because of irregular supply without certainty of vaccine deliveries poor countries cannot keep vast network of vaccination centers and

ancillary facilities including hired contract workers in perpetual condition.

- Pledges to supply Jabs to South Africa by Covax, by China and India need urgent fulfillment.

**Relevant Thought:** Every day, there are to times more boosters administered globally than primary doses in low-income countries. This is a scandal that must stop now.

- **- Tedros Adhanom Ghebreyesus**

## Omicron In India-Testing and Sequencing (Dt: 03.12.2021)

- Stringent covid norms are required for international and domestic air travellers. But Maharashtra has more stringent norms above Centre's Omicron advisory.
- GOI's norms were reasonable, mandating RT-PCR test for high-risk countries and home quarantine for all international travellers for 7 days.
- Overall GDP in July-Sep. quarts exceeded pre-pandemic period in 2019, but in contact intensive sectors e.g. trade and holes which employs many informal workers remained below 2019 mark indicated lost 2 yrs.
- States must camp up RT-PCR tests. Missing S-gene a potential proxy of Omicron can be confirmed by genome sequencing. India should improve genome sequencing.
- Thanks to new testing norms in India more rapid PCR tests with one hour turnaround times unlike regular RT-PCR tests and should be available to travellers. With samples for genome sequencing from airports being dispatched to high throughput labs will help GOI make timely informed decisions.
- States must reserve to allow extraordinary movement curbs under Disaster Management Act and Epidemic Diseases Act for emergency situations. India can't afford more economic shocks. Being smart is better than being hasty.

**Relevant Thought:** If you have ten thousand regulations you destroy all respect for the law.

**- Winston Churchill**

## Don't Delay Boosters (Dt: 04.12.2021)

- IVSACOG has recommended a booster dose for age 40 above, targeting high risk and high exposure individuals against Omicron.
- To achieve 100% adult vay India needs 610 million more doses as of now. States have 220 million, Serum Institute and Bharat Biotech can produce 300 million, plus SII has 100 million of vaccines and production is 35% more than off take. Second dosed, 10 months back, are now 45 million. Hence India's stock and production can compete double dosing of adults and giving booster doses simultaneously.
- Funds for giving booster doses (There are plenty).

i) Only Rs. 19,675 Cr. of Rs. 35000 Cr. budgetary vax procurement done

ii) Till end Oct fiscal of Rs. 12.79 Lakh Cr. are 64% of GOI total receipt will exceed the year's target.

- UK study shows boosters work well with Covishield and Covaxin in trials on booster should be over now Omicron has higher the urgency. We have supplies have money and have the infrastructure. So GOI should not delay.

**Relevant Thought:** The minute you are working with the government, you are dealing with bureaucracy, you are dealing with time lags, you are dealing with rigidity, and you are dealing with a slow pace.

**- Bob Simon**

## Worries On Employment (Dt: 06.12.2021)

- Economic highlight of July-Sep quarter 2021 showed that aggregate economic output erased 2019 level.

- But India's workforce is still struggling. Jobs lost during 1st lockdown were recouped mainly in informal sector. Jan-Mar 2020 to Jan-Mar 2021, proportion of salaried jobs shrank from 50.5% to 48.1%.
- Proxy indicators reported that India's workforce has not yet put the covid impact behind. Private consumption is still below the pre-covid level and workforce is yet to recover fully.
- There is potential damage to human resources Jobs shifting out of the formal sector the upskilling process gets a lot harder and is not possible.
- An immediate need is a relook at fiscal policy to see where it can be tweaked to arrest the shift in jobs to the informal sector.
- It is the quality of human capital that will decide if India makes full use of its demographic dividend.

**Relevant Thought:** Pandemic related disruptions to contact intensive sectors have caused the labour market recovery to significantly lag the output recovery in most countries.

**-Gita Gopinath**

## Tragic Death In Nagaland (Dt: 07.12.2021)

- Army operation by faulty intelligence resulted in tragic death of 14 civilians in Nagaland. Home bound miners died, were non-combatants that has to be the driving point of both army's court of enquiry and Nagaland Government's SIT probe.
- The Draconian law of AFSPA that gives securing forces sweeping powers of arrest and counter-insurgency continues in Jammu and Kashmir, Nagaland parts of Arunachal Pradesh, Assam and Manipur, AFSPA allows security forces to be less circumspect leading to tragedies like "Manipur Malom Massacre" in 2000, which prompted Sharmila to begin hunger strike.
- Anger in Nagaland led to violent protests. With my armor reverting to military junta, refugees and weapons have been flowing into NE This gives regional insurgent groups unwilling to join by ambush

carried out by militants in Manipur on November 13 that killed a colonel, his family and 4 other soldiers.

- Talks are organizing between Naga groups like NSCN (1-M) and the center, aimed at ending insurgency. Army operation in Nagaland must be credibly investigated and AFSPA should be reviewed.

**Relevant Thought:** Security is not a license for people in authority to hide the tactics they would never openly admit to using.

**-Jack Campbell**

## Mandir (Temple) Agitation (Dt: 08.12.2021)

- Another masjid-Mandir dispute is being manufactured in UP.
- BJP suggest a new round of mandir politics via the Shahi Eidgah mosque in Mathura.
- Hindu Mahasabha has more dangerously announced to hold 'Arti' in mosque premises.
- Balia MP, suggest appeal of the Place of Worship (Special Provisions) Act, 1991, which forbids tuning over in any manner a place of worship from one faith to another. A sale exception was made to proceed Balori Masjid-Ranjan-Mabhoomi title suit.
- Argument citing repeal of farm laws by GOI to follow to repeal the worship act is disingenuous.
- SC observation: "This court cannot entertain claims that item from the actions of the Mughal ruler against Hindu places of worship in a court of law to-day."
- Despite this apex court judgement and the 1991 law, a Mathura district court has admitted a civil suit on mosque-mandir issue.
- Mathura is back on the boil become; UP polls are drawing nearer.

**Relevant Thought:** I consider that the anguished soul of India does not today cry for a new temple or a mosque or a gurdwara. What it seeks is a dignified and civilized living for all its people.

**- Somnath Chatterjee**

## India Needs More Vaccines (Dt: 09.12.2021)

- In September, GOI had purchased 66 crore Covishield doses, which carried smoothly upto December.
- In April GOI released Rs. 4500 Cr. as advance to S11 and BB to increase production capacity
- Now SII's predicament has signaled that Covishield will be cut by half with no new purchase orders forth coming from GOI.
- India needs another 58 crore doses to fully vaccinate all adults. Covaxin continues to underperform. Covishield is capable of doing the heavy lifting.
- India Medical Association demanded booster dose for healthcare workers. Like other countries, India will require boosters.
- GOI must reduce the prescribed gap between Covishield doses to accelerate $2^{nd}$ dosing. It was 4-6 weeks originally, then increased to 6-8 weeks and is now pegged at 12-16 weeks.
- WHO has flagged rising infection rates in children in Europe. GOI must publicise guidance to vaccine companies on stocks to be reserved for children so that when below 18 years vaccination being that can quickly cover children with the first dose.
- India needs plenty more vaccines and vax-makers need advance notice. GOI should take need.

**Relevant Thought:** Truly successful decision making relies on a balance between deliberate and instinctive thinking.

**- Malcolm Gladwell**

## Reforms Be Well Drafted (Dt: 10.12.2021)

- Farm agitation is ending, but policymakers must learn to make better changes.
- After GOI conceded their key demands, farmers picketing Delhi's periphery are exiting, although the intent and overarching vision were but the design of legal framework limited the potential impact

of such a far-reaching reform. The poorly designed dispute settlement method was the weakness in the repealed farm package.

- The reform effort of 1991 by capable team of bureaucrats with domain knowledge shepherd the reform through the decade.
- Reforming complex economic structure; the political executive provides the impetus, but implementation will require credible teams work into the need for change.
- A big change was tried in the Railways. Private participating cleaning up to accounts and setting up a regulator with operational autonomy are still pending over 6 years since a committee under Bibek Debroy submitted a report.
- Another reform of IBC is most significant. Creation of a bad bank to help commercial banks offload their NIAs raises questions on the efficacy of IBC. 73% of ongoing resolutions having crossed the extended timeline of 270 days- nudging banks to seek alternatives? GOI needs to ensure this reform realises its full potential.
- Success in future reforms can convince stakeholders by alternant benefits.

**Relevant Thought:** Perseverance is not a long race, it is many short races one after the other.

**-Walter Elliot**

## Jobs/Labour Markets Need Social Security (Dt: 11.12.2021)

- The pandemic'-s most visible impact is increase in employees working remotely.
- Trend in large corporates in India is work contracts HUL (Hindustan Unilever Ltd.) has launched: 'U-Work' and 'Open2U' for employees and gig workers respectively, providing different combinations of flexi-work, financial security and medical benefits.
- This flexi-curity is key to the talent pool that has outgrown the 40-40-40 model (40 hrs a week, 40 weeks a year, for 40 years) which has been blamed for India's failure to either attract investment away from china or grow formal employment.

- Simultaneously Unicorns and Soon corns (white collar tech and managerial) have seen a real war of talent. It follows that new flexi-curity will be attractive and also sinister depending on where one stands in the wanted list of white-collar job market.
- India needs to expand specified higher education to help one move up but only the good economic growth can increase good jobs. Growth in turn is deed to business competitiveness.
- In rich countries, the unemployed have social security, but not in India i.e. thrown to one's own or to the family. It is the big current problem here. Low tax base makes social security unaffordable for Governments. Lack of social security makes employers less willing to experiment with work that impacts innovation.

**Relevant Thought:** I knew who I was this morning, but I have changed a few times since then.

**- Lewis Carroll, Alice in Wonderland**

## Need to Ramp Up Masking (Dt: 13.12.2021)

- Even those with no history of foreign travel, detected with Omicron due to their laxity of mask using. GOI warning and global trend of Infection spurts call for masking.
- Price of masks have reduced. Surgical masks cost Rs. 1 and N-95 masks cost Rs. 20. According to IHME's projections, India's mask usage has dipped to 59% presently after rising through April to 80% of May. In Japan and South Korea, 92% citizens adhere to 92% masking norms.
- Despite high vaccinating rules, US has 1.2 lakh cases daily and Germany and UK around 50,000 a although mortality is low among the vaccinated. India needs masking because of its population size and density.
- Many state governments had levied fines and filed cases under section 188 of the IPC against masked persons. But messages on masking have tapped off as drive of vaccination proceeded.
- States must ramp-up the masking and penalize the violators.

**Relevant Thought:** Health case is vital to all of us some of the time, but public health is vital to all of us all of the time.

**- C Everett Koop**

## GOI To Consider For Boosters (Dt: 14.12.2021)

- Critical question for GOI's consideration of a booster dose are (a) when to start administering and (b) which vaccine to use.
- Like Delta variant's devastation in April and May 2021, it may become an urgency. Nearly 15 crore Citizens- 2.7 cr of them in high exposure or vulnerable category like health care workers and senior citizens.
- In countries recommending boosters, Pfizer's mRNA has become the choice. Covishield was administered to 90% of adults, but apprehension for booster dose may not be of same effective protection. Covaxin's 3rd dose trial results are expected shortly NTAGI is yet to declare about 3rd dose Covishield.
- Covaxin, ZyCov-D, Covovax of SII and Bharat Biotech's intranasal vaccine, Corbevax and Genova's mRNA in phase 2 and 3 trials are the possible candidates for consideration.
- Covovax of SII manufactured in India is already being exported and has done well in UK mix-and-match study with AstraZeneca vaccine (Covishield).
- GOI must initiate mix-and-match studies with Covishield and Covaxin by developing our research capabilities.

  **Relevant Thought:** mRNA sat around for 30 years ..... I always invoke that quote of Julius Caesar that everything of use derives form war.

  **-Dr. David Curiel**

## Social Security For Gig Works (Dt: 15.12.2021)

- On 13.12.21, the Supreme Court agreed to take up a seeking social security for gig and platform workers.

- The Code Social Security, 2020 gave legal identity to Gig Worker, described as "a work arrangement outside the traditional employer-employee relationship" and stated that Gig Workers were entitled to a 'Social Security Fund'.
- During the Covid-lockdown, they were often cut out from receiving benefits extended to other frontline workers. ILO in a 2021 report surveyed around 12,000 Gig Workers globally. The positive side of Gig-Works is the expanded opportunities for people otherwise excluded in traditional work areas. The flip side is the irregularity of work and lack of social protection. Current PIL has a global context framed by developments in economies with a higher standard of protection.
- In 2020, California allowed platforms to classify Gig-Workers kept out of obligatory benefits. In 2021, UK's Supreme Court ruled that Uber must treat its drivers as Workers and not self-employed. EU drafted a bill last week that presumes some of the bloc's Gig Workers are employees and not contractions. It can cover upto 10% of 28 million workers. India has large informal working.
- Almost 15 months after Social Security Code was passed by Parliament, implementation has been delayed as accompanying notification is not in place. The Government must contribute to a Social Security Fund but also provide for as employer's contribution.

  **Relevant Thought:** Power has only one duty to secure social welfare of the people.

  **-Benjamin Disraeli**

## UP Looks Advantage For BJP (Dt: 16.12.2021)

- Project unveiling spree with religious messaging of Prime Minister, Narendra Modi in UP is an advantage for BJP in 2022 polls.
- Akhilesh Yadav's 'Vijay Yatra' crisscrossing UP makes it clear that SP is BJP's biggest challenger.
- Covid pandemic impact may play a role in addition to usual metrics of caste, community, and sub-region in UP.

- Yogi Adityanath, CM as showcased by grand ceremonies centered around the 'Jewar Airport', the 'Purvanchal Expressway', the 'Kashi Vishwanath' advantage of having some party govern the Centre and state as double engine, delivering some welfare schemes successfully and micro cast managements are indications in favour for BJP.
- BJP appears ahead as indicated by opinion polls as well.
- Akhilesh is focused on cast census demand and unemployment, farmer's wrath, cornering BSP's Dalit and Muslim votes assuming Mayawati appears listless.
- The Congress helmed by Priyanka Gandhi targeting of Women Voters does not look convincing.

**Relevant Thought:** Wars and elections are both too big and too small to matter in the long run. The daily work that goes on, it adds up.

**- Barbara Kingsolver**

## Bold Industrial Policy: Semiconductor (Dt: 17.12.2021)

- Semiconductors are world's 4th most traded product and its manufacture is in limited countries.
- On dt. 15.12.21, GoI announced a Rs. 76,000 crore ($10 billion) package fox to manufacture in India. The aim is to create design and manufacturing of semiconductors.
- It has 3 feature (i) complexity: manufacturing these products needs 300 different high technology inputs (ii) It has highly concentrated global supply chain in the US, Europe and East Asia, where there is extraordinary degree of specialization. In just 2 countries-Taiwan and South Korea, most advanced (below 10 nanometers) 100% semiconductor manufacturing facilities are located. (iii) The product has largest investment in both Research and Development and manufacturing among all industries. Over the next decade, about Rs. 2,50,000 crore ($ 3 trillion) in investment will be needed.
- GoI and states will have to select and focus on parts of the supply chain to encourage. Semiconductor foundries are world's most expensive factories, which fabricate, to lower the risk, India should

look at backend of manufacturing will follow. Simultaneously GoI needs to leverage.

- Indian engineers in Chip Design.

**Relevant Thought:** Semiconductor growth is driven by very few absolute killer applications, and these come and go.

**- Kurt Sievers**

## Delhi NCR's Air Clean Up (Dt: 18.12.2021)

- Supreme Court had directed CAQM (Commission for Air Quality Management) to receive suggestions from public and experts to find a long term solution. The Solicitor General of India, Shri. Tushar Mehta appearing for the Centre and CAQM told the court that an expert committee is working to find a solution. On 16.1.221, SC expressed satisfaction over the measures taken by CAQM.
- According to IQ Air Visual's 2019 "World Air Quality Report", 21 of world's 30 cities with worst air pollution are in India. Six Indian cities are in top 10. Delhi-NCR's average levels of most dangerous airborne particles, PM 2.5 are 14 times the WHO's recommended limit.
- Inability to monitor and control exemplifies lock of action plan, political will and weak governance systems Delhi air is always bad and worse in winter.
- Primary source of pollution in Delhi are Vehicle exhaust heavy industry small-scale industries, suspended dust, open waste burning, combustion of fuel for cooking, lighting, heating, and diesel generator sets. The problem is compounded by meteorological dust storms, forest fires and open-field fires.
- Tacking these require a bold Government., a unified Centre-state front, an independent agency and an involved citizenry.

## Policy Of Scrapping Old Cars (Dt: 18.12.2021)

- The Delhi Government will deregisters diesel vehicles that have completed 10 years. This came in effect to an old order of National

Green Tribunal that was passed 3 years ago by Supreme Court. If the vehicle is not over 15-years old, they can get a no-objection certificate from Delhi and have it registered on a neighboring state.

- In case of vehicular pollution, the only matter is tailpipe emission, not the age of a vehicle. This should be the focus of the exercise to improve air quality in India.
- India notified a national vehicle scrapping policy in September 2021. It relies on incentives to phase out old vehicles. GOI in Parliament has said that the policy's aims include taking "Unfit polluting vehicles" off the road. The best way to do it is to focus on tailpipe emissions and make it mandatory for older vehicles periodic fitness checks. Scrapping old cars is bold policy.
- These measures will work by strict enforcement of a tightly aligned policy goal.

**Relevant Thought:** An economist is a scoundrel who tells you the way things are rather than the way you want them to be.

**- William D Nordhaus**

## Inflation Challenge For India

**(Dt: 20.12.2021)**

---

- The last global lead line of 'Inflation' happened in 1970s.
- Now the underlying causes of inflation are different.
- The 3 central banks, US Federal Reserve, Bank of England and RBI have a grip on the issue. None of the banks have crossed the threshold of full economic recovery from the pandemic, but they have shifted position.
- BOE increased 2%-point interest to combat inflation in November 2021 us Fed's chairman indicated that they would stop classifying higher inflation as 'transitory'. In India, WPI in November, 2021 was 14.23% a 12 year high.
- The underlying causes are pressure from both demand and supply. The developed economies have unrolled massive fiscal support, during the pandemic. However, as economics began normalisation

supply disruption pushed up price level of manufactured products, worsened the digital structure products such as semiconductors.

- India cannot insulate itself, as supply chains are import dependent for inputs. RBI therefore should get trickier in 2022 as we have not recovered from Covid shock. RBI over last 2 years used both interest rate adjustments and liquidity tools to push down market interest rates to low level. The challenges will be governed by the US Fed changes, debt markets and foreign exchanges. 2022 is challenge for India's economy.

**Relevant Thought:** The Government. will always tell you that it wants low inflation. The real issue is the horizon over which to bring inflation down.

**- Raghuram Ranjan**

## Two Sacrilegious Lynching In Punjab (Dt: 21.12.2021)

- Two lynching incidents took place as a sacrilegious conduct; one at the Golden Temple and other at Kapurthala Gurdwara. Desecrating a place of worship is reprehensible, but mob lynching for the same is more awful. Above all, the police inaction and politicians failing to condemn are more disturbing. Particularly a prominent leader of a famous national political party calls it as "public execution of the sacrilege accused." another leader says, "there is a conspiracy". Such statements can encourage more mob action.

- Some even argued that police and CBI failure to solve the 2015 sacrilege incidents, which remain a wound for many Sikhs, have created such violent mob action.

- Signals for politicians and administration seem to suggest and punishing them seem as remote in Punjab as they are at other states where police wink at violence carried out in the name of religion, that has political backers.

- In Punjab dark possibilities have added dimension being narcotics, bordering Pakistan Hindu-Sikh divides etc. getting exploited as election campaigns heat up, plus worry of the ghost of militancy and to top of it, Punjab does not even have a full time DGP.

**Relevant Thought:** There is no grievance that is a fit object of redress by mob law.

- **Abraham Lincoln**

## Electoral Roll Data Linkage To Aadhar (Dt: 22.12.2021)

- RP-Representation of the People Act got amended by passing in both Houses of Parliament requiring voters to furnish their Aadhar number to electoral registration officers. This happened in few hours without debate.
- It can bar people from being registered as voters form more than one constituency and prevents bogus voting.
- Union Law Minister, Shri. Kiran Rijiju claimed that the 3 tests of (a) legality (b) need (c) proportionality are now used to assess the permissible limits of invasion of privacy.
- Legality requirements to meet private safeguards would have been substantiated through discussion in Parliament having further fine-tuning of the Act's provisions.
- The bill is essentially a fest of identity between details of voter ID and Aadhar card.
- RP Act's new section 23 (b) allows those unable to furnish Aadhar for "prescribed" reasons to produce alternate documents. The poor whose details may vary, could be affected. While Rijju said linking is voluntary and not mandatory, amendments say electoral officers **"may"** ask for Aadhar.
- Further section 23(5) suggests that GOI could notify a date by which every person in the electoral roll **"may"** intimate his/her Aadhar number to authorities. The worry would be what happens if one does not do this?
- The change to such electoral rolls should be foolproof and abuse proof.

**Relevant Thought**: It is better to debate a question without settling it than to settle a question without debating it.

**- Joseph Joubert**

## Jammu and Kashmir Delimitation (Dt: 23.12.2021)

- J and K delimitation commission carried out delimitation with the result that Jammu is to get 6 more seats in the proposed assembly and Kashmir will be given one more i.e. 43 seats for Jammu and 47 to Kashmir in a 90-member assembly. Kashmir politicians are feeling that their region got a raw deal.
- Jammu and Kashmir Reorganization Act, 2019 sets the terms of the commission. In addition to population, other aspects such as physical features, communication and conveniences were to be considered in the delimitation exercise.
- Andhra Pradesh bifurcation has 2014 AP Reorganization Law that states to increase assembly seats, but that exercise has been put off till the first census after 2026 when there can be a national delimitation exercise.
- Chief Election Commissioner observed that delimitation must reflect political aspirations. Therefore, the Commission now needs to engage politicians from Kashmir.
- Reactions to this exercise will need to rethink the forthcoming national delimitation exercise. Constitution initially linked Lok Sabha seats to a state's population. Subsequent amendments froze the population reference point to 1971 census till 1$^{st}$ census after 2026 means to protect law fertility states.
- A national delimitation is best to be avoided for dangerous consequences.

**Relevant Thought**: It is of no use to discover our own faults and infirmities unless the discovery prompts us to amendment.

**- John Adams**

## WHO For Boosters 'GOI' Unclear (Dt: 24.12.2021)

- SAG (WHO's strategic Advisory Group of Experts) has recognised 6 months after 2$^{nd}$ dose and called for "targeted" administration of boosters. India's stand is still not clear.

- For healthcare workers, senior citizens, and those with comorbidities; a booster dose ahead of a feared 3rd wave would be rational and science-driven approach.
- As per AstraZeneca; Oxford study suggests (yet to be published) that a 3-dose course of Covishield (its vaccine) maintains neutralizing antibody levels against Omicron.
- CMC (Christian Medical College) Vellore is undertaking mix-and-match of Covishield and Covaxin to study there performance as booster.
- SII and Biological E using there Covishield and Corbevax jabs are booster dose have been rejected.
- No report is from NTAGI (Nat'/Technical Advisory Group on Immunisation) approving mix-match studies in Indian pipelines as a collaborative exercise between ICMR and vax manufacturers.
- West has growing reliance on "MRNA" vaccines, but are not available in India.
- GOI must declare the booster policy without delay.

**Relevant Thoughts:** The value of a decision as a precedent is very much enhanced by the care with which it has been considered.

**-Samuel Freeman Miller**

## Omicron Complicates Upcoming Polls (Dt: 25.12.2021)

- When elections are due in Punjab, Uttarakhand, U.P., GOA and Manipur, Omicron is also at peak i.e. in early February i.e. according toe IIT, Kanpur study and forecast. Allahabad High Court's observation on UP polls whether should be deferred is to be mulcover.
- In last elections there was failure to enforce social distancing norms at election rallies No party really took to virtual rallies.
- India's smartphone base (83 crore in 2022) remains an opportunity, that most parties are not exploiting enough.

- EC may consider deferring election if a 3rd wave gains pace. Elections necessary for democracy can wait a bit to tide over a public health emergency.
- The terms of all 5 assemblies are getting over and options are available like Presidents Rule or Parliament extending assembly term or a caretaker CM continuing. Except Punjab all others are ruled by BJP, So EC's decision may get easier. EC at election time must take efforts to safeguard people form the risks.

**Relevant Thought**: One of the tests of leadership is the ability to recognize a problem before it becomes an emergency.

**-Arnold H Glasow**

## Details On Boosters (Dt: 27.12.2021)

- PM, Narendra Modi announced on X mass Day that children's vaccination for 15-18 years of age is approved and will start from January 10, 2022.
- But details for India's 3rd dose is booster is yet not clear. The regulator has authorized 2 vaccines for children –Cadila's ZyCoV-D and Bharat Biltch's Covaxin. In addition, 3 more vaccines are in clinical trials in India for Children's Job.
- India has other option Covovax, a protein vaccine manufactured by serum, received WHO authorization on Dec, 17. Two other vaccines in regulatory pipeline are Bharat Biotech's intra-nasal vaccine and Genova's mRNA vaccine.
- Whether adults will receive the same double dosed vaccine as there is 3rd dose is yet not clarified. Which vaccine will be used as boosters for Covaxin and Covishield? If it is the same job, questions remain as it will be a decision based on virtually no publicity available local data. And when new vax ave available, will they be allowed as boosters for Covishield and Covaxin double doses?
- The booster program must be finalized and rapidly executed based on expert reviewed and publicly available scientific conclusions.

**Relevant Thought**: Prevention is better than cure.

**- Desiderus Erasmus**

## Inadequate Research On Pandemic (Dt: 28.12.2021)

- India will embark on booster vaccine in beginning of January; but details are not in public domain. South Africa's identification of Omicron, similar efforts of UK scientists, studies conducted by US Europe and Israel are examples of Government and science on pandemic.
- Although India developed its own Covid vaccine, become a non-player in carrying out local studies on vaccination drive and critical information on jobs.
- CMC, Vellore is studying a mix match regiment fox the first two doses using Covishield and Covaxin and dials also include booster doses. This trial has begun since few months, but before India starts its booster program, the results should have been out and conclusion drawn.
- Many more such studies should have happened. GOI should have shared its data with India's scientific community. This was brought to Government's notice in April by around 900 scientists asking for more transparency. Opening up ICMR's extensive data on testing, to India's scientific community would have yielded insightful studies.
- UK does not allow Astra Zeneca as a booster for double dosed but in India if Covishield is used as a booster, what is the scientific basis? Government's effort for independent studies and utilization of scientific community has been absent.

**Relevant Thought**: When you have a virus which is asymptomatic and can cross the species barrier that makes it impossible to get rid of.

**- Gagondeep Kang.**

## New Vaccines and Anti-Covid Pill (Dt: 29.12.2021)

- Finally, the Union health ministry has advised to adapt both standard and imported S-gene drop RT-PCR test kits to detect Omicron cases. Such dual testing obviates the need to send all Covid positive samples for genome sequencing, which is time consuming.

- Also, the regulator approved EUA to SIIs Covovax and Biological E's **Corbevax** vaccines, and also granting permission to manufacture and market anti-Covid pill **Molnupiravir** for restricted use in patient with Covid having high risk of disease progression.
- **Covovax** is Novovax's recombinant nanoparticle protein-based Indian vaccine and 200 million doses expected between Aug, 21 **Corbevax** too is indigenous protein-based and is aiming to hit production of 100 million doses per month by February.
- **Molnupiravir** pill is to reduce risk of hospitalization or death among adults with mild to moderate Covid by 30%. Its developer Merck has already shared the license with 8 Indian generic drug makers. Therefore, GOI should stockpile the drug and release it both through the public health system and private channels.

## Denial Of FCRA Renewal (Dt: 29.12.2021)

- Union Home Ministry refused application for renewal of FCRA (Foreign Contribution Regulation Act) registration. This law is intended to check "activities detrimental to the national interest" and if any NGO is being accused of this, evidence must be provided.
- Amnesty International exited the country last year due to its financial choking and other prominent civil liberty, human rights and charitable groups facing similar straits.
- From food to education oxygen to plasma their services remain invaluable as the state is not always there for everyone.
- MOC-Mother Teresa works among the sick and the poor. A suspicion it confronted today. In the FIR against one of MOC's children's homes in Vadodara this month followed allegations of religious conversions. This accusation can be debated and litigated but cannot be touchtone for funding of important services and not for axing global supply serving the needy.
- Adverse in puts or FIRs on allegation of conversion do not really constitute activities "detrimental to national interest". On present known facts, MOC should not be denied FCRA renewal.

**Relevant Thought**: May be Christmas, the Grinch thought, does not come from a store.

- **Dr Seuss**

## NEET-PG Fiasco (Dt: 30.12.2021)

- Resident doctors protested over delayed NEET PG counseling. NEET-PG exams originally stated for January were postponed to April and later to September. But intake of fresh batch got delayed further because neither GOI nor SC (Supr. Court) thought through the impact of their decisions.
- After the Centre introduced OBC and EWS reservation in all-India quota seats and fixed a Rs. 8 Lakh creamy layer limit for both categories, SC took up petitions challenging these policies.
- Due to judicial and administrative proceedings, on November 25, GOI asked for 4 Weeks to revisit the EWS income criteria and the matter is now listed for Jan, 6. The result is that PG-NEET counseling for freshers is delayed and resident doctors are overburdened. Career academic progression and work life balance are real issues for professionals.
- Income ceiling for EWS/OBC are policy issue for Government. SC should be conscious of academic time loss by students, but judicial process follow their own fine frame.
- Coming March, next NEET PG exam are due. PG institutes will have to admit 2 batches in quick succession putting an unwanted strain on medical education.
- This avoidable crisis should be lesson for courts.

## Rallies, Testing and Hospital Data (Dt: 31.12.2021)

- There is steep growth rate of Covid cases. Curbs are not on political rallies where unmasked crowds without social distancing are freely moving, But only on metropolitan citizens. Election commission should not be cowed by Netas.

- Even political parties can combine moting and messaging by fee distribution of masks in colours of their party flags.
- Government. should speed up testing only 12 lakh tests were conducted nationally on Dec 29 against an average of 11 lakh daily tests in early December.
- Government's suggestion of dual RT-PCR testing on samples first with regular kit, which if positive should be followed with an S-gene drop testing kit will help better gauge the Omicron spread and also conserve the currently scarce S-gene drop test kits. But states are yet to follow through this.
- India's Omicron number of around 1000 is most probably a huge undercount, limited by our ability to do genomic sequencing. So dual RT-PCR is vital.
- Tracking and publishing hospitalization data like ICU bed occupancy must start immediately to help the healthcare system.

**Relevant Thought**: One of the reasons people hate politics is that truth is rarely a politician's objective. Election and Power are.

**- Cal Thomas**

## Optimistic New Year 2022 (Dt: 01.01.2022)

- In New Year 2022, we can hope the Omicron wave remains mild. India now has bunch of vaccines and is heading towards dose of full vaccination. Breakthrough drugs are also on their way by good co-operation of global science and domestic manufacturer.
- Omicron probably won't be tragic like delta. Assembly elections should not meet super spreading as was in 2021. EC should enforce covid safely in election rallies with cooperation of political parties. Vicious battles over those past dead leaders, debates and disputes on religions are at the cost of progress (Vikas).
- Youths need job, not polarized history lessons, rising the economy, fighting the inflation, and keeping the virus in check etc. are the real issues and wish lists for India is the year 2022 begins.

**Relevant Thought**: Finding out what connects us, reveling in our differences; this is the process that brings us closer, that gives us a world of shared values, of meaningful community.

**- Bell Hooks**

## Covaxin Vaccine For Children (Dt: 03.01.2022)

- Covaxin vaccination for teenagers (15 -18 yrs) begins today 3rd Jan. as a great relief by schools and parents. Covaxin is the only vaccine for children now.
- Although DNA-based indigenous vaccine ZyCov-D from Zydus Cadila was approved for 12 – 18 year olds, surprisingly did not wave the cut.
- Among adults Covaxin's off take was poor i.e. 2 crore doses last month against 18 crore Covishield jobs. Hence, BB must meet target of 15-18 age group around Rs. 10 crore now onwards.
- Further, NTAGI's recommendation for mix-match of Covaxin and Covishield for 3rd dose and 2 other vaccines recently approved as Covovax and Corbevax are awaited and may join the adult vaccination drive.
- All school going children (5-14 years age) estimated around Rs. 24 crore must be jobbed.
- Supply constraints are apprehended. Also, social media's misinformation propagated by anti-vaxxer sections is another concern for which GOI should be alert.
- GOI should publish information on how many Covaxin doses are available alongside timeline for vaccinating younger children.

**Relevant Thought**: The saddest aspect of life right now is that science gathers knowledge faster than society gathers wisdom.

**- Isaac Asimov**

## Communal Bullies and Hatemongers (Dt: 04.01.2022)

- Hate speech by (a) Dharm Sansad at Haridwar and (b) Cyber harassment of Muslim women through app called 'Bulli Bai' are under probe investigation by Uttarakhand's SIT and Mumbai, Delhi police respectively.
- In Dharm Sansad, the hate speed offence was registered by local police only after Muslims logged complaints, but could have been by SUO motu investigation.
- Ignoring violent anti-minority statements and actions by terming them as products of fringe movement is just a dodge. They are not on the fringe.
- Mob actions in the name of majority religion have been on rise. Preventing Namaz in Gurgaon, attacks on churches around the country and violence against traders from minority communities are such events.
- None of these has seen quick, firm police response, nor condemnation by any governing politicians.
- Only government signals, severe judicial strictures or once in a while, a storm of public criticism can force cops to act in such cases.
- Now the above police action in 3 states can have a chance to send effective messages to hate mongers, cyber bullies.

**Relevant Thought**: There is a fine line between free speech and hate speech. Free speech encourages debate whereas hate speech incites violence.

**- Newton Lee**

## Freebies Before Election (Dt: 05.01.2022)

- Before state elections, politicians are tempting the electorate with SOPs.
- Punjab Congress chief has promised Rs. 5,000 to Rs 20,000 for girl children in classes 5 to 12, free e-scooters for female college goers

and interest-free loans for their higher studies besides Rs 2000 per month for women homemakers.

- AAP in Punjab, Goa and Uttarakhand had promised Rs. 1000 per month for all women.
- SP in UP announced free electricity for irrigation and first 300 units free for households.
- BJP in UP transferred cash bonanza of Rs 2,000 PM-Kisan tranche, Rs 1,000 Crore for self-help groups targeting around 16 lakh women, Rs. 1,100 to primary school students for buying school gear, and Rs 2,000 to 1 lakh girl children.
- Some cash transfers are good policy like PM-Kisan and Tamil Nadu's Amma Canteens. But many freebies have massively distortionary.
- When politicians promise SOPs, often fiscal constraints force governments in raising new taxes, a sign of strained finance.

**Relevant Thought**: Well-designed subsidies help the poor make the best of whatever opportunities they have; poorly designed ones either do very little or actually make things worse for them.

**- Abhijit Banerjee**

## Managing Current Covid Surge (Dt: 06.01.2022)

- This is the 3rd year of the pandemic in world over Experience of 2nd wave in 2021 of lockdowns need to be effectively coped with by the states' municipal corporations etc.
- Daily caseload increased 46% in a day to touch 9,184 on Dec, 28, National daily caseload reached 58,097 between January 4th and 5th, accompanied with daily positivity rate 4.18% from just 0.73% a month ago.
- Some states have responded by curbing mobility. Delhi has night curfew to be supplemented by weekend curfew, Tamil Nadu has night curfew with full lockdown on Sundays, West Bengal has limited flights from Delhi and Mumbai to 3 times a week.

- Around 65% adult population is fully vaccinated and over 8 million children in 15-18 age group have been administered a single dose.
- More sophisticated approach is required by all Governments impose a disproportionate cast on the most economically vulnerable segments and not really curb infections.
- Maharashtra is using Covid bed vacancy as a measure to choose policy options. It seems the approach makes sense.
- A smarter approach with enforcement of masks and capacity restrictions in public spaces will help controlling the spread of infections and limiting the economic fallout.

**Relevant Thought**: The one who adopts his policy to the times prospers, and likewise that the one whose policy clashes with the demands of time does not.

**-Niccolo Machiavelli**

## Vaccination Coverage In India (Dt: 07.01.2022)

- Around 90% of vaccine recipients are of Covishield. SIT has no problem in raising Covishield production Underperforming BB has enough for 3rd doses of those double dosed with Covaxin.
- GOI approved 3rd (booster) dose after 9 months of 2nd dose, is now questioned, could have been more ambitions; as suggested by many global studies-on-immunity to reduce it to 6 months, and group of 45 age and above would be 3rd dosed much faster.
- The booster dose now has to start form Jan, 10 launching. The 9-month gap makes 1.26 crore people who received 2nd dose by April 10 in 2021. Relaxing to a 6-months gap for 45 year olds and above would make 6.8 crore eligible for 3rd dose on same day.
- GOI cited 9 months after 2nd job, but UK Health Security Agency study shows that 3rd shot has 88% protection from hospitalization against Omicron while this drops to 52% for those who got 2nd job over 6 months ago.
- India should reassess the cutoff date and age ceiling. Similarly, GOI look at relaxing the age bar (15-18) for children vaccination.

- Covaxin has been approved for those are 12 and trial have been conducted for children over 2 yrs. Clearance for vaccination above 12 must come soon. other countries moved on booster doses for children.
- Mix and match trials on BB's intranasal vaccine and corbevax and covovax booster trials should be expedited.

**Relevant Thought**: There is one thing we all can do to end the pandemic: that is getting vaccinated. So get vaccinated and we will get through this faster.

**- Justin Trudeau**

## Drugs and Vaccinations For Covid (Dt: 08.01.2022)

- After 9 months of 2nd dose of Covishield/Covaxin w.e.f. 3rd booster dose.
- But globally 6 months after 2nd dose, 3rd Booster
- Above 45 years and 6 months after 2nd dose =?
- 3 Jan, 2022 launched 15-18 years Vaccination by Covaxin.
- DNA based 'ZyCoV' of Zydus approved 12-18 years=?
- Mix-Match 'Covishield' and 'Covaxin' (NTAGI approved)=?
- 'Covaxin' approved from 12years and trial over 2 years yet to be launched=?
- 'Corbevax' of M/S Biological-E for EUA- adult vaccination=?
- 'Covovax' of SII for EUA-adult vaccination=?
- Mix and Match trials, on BB's 'Intranasal Vaccine' and biological E's 'Corbevax'
- Dual RT-PCR-1st with standard regular kit for Omicron and S-gene drop test=Not followed
- India's records: Are undercount by our limited ability to do Genome Sequencing.

- 'Molnupiravir'-the anti-covid pill approved but not getting recommended?
- 2 -Deoxy- D Glucose(2-DG)-Covid-19 drug developed by DRDO + Dr. Reddy Lab and approved by DCGI-May2021(Anti Covid Medicine in powder form)

## 2022 GDP Recovery (Dt: 08.01.2022)

- Government shows the economy has bounced back to the pre-pandemic level. GDP is expected to grow by 9.2% to Rs. 147.53 lakh crore or about $3.2 trillion. GDP estimate for 21-22 is 1.26% is higher than that of 2019-20, the last pre-pandemic year.
- But private consumption continues to be lower than what was recorded 24 yrs ago. It indicates the recovery will be uneven and economy will be difficult to come back on track.
- The unevenness is captured by the performance of the trade transport and logistics sector. The forecast is Rs. 24.70 lakh crore in 2021-22 8.4% lower than the level 2 years ago. The weakness here is private consumption; which is forecast to be Rs. 80.80 lakh crore in 2021-22, 2.8% power than pre-pandemic level.
- The positive aspect is the recovery in fixed investment which is estimated to be Rs. 48.51 lakh crore this year, 2.5% higher than pre-pandemic level.
- The advance estimate was compiled without considering impact of ongoing 3rd wave of Covid-19 infections. The policy is without considering lockdowns curfews and contact-intensive sectors getting worst hit.

**Relevant Thought**: Aggregate GDP has passed 2019 levels, but consumption and stressed sectors remain below it pointing to income loss that still has to be made up.

**– Ashima Goyal**

- International Trade: Four mutually reinforcing reforms by the Government in past 5 years have been initiated.
- Insolvency and bankruptcy code
- Goods and Services Tax
- Labour Codes
- A global competitive corporate profit tax with impressive progress in building both physical and digital infrastructure have laid foundation of robust growth in coming two decades.
- The impact of these can be considerably enhanced by access to the world markets for entrepreneurs white simultaneously exposing them to global competition. One avenue to achieve this objective is FTA (Free trade agreements) with EU, UK, Canada, Australia, and UAE.
- Duty free access for Indian products to these large markets will accelerate growth. At least 90% of trade should be covered under liberalization.
- Rewrite the SEZ (Special economic Zone) Law making Indian manufacturer globally competitive.
- Doing high custom duty down.
- Reform in higher education by HECI Act (Higher Education Commission of India) Abolish UGC give academic and administrative autonomy to higher education leading institutions white providing them bulk of funding.
- Open the door to foreign universities to establish campus and the domestic institutions to do the same abroad.
- AICT and NCTE should be subsumed in HECI
- Finally, research should by moved to universities from dysfunctional councils e.g. ICSSR (Indian council of Social Science Research).

## Poll Campaigns In Surging Covid (Dt: 10.01.2022)

- Five states (UP, Punjab, Uttarakhand, Manipur and Goa) shall go for assembly polls. Electoral mobilisation can spread infections faster. Therefore, EC's one week moratorium till Jan 15 on physical rallies and roadshows is welcome. EG should have option of extending no-rallies rule of situation demands.
- Parties should rewrite their campaign and concentrate on online campaigning and doorsteps visits in groups of 5 or less which EC has allowed. Star campaigners should switch to virtual rallies and smart phones penetration, by messages etc., from grassroots workers.
- This election will be a good measure by voters assessing the economy whether in good health by some macro measures or has worry spots of unemployment and not recovered consumption. Also, test will be whether farmers groups have real electoral power in Punjab and parts of UP.
- Coming to Polls- BJP is incumbent in 4 states. Congress faces grave question on its national relevance and taking on BJP in 3 states.
- Regional Parties- SP in UP, AAP in Punjab and Goa and DMC in Goa and Manipur are fighting BJP and Congress.
- During covid, EC must hold party leaders responsible for cadre's violations.

**Relevant Thought**: In time of crisis, the incumbent suffers and the bigger the crisis, the greater the punishment inflicted on those in power unless they do something that makes a change.

**-Tariq Ali**

## Bank Probes – CBI, CVC and CAG Risks (Dt: 11.01.2022)

- The incentive structure influencing PSBs (Public Sector Banks) is under positive changes.
- CVC (Central Vigilance Commission) has amended rules to minimize the possibility of CBI taking unilateral decisions on investigation into alleged bank frauds.

- Separately, Bankers have asked GOI to have 'Sunset' period for investigations subject to conditions.
- GOI should consider this favorably and revisit its entire incentive structure that influences credit disbursal in PSBs, and does not fritter away taxpayer investments.
- BSBs are with regulatory layers: 3Cs-CBI, CVC and CAG.
- The culture of distrust has extracted a cost on both the financial sector and the real economy.
- Stigma around NPAs has incentivised creative ways to tide then, consequently resulting in large losses India's PSBs go through risk aversion that are disconnected with their balance sheets. The divergence in performance of private banks and PSBs is partly to do with PSB's incentive structure.
- The solution is GOI to stick to policy making and the incentives for bankers need to change. Encouraging lateral entry in upper echelons be stopped and instead 3Cs should factor bank chiefs in decision making.

**Relevant Thought**: The proper study of mankind is the science of design.

**– Herbert A Simen**

## Equity Stake In Vodafone (Dt: 12.01.2022)

- ON 10 January 22 Vodafone Idea's governing board opted to make GOI the company's targets share holder.
- Industry bailout package offered by GOI in last September was deferment in payment of spectrum and adjusted gross revenue (AGR) dues. The interest arising out of the deferred payment could be paid to GOI in the form of equity shares.
- GOI should accept decisions of 2 companies. It will own 35.8% of Vodafone and 9.55% of Tata Tele. It is not nationalization; instead, it is a short-term support to insulate the economy from implosion of a large firm. Such temporary support has precedent in India and elsewhere.

- The U.S. Government supported G.M. and Chrysler and held 61% in G.M. providing short term support to Vodafone and Tata Tele is justified. GOI should how however keep away from operation as it has poor record in telecom business BSNL and MTNL having cumulative losses of rupees 47508 crore.
- GOI will get opportunity to exit at a profit. The real gain is insulating the economy when it is still recovering from the pandemic induced shock.

**Relevant Thought**: There has rarely been a less loved or more necessary emergency program than TARP.

**- Barack Obama**

## UP State Poll Gets Interesting (Dt: 13.01.2022)

- Resignation of 2 UP cabinet ministers and 4 legislators have shaken BJP
- Crossover of BSP MLAs to SP and BJP
- Congress losing the prominent western UP face to SP.
- Hence all pointing to SP Vs BJP big fight.
- SP is creating fissures in BJP's umbrella OBC coalition which includes MBC (most backward class), may hit BJP, where it hurts most.
- SP Borrows BJP's tactics of building a wide social coalition.
- Partnering BSP to net Jatav notes consolidation of upper caste non-Jatav, non-Yadav Hindu votes etc. are BJP's 40% vote banks.
- SP has realized its limitation of Muslim Yadav vase in comparison to BJP.
- SP's revived alliance with Jat-dominated RLD has gained amid western UP farm agitation.
- SP has also approached small parties of Kurmis, Mauryas and Nonias.

- A split in Yadav votes was averted by mending fences with Akhilesh Yadav's estranged uncle Shivpal Yadav.
- BJP had reshuffled cabinet last year with 270 BC, 12 Dalit MPs the extension of OBC reservation to NEET all-India cnsucd

**Relevant Thought**: The magician and politician have much in common. They both have to draw our attention always from what they are really doing.

**- Ben Okri**

## Omicron-powered 3rd Wave (Dt: 14.01.2022)

- Covid 3rd wave with Omicron is spreading very fast. National Test Positivity Rate is 12% and reached 25% in some large cities. Daily testing increased from 11 lakh to 20 lakh now but the number is still inadequate. Most testing concentrates to metro areas Reported figures, therefore are underestimates. Also, there are unreported infections by home testing.
- 1st We should have much more data, like other countries most matters to have data on no of hospitalization and hospital caseload. Hospitalisation figures form Delhi and Mumbai show: no shortage of $O_2$, ICU and ventilator beads yet.
- 2nd Data required on national and regional break up of hospitalization by the status of vaccination.
- Do partially vaccinated or unvaccinated persons need hospital care?
- In Mumbai, unvaccinated accounted for 96% of admissions for $O_2$ beds. Such data should be collated and published nation – wide Even after 2yrs living with Covid, India has not managed the system.
- 3rd GOI should now reduce the time between 2 Covishield doses so that large partially vaccinated can shrink. This group should be seriously targeted by state Government, which is not being done.
- 4th Children's vaccination has slowed down after a brisk start. It is time to seriously consider door to door vaccination.

**Relevant Thought**: You never let a serious crisis go to waste. And what I mean by that is it's an opportunity to do things you think you could not do before.

**– Rahim Emanuel**

## Vaccination Option For Livelihood (Dt: 15.01.2022)

- Governments across the world are mandating individual vaccination to limit health risks. In US, the Supreme Court overturned Government's vaccine mandate for large companies, but upheld it for healthcare workers.
- In France, lawmakers have upheld tighter vaccine pass for access to public settings e.g. restaurants and trains In Canada's Quebec province, Government announced
- Vaccines lower the risk of hospitalization and death. In Delhi Between 9 Jan to 12 Jan about 72% of the 97 Covid deaths were among the cenvacinated.
- In normal times, vaccination can be of individual's choice, but in case of respiratory pandemic, the choice to avoid vaccination can impede other's mobility and livelihood which means that their choice has consequence for others.
- France, now has decided that only vaccination will be accepted and it is a strong disincentive against remaining unvaccinated.
- Vaccination in India need not be mandatory but the unvaccinated should not have the same privileges if they pose a risk to the freedom and livelihood of others.

**Relevant Thought**: The unvaccinated, I really want to piss them off. And so, we are going to continue doing so until the end.

**- Emmanuel Macron**

## UP Election Ticket Distribution (Dt: 17.01.2022)

- In UP state election caste is overriding factor for candidate selection. BJP has given OBC 44 out of 107 tickets in its first list. SP has different formula as Muslims + Yadav + other castes and BSP as Dalit + other castes against Hindutva + caste.

- SP (Akhilesh Yadav) has been dangling the promise of a caste census as a sort of superglue for all the governance cracks in the state.
- A chilling data point is that UP had fewer employed people at December 2021 than Dec 2016. The solution in dividing up jobs as well as educational scots by actual caste numbers is a failure of common sense and policy imagination.
- This is a vicious circle where a Neta (leader) interest is in digging social divisions even deeper than religious polarization.
- Ultimately, whoever forms the government will face a major trust deficit form certain castes form day one.

**Relevant Thought**: Caste has become much more powerful in certain respects, than it ever was in pre-British times.

**- MN Srinivas, 1957**

## Jabs For The Kids (Dt: 18.01.2022)

- During last two Covid waves Indian students suffered one of the longest school closures in the world. Now Omicron forces different state regulations upon them.
- In India the vaccination for under-18 age was initiated one year after Israel, 9 months after US and 6 months after UK.
- Within 13 days of vaccination to 15-17 age group, 45% of 7.4 crore have got their 1st dose. Nest about 7.12 crore of the 12-14 age group will have their turn.
- NTAGI (National Technical Advisory Group on Immunisation) chairman has indicated that only after completion of double-dosing of 1st group, will vaccination open for the 2nd group around February-end or early March. By this, the children aged 5-11 years of about 16.2 crore for whom no vaccine is authorized yet, will be waiting for vaccine well into 2nd half of 2022.

- States are suffering in managing schools for last 2 yrs. rocking teacher supports, not reconfiguring syllabi without amped-u learning recovery programs etc.,
- Covaxin supply is around 6 crore a month which children have to split with adults' regular jobs and boosters. Between Dec 29 and Jan 17 of 5.6 crore doses of Covaxin administered, 15-17 yrs account for 3.45 crore doses. So Covaxin alone can't get our kids jabbed fast.
- Corbevax and Covovax trials are still underway.
- ZyCoV-D was approved EUA for 12 yrs and above in August 2021 but not yet being in service.

**Relevant Thought**: It seems ridiculous to say that a year of disruption will last the rest of their life. But given that we fail in normal times, I don't know how we think we are going to catch us this time.

**- Anna Vignoles**

## Inequality and Economic Growth (Dt: 19.01.2022)

- Oxfam International has brought out report on 'Inequality' in India based on measurement of wealth and not by income. Hence their solutions are unworkable.
- Oxfam has made 3 suggestions; (i) to ask for better measurements and more regular ones (ii) the other two are taxation: Wealth Tax and (iii) a temporary 1% surcharge on the richest 10%.
- India had levied Wealth Tax in past; which was published in 2015 Union Budget as it had no impact. To compensate its abolition, a surcharge on income above Rs. 1 crore was levied.
- There are practical difficulties in taxing wealth; which has also been influenced by more than a decade of loose monetary policies of major central banks that are trying to boost economic growth.
- What really matters is economic growth and the creation of pathways is economic growth and the creation of pathways to economic mobility.

- Post 1991, the rise in India's economic growth lifted millions out of poverty even as inequality widened. Policy needs to focus on obstacles to growth. US billionaires fid not inherit their wealth. Their ideas created their wealth and millions of other jobs and opportunities. That is what India needs. Policy focus should be on creating pathways of economic mobility, not messy taxation laws

  **Relevant Thought**: I think inequality is fine, as long as it is in the common interest.

  **-Thomas Piketty**

## India's Statistical System (Dt: 20.01.2022)

- Divergence between same states' official covid toll and the higher number of compensation claims accepted by them has raised questions on India's mortality statistics.
- Supreme Court(SC) questioned GOI on starvation deaths, while hearing a plea for a national policy on community kitchens, which is an unsatisfactory state of affairs.
- Virtual statistics of population in India began in $19^{th}$ century and recording of these details in 1969 was made mandatory.
- Civil registration system (CRS) is overseen by GOI on births and deaths, but the quality varies sharply across states. In CRS 2019, India has 8.3 million deaths of which 92% were registered. When it comes to medically certified, lower proportion that 21.1% and 22% recorded in preceding years.
- To combat malnutrition, consumer price index, poverty estimates etc. depend on accurate data. Absence of relevant statistics is the primary problem in India.

**Relevant Thought**: Facts are stubborn things, but statistics are pliable.

**-Mark Twain**

## Premature Fiscal Tightening (Dt: 21.01.2022)

- Indi's economic challenges have multiplied as to revive economy in the midst of economic contraction and simultaneously to focus on high retail inflation.
- A popular gauge of inflationary pressure is the price of Indian basket of crude, which is now around $87 a barrel higher about 50% over the last year.
- Therefore RBI and GOI should simultaneously support economic growth and cope with upward pressure on retail inflation.
- Monetary policy, to revive the economy has been the central bank's policy rate at 4% been lower than retail inflation for long periods and market interest rates have been pulled down by expanding liquidity. Consequently, in last 2 years, deposit rate of banks for fresh inflows have fallen by 2.13% and average lending rates for new loans are now 1.97% lower.
- Over last 2 months, the gap between interest rates on short-term and long-term rows has widened and the expectation that there will be substantial borrowing by GOI and states. This should not deter GOI or states. Both contact-intensive services and private consumption remain below pre-pandemic levels.
- Core inflation is around 6% higher GDP growth will improve the deficit parameters of GOI and states.
- It will be parameter to lighten fiscal policy further as RBI may have to read just for inflation and financial market's behavior.
- Government spending can crowd-in private business and investments.

**Relevant Thought**: You care about the deficit because it allows you to do things you do to need to do to help people who are suffering.

**-Christina Ramer**

## Women's Property Rights (Dt: 22.01.2022)

- The Supreme Court has ruled that daughters will have equal rights to their father's property even prior to enactment of the HSA (Hindu Succession Act) of 1956.
- It clarified that if a property of a male Hindu dying intestate is a self-acquired property or obtained in partition of a coparcenary or family property, the same would devolve by inheritance to daughters and not by survivorship as was the case before 1956.
- National Family Health Survey-5 says that 43% of women respondents reported owning house/land alone or jointly. But doubt remains about women's ability to actually access and control property. A 2020 University of Manchester working paper found barely 16% of women are in rural landowning.
- States such as Punjab, Haryana, UP and even Delhi have regressive inheritance provisions. In UP since 2016, married daughters are not considered primary heirs. Haryana twice dried to take away the progressive rights given to women through HSA. Ground-level resistance to register land for women continue in several states.
- Thus women empowerment and property rights remain an unfinished project.

**Relevant Thought**: If society will not admit of women's free development, then society must be remodeled.

**-Elizabeth Blackwell**

## Dynamic Politics in Assembly Elections (Dt: 24.01.2022)

- Many political families are upcoming five states Assembly Elections.
- Akhilesh Yadav in UP marginalised in family, public sum for being a family enterprise. His sister-in-law Apama Yadav with no future in SP has joined BJP.
- The Badal family domination of Akali Dal in Punjab is yielding diminishing return to a movement.
- Dynastic succession is a reality in India accept BJP, CPM and CPI.

- BJP is sharpening "Parivarvaad" against the five namely M. Karuranidhi, K Chandrashekhar Rao, Sharad Pawar, Bal Thakrey, Mulayam Singh, Lalu Prasad and Mamta Banerjee.
- Political elites down district level are prolonging own fiefdoms.
- In Punjab and Uttarakhand Congress is attempting one family one ticket rule discomfiting Channi and Harish Rawat.
- BJP likewise denied Panaji seat to Manohar Parikar's son.
- Indian politics and its economy need reforms that improves opportunities for the youth.

**Relevant Thought**: **O**ur country has certain problems. We are dynasty lovers. We love the fact that this guy comes from this family and we start giving them concessions.

**-K.K. Menon**

## Germany Navy Chieftain Comments (Dt: 25.01.2022)

- Germany's Navy Chief, Vice-Admiral Key-Achim Schoen back had to resign for comments he made at an event in India. He said Kiev (Capital of Ukraine) would not regain the Crimean Peninsula that Moscow had seized in 2014.
- Russia recently has amassed 1lak troops along Ukrainian border as a part winter exercise. Ukraine and the West fear this is a preparation for a full-scale Russian invasion. Moscow has long objected to NATO's eastward expansion.
- Provoking Russia will be counterproductive for NATO. Russia has enough military depth and it provides 40% national gas supplies to Europe, hence can turmoil European economy. Therefore, NATO needs to adopt a strategy to deal with Russia. Schoenbach's analysis is right that China is the biggest threat and not Russia.
- China with its vast economic and technological powers is the biggest threat to global order.
- Teamed with China Russia can be a serious disrupter and further Beijing's interests.

- Thus a better approach will be by NATO to work out a modes vivendi with Russia in Europe and drive a wedge between Moscow and Beijing.

**Relevant Thought**: Putin needs strong moves to keep the country as one. In Russia, if you don't centralize power, you have the risk of losing the country. **-Anantly Karpav**

## Learning Response to Covid (Dt: 26.01.2022)

- New Covid cases on Dec. 24, 2021 was 7189 and daily positive rate of tasting was 0.65%. After a month, the daily case load increased 36 fold to 2.55 lakh with a positivity rate of 15.52%. both medical infrastructure and economic activity were not disrupted. Even during the current wave of last four weeks, India has absorbed lessons of 1st 2 waves and has good response.
- The 1st wave taught us that infection peaks vary across reason and homogeneous national response has unwanted economic cost.
- In 2nd wave, mobility restrictions were calibrated to limit economic damage by linking to vacant Covid beds.
- School closures were resumed in Maharashtra and West Bengal with in-person classes.
- 60% adults been fully vaccinated has lowered stress on healthcare infrastructure. But still, in domestic research and data collection, things need to be better.
- Genome sequencing of samples is inadequate.
- Availability of more granular data are necessary to help states further refine their responses.
- Indian research needs better coordination from GOI that should take the lead in raising standards.

**Relevant Thought**: We may have stopped the epidemic's exponential growth but we have by no means stopped the virus.

**- Richard Hatchett**

## Targeting Major Voter Turnout (Dt: 27.01.2022)

- Prime Minister, PM Modi has asked citizens and party workers to achieve 75% voter turnout in upcoming elections.
- Chief Election Commissioner Sushil Chandra said India now has 95 crore voters that trumps over US, the 2nd large democracy.
- Framers of constitution weighed in favour of a central, independent constitutional body to oversee elections. This works better than US model of decentralized electoral process. India has easier enrolment and improved access to voting for citizens at the margins. Commission's self-correction like crackdown on large election rallies is praised worthy.
- Another impressive achievement of EC is special attention to improve women enrolment and increased female participation in elections. Now even political parties are helping for this.
- Concern is Urban voters are not pulling enough to cast vote Data of Mumbai, Delhi, Chennai, Bengaluru and Hyderabad proves that.
- Great concern is though migrants on the rise in cities, but they are losing their votes at both sources and destinations. EC must evolve strategies so that migrants don't lose out on voting day.

**Relevant Thought**: The most important office and the one which all of us can and should fill, is that of private citizen.

**-Louis Brandeis**

## Booster (3rd Dose) To All Adults (Dt: 28.01.2022)

- GOI should extend the 3rd dose booster programme to all adults. Major countries have introduced booster. shots to all adults including children.
- Efficacy studies of BB's under-trial Intranasal vax, Corovax or Corbevax as boosters should be publicized.
- Israel and UK indicate 3rd dose vax is useful and protection is high 83% whereas 2 dose protection is 64%.

- Union health secretary has said, in April 2021 that 88% of all Covid deaths were in 45+ age groups and in Oct, 2020 he had said 35% of fatalities were in 45-60 age group and 53% in 60+ group.
- Diabetes Hypertension and Heart disease in 2020 is British journal, BMJ showed that these in case of 60-70 age group are marginally higher than those of 40-60 age group.
- More Indians in 45-60 age groups work, and travel for work than those in 60+ groups. Therefore 45-60 age group should be considered high risk category.
- Hence booster to all adults should be decided.

**Relevant Thought**: We learnt a lot about the third shot before the rest. And we saw its amazing effect reducing illness in the most impressive way.

**- Golia Rahav**

## Worst Hit Restaurants In Lockdowns (Dt: 29.01.2022)

- Unlike earlier years, states this time have not let restrictions linger although daily infections are around average 2.5 lakh. It is a relief for India's beleaguered contract intensive eateries. This sector (Restaurants and Eateries) has been worst hit over last 2 years. NRAI (National Restaurant Association of India) last year estimated that 25% restaurants are out of business and 2.4 million employees leading to retrenchment.
- Differentiating between essential and other activities to decide on shutdowns should be avoided. Every activity generates jobs and arbitary demarcations undermine livelihoods. Gyms are worst hit by shout downs. Average Indian small sized business cannot survive prolonged shutdowns. These are the source of employment for low skilled and unskilled youth.
- Large scale closures of restaurants have long term consequences in India's job market.
- Governments should avoid closures based on incidence of infection; rather should focus on keeping healthcare infrastructure prepared.

**Relevant Thought**: Discretion is the perfection of reason, and a guide to us in all the duties of life.

**- Walter Scot**

## West UP Election Campaign (Dt: 31.01.2022)

- UP has 403 assembly seats. The first two rounds of polling begins on 10 Sep UP will have focus predominantly on Western UP, which contributes about 73 seats. The theme of campaign here are identity and economic issues by public opeman.
- Highlight of current campaigning is to attract Jat voters they have been integral to BJPs social alliance in UP. Jat farmers were against the agriculture reform and part of agitation. West UP's agrarian economy is dependent on Government's price support on 2 key corps, wheat and sugarcane.
- Significant Muslim population has a big population has big polarisation.
- Critical question is whether BJP's social coalition or SP and RLD alliance will be the winner.
- Outstanding sugarcane dues to farmers owed by sugar mills and disgruntlement over ticket distribution will affect the dynamics.
- Home minister Amit Shah is on door to door campaign for BJP.
- Political parties are not on economic problems. Promises revolve around free electricity, corps for sugarcane payments. For millions of young job seekers in UP, election does not offer much.

**Relevant Thought**: Politics is the art of choosing between the disastrous and the unpalatable.

**- John Kenneth Galbraith**

## Message of Economic Survey (Dt: 01.02.2022)

- Key message of economic survey is that in 2022-23, the economy is expected to grow between 8 to 8.5% mainly on account of vaccination normally, exports and physical space for GOI investment.

- Survey expects monsoon to be normal.
- It assumed global key control banks will ensure that financial markets don't panic during liquidity tightening.
- It says, average price of oil will drift down from current $89/barrel to an average of $70 to $75.
- GOI assumes that pandemics economic cost is temporary and vulnerable economic segments will bounce back.
- But data on both 'Employment and Overall Consumption' shows private consumption in 2021-22 is not expected to reach the level that existed 2 years ago though the overall GDP will be higher.
- Urban employment shows jobs have shifted to the informal sector according to GOI's quarterly surveys. In Jan-Mar 2021 survey there is 2.4% points dip even a year in the formal sector jobs to 48.1%.
- CMIE data covers period till Sep-Dec 2021. It shows that over 2 years there is more than 2% points fall in labour force to 40.3% of population.
- People drop out of labour market and informal sector jobs offer low and uncertain income. Consumption has not kept pace with overall GDP. Even banks have funds, industry waits for demands.
- Recovery in GDP will be by physical space arising from buoyant revenue. Recovery has been good, but worries remain.

**Relevant Thought**: A monitory policy stance tightens more broadly this year economics will need to adopt to a global environment of higher interest rates.

**-Gita Gopinath**

## FM's Big Bet Budget (Dt: 02.02.2022)

- FM Nirmala Sitharaman's 4th budget dt. 01.02.2022 in Parliament revealed to keep momentum of economic recovery with 35%

increase in Government spending on asset creation and appeared to be banking on growth, and is ready to risk high inflation.

- RBI's MPC may hike fuel price, but should be done gently.
- To encourage private investment; Budget offers stability in direct tax regime.
- She acknowledged that economic recovery is uneven by extending credit guarantee for MSMEs and focusing on that.
- How to have money for huge hike in Cadex?
- **First,** by increase in tax revenue; **Second** by switching from welfare spending to investment. Allocation to food subsidy and MONREGA have been lowered. Spending on vaccines and Air India will fall in 2022-23.
- Two Assumptions: **First** – There will be no more shocks. **Second-** Growth will reduce need for high targeted support.
- **30% Tax on gains from Crypto Assets** – is a smart call as is making the new tax applicable from March 2023 which will give time to Crypto Asset holders to adjust their portfolios.
- Aside the Crypto more, if RBI launches digital currency in next financial year, India will move up the block chain technology ladder.
- GOI seems taken that it is not best time to sell assets and privatization.
- It's a good budget if GOI can spend all the capex budgeted for.

**Relevant Thought**: We are sure to achieve the numbers. If anything, we will probably better them.

**-Nirmala Sitharaman**

## Digital Rupees In 2022-23 By RBI (Dt: 03.02.2022)

- The budget stated that RBI will issue digital rupees during 2022-23, i.e. its own Central Bank Digital Currency(CBDC). It is a digital form of paper currency. Globally private products on CBDC have been underway since 2014.

- India today is with digital retail payment system that runs 24/7 and transfers real time. Digital payments are catching on fast while cash is preferred made of payments for transactions up to Rs.500 and digital payments are more popular for higher amounts.
- There is no real incentive to switch to CBDC as retail transactions are already done digitally.
- What are the implications of CBDC for banking system is not entirely clear. If there is partial shift always from bank deposits to CBDC, what is the role of banks in credit creation? By extension, What is the implication for monetary policy?
- Sweden's Riks bank launched e-krona project in 2017 and is still studying its need and potential impact on Sweden's economy.
- CDDC for India may be inevitable; rather it is about the need to be flexible.

**Relevant Thought**: We probably overestimate how much there is new in this debate for CBDC.

**-Hyun Song Shin**

## Tax Reform To Simpler Regime (Dt: 04.02.2022)

- India has reputation of a litigation prone tax jurisdiction. Now the tax policy reform is to more towards a simper regime, without exemptions and of low rates, which will drastically reduce litigation and be a fairer one. Litigation has kept mounting The cause for litigation, abundance of loopholes limits the tax collection
- Sovereign Government face limitations in selling tax rates on companies because capital is mobile. Hence rich countries to get major economies, agree to minimum tax rate. A shift to a simpler tax regime will reduce the litigations and thereby, attract more investment.
- 75% of returns filed are for income blow Rs. 5 lakh. Two separate reforms are needed here: (a) the threshold for tax (b) Income of Rs. 2.5 lakh need to be indexed to inflation. The current floor since July 2014; the inflation has lowered the tax threshold. Which is a

regressive development. Linking it with inflation makes it fairer and removes unwarranted discretionary power.

- This step needs to move to a regime without exemptions save for everyone's retirement savings and making a simple process of filling returns. All there have been addressed in GOI's tax reform reports that should be made public.

**Relevant Thought**: What I want to do is create more taxpayers, not more taxes.

**-Geoff Davis**

## Diplomatic Boycott Beijing Winter Olympics (Dt: 05.02.2022)

- India boycotted the Beijing Winter Olympics diplomatically. It is a right decision of GOI.
- China made a PLA regiment commander involved in the 2020 Galan clashes with India as the torch bearer in Olympic relay. It is a politicization of Games by China.
- Before India the US, UK, Canada, Australia, Estonia, Lithuania, Belgium, Kosovo and Denmark have announced boycotts of the Games citing China's human rights violation. Put together these countries constitute 35% of global GDP.
- Add to this, well developed countries like Japan and in Asian grouping who have turbulent relations with China give a message that China's political and security misadventures will be costly economically.
- India aligned with major democracies on this issue and the US welcomed the decision.
- Putin and Xi both met before the winter Games began may have made it a tricky for India, given that we still need Moscow's weapons. But Russia too needs India's arms orders. So, India rightly proceeds in China strategy.

**Relevant Thought**: Everybody knows politics is a contact sport.

**-Barack Obama (US president 2009-2017)**

## Voice of India: Lata Mangeshkar (Dt: 06.02.2022)

- We are greatly shocked with the sad demise of Lata Mangeshkar, the nightingale of India on 6th February 2022. Her democratizing voice is ever present in the soundtrack of our everyday lives like the air, we breath. She transcended generations and she has nearly 15 million followers. She represented an unwavering dedication towards attaining excellence in uncompromising work-ethic, devotion to meticulousness and unmatched talent.
- in 1974, Michael Foot, British Labour Party Leader introduced her as "The Voice Of India" before her famous Royal Albert Hall performance in London. It is well known that Lata's rendition of "Ae Mere Vatan Ke Logon" made Jawaharlal Nehru weep.
- It was her voice and ability to stay unsullied by the march of time. Lata's finest songs came at the junction of pain and longing and evoke a woman. She has sung songs of every genre; melancholic wistfulness is what she did best.
- Her voice has the universality of appeal, the ageless ability to speak the truth and like water, is able to quench a thirst in a way that nothing else can. Her songs communicate with the hearts of emotions that seem to evoke for which she was the preferred choice of so many music directions however diverse their styles might be.
- Lata Mangeshkar did not belong to any one era. Her music will continue to cast spells as it always has.

**Rely Thought:** I won't ever stop singing.

**-Lata Mangeshkar**

## Job Quotas for Locals (Dt: 08.02.2022)

- Supreme Court is to hear this week a case that will test constitutionality of Haryana's new Law of 75% reservation of private sector jobs for locals, subject to monthly salary cap of Rs. 30000.
- Andhra Pradesh's assembly passed a similar Law last year. Jharkhand's assembly followed suit. Punjab is set to replicate Haryana's approach catching this idea as one of election promises.

- Haryana Other than domicile reservation has covers not just corporations, but also trusts, societies and partnerships.
- Domicile based reservation in private sector violates fundamental rights of citizens from other states.
- It is GOI's duty to push back against nativism and attempts to erect barriers to labour mobility.
- India's path to economic prosperity depends on giving the private sector the space to make appropriate choices and migration runs the labour market and keeps wages competitive. Therefore, Nativism is against both labour and capital.
- States need to work with industry on programs that impart skills and make local youth more employable. This way, everyone will gain.

**Relevant Thought:** If you do not change direction, you may end up where you are heading. - Lao Tzu (Ancient Chinese philosopher and writer)

## 2002 Privatization of HZL (Dt: 09.02.2022)

- India has low trust environment and ill-equipped investigation was the focus on 7th Feb, 22 in Supreme Court (SC).
- GOI plans a review potion of an SC judgment of Nov 2021 directing CBI to file FIR in the 2002 privatization of Hindustan Zinc. (HZL). GOI's argument claimed that fundamental facts presented CBI were factually incorrect and this was the result of 'intricate commercial processes" being examined by investigating officers.
- Quality of work in agencies; CBI, CBC and CAG have sometimes led to delays and substantial economic costs. Price for it is borne largely by citizens.
- Six years after SC cancelled 122 telecom licenses, a CBI court acquitted all the accused and said matters were "conjectured". Reverberations of those events in telecom sector are still being felt.
- GOI's present position on HZL privatization hopefully will be followed to sell its residual stake of 29.6% soon. It is almost a decade since a decision to sell was taken. This is an example of delay that imposes costs on the exchequer.

- GOI continues with 2 conflicting votes, commercial operations in different sectors and policy making for the same. To ensure a sharp focus on right policies, it is important to retreat form commercial operations.

**Relevant Thought:** It is impossible to go through life without trust: that is to be imprisoned in the worst cell of all, oneself.

**-Graham Greene**

## Populist Poll Manifestos (Dt: 10.02.2022)

- FM's budget drew praise for populism in election season for its spending pattern and the state will have economic growth.
- Election manifestos by political parties for assembly election have compete disconnect in the economic approach of GOI and next Governments in the 5 states. It is only the wild populism.
- BJP being the incumbent in 4 of 5 states, its manifestos are trying to woo the electorate on populist promises. In UP it has promised free electricity, 2 free LPG cylinders and 20 million smart phones and tablets for students. In Punjab, BJP promises MSP for fruits and vegetables and loan waivers and free electricity.
- AAP has promised to open the coffers, hence to the free electricity and monthly income transfer bandwagon.
- Congress and SP have usual promise of free electricity. Congress has announced direct money transfers to homemakers and pensioners.
- The problem with these promises is the state budgets will have to accommodate these populist promises. In order to fulfill election promises, budgets will have to cut back on something, i.e. public investment or capital expenditure, which create enabling environment for economic growth and leads to jobs. Therefore, poll manifestos are wildly populist and contradict FM's growth push.

**Relevant Thought:** The fault, dear Brutus is not in our stars, but in ourselves.

**- William Shakespeare**

## Redefining Covid Policy (Dt: 11.02.2022)

- Many countries are lifting restrictions and easing rules in today's new phase of pandemic. Those are Australia, South Korea, Norway, South Africa, UK and US.
- From Feb 14, India will require international passengers from 82 countries to only upload their full vaccination status and will stop 7 day home quarantine. Such moderations are guided by (a) Vaccination and (b) to build back economy, education and normal life.
- UK seems to end the requirement to self-isolate after testing positive likewise there is rollback of mask advisories in various parts of US.
- Indian and East Asian neighbours practice wide spread making as an inexpensive and effective prevention.
- Sweden has gone ahead-stop mass testing stop daily release of inflection numbers and redefines Covid as one where infection is followed by hospitalization.
- India's adult vaccination has been a big achievement with 77% fully jabbed. Children vaccination is on. The 2nd dose has to be speeded up to clear 5-14 age vaccination and quickly extend booster to those above 45 years. These will be big steps towards full normalcy. Millions of poor Indians with low income depend on brisk economic activity outdoors for their livelihood.

**Relevant Thought:** The pandemic is not over, but has entered a totally new phase.

**-Magdalena Andersson**

## Hippocratic Oath Vs Charak Shapath (Dt: 12.02.2022)

- NMC (Nat's Medical Commission) has reportedly decided to replace the Hippocratic Oath in medical colleges with the Charak Shapath.
- The Hippocratic Oath is a worldwide rite of passage for medical students in modern medicine. As India has its own rich heritage n

medicine, therefore borrowing an oath with roots in ancient Greece does not make sense.

- Charak Shapath is derived from Maharshi Charak's 'Charak Sanhita' essentially enjoin medical practitioners to put patients first, respect their privacy and practice with the best of judgment. Thus, it hardly makes any differences which oath is administered.
- NMC came into being in 2020 and its aims include improving access to quality medical education and ensuring availability of adequate medical professionals.
- $15^{th}$ Finance Commission made public that every allopathic doctor in India caters to 1,522 people against WHO norms of 1;1000. Shortage of trained nurses is with ratio 1:670 against WHO norms of 1:300. NMC's effort should be directed at improving these numbers. The focus should be on rigorous scientific standardization of thee streams. NMC should boost actual medical infrastructure in the country especially in light of Covid. The type of oath administered to medical students is irrelevant.

**Relevant Thought:** The physician's highest calling, his only calling, is to make sick people healthy to heal, as it is termed.

**- Samuel Hahnemann**

## NSE Recurring Problems and Governance (Dt: 14.02.2022)

- To prevent archaic market practices, securities trading frauds and circulations of bogus physical shares; NSE (National Stock Exchange) started operation in 1993. It was followed by a centralized clearing house.
- Market and its practices registered a quantum improvement.
- Sebi had announced punishment to NSE and its 2 members of founding team. Sebi a year ago age imposed a penalty on NSE and its informer leads in the co-location case. Last week, penalties and temporary bars in another case pointed to a serious breakdown of governance.

- NSE was the world's largest derivatives exchange in terms of contracts traded. It is highly profitable-net profit of Rs 3,573 crore on an income of Rs 6,202 crore in FY 2020-2021.
- The latest problem is NSE's executive head between April 2013 and December 2016 sent out confidential information at a time when the exchange was looking to lunch an IPO. Inter twined is the appointment of an ill-equipped consultant who was given substantial executive powers which received board approval. And a mysterious 'Guru' received confidential details of NSE.
- An efficient capital market is a must for modern economy. Therefore, a deeper investigation in NSE is essential. NSE's IPO has been delayed due to co-location problem. Detailed investigation and follow up regulatory action are needed.

**Relevant Thought:** We live in a fantasy world, a world of illusion. The great task in life is to find reality.

**-Iris Murdoch**

## Opposition Planning Federalism Meet (Dt: 14.02.2022)

- Oppositions CM's of Telangana (KCR), West Bengal (Mamata) and Tamil Nadu (Stalin) are planning a Delhi meet on 'Federalism' Principle of federalism should be articulated through governance and best practices.
- India's vaccination PDS (Public Distribution System) is a good example of federalism i.e. GOI being procurer distributing equitable to states. GST is also a good example.
- Bypassing federalism is farm reform. Had the views of states sought explaining costs of procurement system and the local response to it, agriculture may have actually witnessed a change.
- States have pointed that centre-state revenue share hides distortions that cess and surcharges create in favour of the centre. After the first national lockdown, centre should have covered the revenue shortfall of states.

- Centre's recent decisions of posting of IAS and IPS officers are to its advantage. A federal discussion on it would have first recognised the shortage of officers and UPSC intake must sharply go up.
- Inter-state councils are also very useful.
- Delhi meet on federalism can be a good initiative.

**Relevant Thought:** Democracy is an experimental system. I like it when states dry out new ideas. I think we ought to expand, not contract, our federalist system. **-Alex Tabarrok**

## Home Buyer – A financial Creditor (Dt: 16.02.2022)

- A home buyer is a financial creditor of real estate projects as payments are made well before delivery of the house. There was no protection form delays in delivery or cheating by the developers.
- In 2016, two laws were passed: (a) IBC (Insolvency and bankruptcy Code) (b) Real Estate (Regulation and Development) Act (RERA) consequent SC (Supreme Court) judgment have reinforced home-buyer with protection. On 14.02.2022 Monday apex court judgment held that if there is a conflict between RERA and SARFAESI, a 20 year-old legislation to protect financial creditors the former will prevail. Yet the event of last 6 yrs has been half-hearted protection.
- In Aug, 2018, the parliament a mended IBC to treat home-buyers as financial creditors; as a big step. But IBC priorities payments to secured creditors such as banks and not home-buyers in priority. GOI depends on buyer-builder agreement. Agreement that confers secured creditor status on buyers is unlikely.
- IN Aug, 2019, SC verdict held that IBC shall take precedence over RERA in case of a conflict putting secured creditors in pole position.
- In March, 2020, IBC amendment made it necessary for home-buyers to get a quorum to trigger the code. It was made to prevent frivolous cases, but once again over looked the asymmetry of power between buyers and builders. Therefore, of three stakeholders, buyer's builders and banks, it is buyer who bears most risk and the unfulfilled contracts b builders needs to be sorted.

**Relevant Thought: Hope is being able to see that there is light despite all of the darkness.**

**-Desmond Tutu**

## IITs Expanding Abroad (Dt: 17.02.2022)

- IITs may open up in Britain is good news for international expansion. They should prepare a competitive education in advanced market.
- IIT's success in India is due to smart meritorious students prepare for months and get in ferociously competitive exams, and shine even with less qualitative teaching, research and old institutions. CAG audit in 2019 found 8 new IITs are in deformable condition Lack of proper infrastructure, land, labs, little research and zero patents even after 5 years, are their status. The audit indicts the governing bodies for poor stewardship. Hence much action is needed for foreign expansion.
- In 2010, Union cabinet had approved foreign universities to set up branches here. Then IIT, Bombay worked on opening an applied science campus in New York City, but the project has borne no fruit NEP, 2020 indicates and budget 2022 suggests that top foreign university will soon operate in Gujarat's GIFT City without having restrictive domestic rules and create institutions of excellence.
- NEP has proposed a reformed higher education regulator which can help for university reforms.

**Relevant Thought: It is not that they can't see the solution. It is that they can't see the problem.**

**-Gilbert K Chesterton**

## Low Legislative Sittings (Dt: 18.02.2022)

- State legislative assemblies have 30 sittings a year over past decade. States of high electoral politics have considerably fewer sittings than national average. Among them are Punjab, Haryana and Delhi assemblies meet less than 20 days a year. Andhra Pradesh, Telangana and UP meet 25 a year. Lok Sabha has just 63 sittings poorer than national chambers of democracies like US, UK, Japan Canada and Germany.

- Legislators (MP and MLAs) thus are not spending enough time in debating laws and governance issues. CJI recently highlighted about poor drafting of laws that lead to controversies over interpretation and litigation.
- State and central executives feel unconstrained by the legislature only 13% bills of current 17th Lok Sabha were referred to standing committee, compared to 27% in previous one and 60% during 15th Lok Sabha.
- Therefore, India needs a minimum of 100 sitting a year and majority of MLAs or MPs from each party must present in those sittings. Legislatures continue to remain unimportant in governance, shows the decline in quality of democracy. Leaders must understand the democracy is at stake.

**Relevant Thought:** The principles of free constitution are irrecoverably lost, when the legislative power is nominated by the executive. Edward Gibbon (English Historian)

## India's Fine Balance On Ukraine Crisis (Dt: 19.02.2022)

- India is under pressure from US to take a clear stand on Ukraine crisis. India has rightly maintained a fine balance, sticking to the position in UN to defuse tensions through dialogue New Delhi can't ignore the bilateral ties with Russia and the deep defence ties with it. US desires that India should view Russia-Ukraine matter the same way as it views China's expansionist design in Asia.
- China is an immediate threat for India, Ukraine does not fall into same category. In past America had little time for India's position on Pak-sponsored terrorism when Pakistan was an US strategic priority.
- China's actions are threating global stability for which Quad was created to reinforce rule-based order.
- Russia has strategic and economic compact with China. US should create space between Russia and China, nullifying their combined

threat. Principles alone don't move for strategic choices, aligning interests do. On China, India and US interests align.

**Relevant Thought:** Foreign policy should not be justified through waking oneself feed good, but through results that have tangible consequences.

**-Zbigniew Brzezinski**

## Unpredictable 2024 National Polls (Dt: 21.02.2022)

- Telangana CM (KCR) meeting Maharashtra CM Udhav Thackeray and NCP supremo Sharad Power shows attempt by regional parties to have alternative to BJP's national dominance.
- Ongoing 5 state assembly elections are witnessing SP in UP, AAP in Punjab and NPP in Manipur offer resistance to BJP, and congress.
- Voters in some states will distinguish between a vote for Modi in national level and BJP in states, which may work adversely to BJP; as it has happened in Haryana, Jharkhand, Maharashtra, Delhi and Bengal post 2019 LS win.
- TMC and AAP are attempting national alternative to Modi by testing waters in multiple states.
- Some regional parties have their struggle in LS polls even against Congress.
- In Kerala, CPM though dominates in assembly and panchayats was decimated by congress-led UDF in 2019.
- Gujrat, HP, Karnataka, MP, Rajasthan, Chhattisgarh and Telengana are all poised to intense contestation.
- Hence, revitalization of BJP or congress in 2024 national polls is unpredictable.

**Relevant Thought:** No government can be long secure without a formidable opposition.

**-Benjamin Disraeli**

## Job Reservations for Locals (Dt: 22.02.2022)

- Haryana Government has taken decision to legislate reservation of jobs for locals in the private sector. The case rests on 2 pillars: it is states responsibility to provide jobs and the advent of GST has catalyzed this policy.
- GST did impact states with large manufacturing base that incurred costs to encourage industrialization. The issue was addressed and compensation provided therefore it is incorrect to use GST as a reason to provide domicile-based reservation in private sector.
- Today's 4th industrial revolution is accelerating automation of manufacturing process, and need for labour is declining. World Bank said that between 1994 and 1211, the share of manufacturing in employment declined in most countries.
- Azim Premji University research found Rs. 1crore investment in 1994 could absorb 33 factory workers, but by 2015, the figure is just and workers. Job reservation to locals is not going to reverse the trend. Instead, it will harm entire country by sparking chain reaction across states.
- Hence, Haryana's focus should be on creating opportunities for locals, by making quality of human capital on technological, investing in education, skilling programs to make youths employable.

**Relevant Thought:** The increase of technical efficiency has been taking place faster than we can deal with problem of labour absorption.

**-JM Keynes**

## Russia Occupied Eastern Ukraine (Dt: 23.02.2022)

- Russian troops entered Ukraine and freed occupied two areas; Donetsk and Luhansk making a dangerous precedence of breaking global norms.
- US and EU have responded with targeted sanctions. Germany has halted nard stream 2 pipeline which is meant for Russian gas export to Berlin.

- Targeted sanctions would be a face saver for NATO while not forcing Russian economy altogether and is a delicate balance.
- Escalation will not help the rest of the world and oil prices are facing high with inflations rising. The only way to ensure solution is to reduce trust deficit between US-led West and Russia.
- India has rightly taken a neutral approach to the Ukraine crisis.
- But should Russia escalate going further into Ukraine, it would be difficult to balance a neutral position by India keeping ties with both US and Russia while facing huge threat from China. Hence New Delhi must try hard that there is no exaction.

**Relevant Thought:** Multilateralism is on its deathbed ... It has been assaulted today, as it has been by other powerful states in the recent past.

- Martin Kimani, Kenyan Ambassador to UN

## Fiscal Cushion and Fuel Taxes (Dt: 24.02.2022)

- As Ukraine crisis deepens, the crude oil price rises to $100. GOI should reduce its fuel taxes to offset the impact of increase in cost of crude.
- Between FY 15 and FY 21 GOI collected about Rs. 16.7 lakh crore through excise duty on petroleum products and most of it was retained by GOI. Therefore, today GOI has the fiscal cushion to lower fuel taxes and hold up private consumption.
- In India, a round 80 of every 100 passenger vehicles sold are two wheelers running on petrol fuel price increase affects a vulnerable population that is already suffering for inflation in articles other than food and fuel. Higher fuel price will keep consumption weak and undermine promise of a growth-oriented budget.
- There is scope to reduce fuel price as the budget was conservative in revenue estimates Gross tax collection for FY-23 expected to increase *by 9.6%) to Rs. 27.6 lakhs crore, a level lower than growth in nominal GDP of 11.1 %. GOI should slash fuel taxes and insulate the economy from Ukraine's impact on energy market.

**Relevant Thought:** Intelligence is the ability to adapt to change.

**- Stephen Hawking**

## Putin's Invasion of Ukraine (Dt: 25.02.2022)

- Vladimir Putin has invaded Ukraine. Rise of Oil and gas price will affect all but not much to Russia. Energy-rich Russia will have customer China than the West. Diplomatically Putin proved that noble words on global rules and sanction won't stop him to attach. He seems to look at regime change in Kyiv.
- US had already taken hit by withdrawing from Afghanistan and has limitations; So there is a bleak new uncertainty.
- For India there are several implications. US EU and Ukraine put pressure on India to talk to Russia. PM Modi told to Putin that violence must cease.
- India's relationship with US-led West is more important than before. Imran Khan's Moscow visit is for attempting Pakistan be made a player in China led axis, but can't be done against India-Russia relationship.
- Tough US sanctions on Russia may impact India's defence supply line as well as future acquisitions like the S-400 missile system.
- US, EU, India and rest of world will suffer high oil and gas prices indefinitely. Current account deficit will widen, inflation will spike, rupee will weaken, India's stock market will be hit. GOI should prepare for stormy days.

**Relevant Thought:** Bombing another city, killing people, destroying society, undoing accomplishment, shattering ties, Again, this again this.

**– Sarah Schulman**

## Dependency On Russian Arms Unviable (Dt: 26.02.2022)

- Military platforms of Russian origin constitute 50% of India's overall military assets and cut across all 3 services. Over 90% of Indian arm's 3000 plus main battle tanks are Russian T-72 and T-90s. India also in advanced talks to procure another 464 Russian T-90 MS tanks. India's air force fighter squadrons comprise Russian aircraft like 272 SU-30 MKL. The Indian Navy has a Russian aircraft carrier

(INS Vikramaditya) and 9 Russian diesel electric submarines among other platforms.

- All of these require periodic upgrades, maintenance spare parts and ancillary support. These will be difficult to obtain under new sanctions regime. As soon as CAATSA bites, India's plans on S-400 missile systems and other acquisitions will be paralyzed.
- India tried to diversity its defence imports over last 15 years by purchase of Rafale from France. But by price and technology Russian platforms remained the preferred choice. Make-in-India defence plan was ill-executed.
- With Russia in US crosshairs, Russia getting close to China and Pakistan sequencing in India needs to find alternatives now. Inviting western arm manufacturers and doing indigenisation are the obvious steps.

**Relevant Thought:** Invincibility lies in the defence; the possibility of victory in the attack.

**– Sun Tzu**

## Economic Fallout Of Ukraine Conflict (Dt: 28.02.2022)

- Since 4th February, Russian invasion continues on Ukraine and the economic fallout on India are beginning to emerge. Immediate hit has come through a surge in crude oil price $ 100/barrel, will have inflation. Another impact is likely to be felt on cooking oil prices as Ukraine and Russia together dominate sunflower oil exports.
- FM, Nirmala Sitharaman has indicated that this conflict will challenge India's development. Budget had assumption of average oil price $ 70-75 to be elevated, but has crossed.
- Now during weak private consumption period, the conflict has coined which is an unusual situation. Hence GOI should immediately reduce retail fuel taxes.
- Western response to Russia is economic sanctions to squeeze its economic base. Russian banks will be ejected from SWIFT payment system. India's hydrocarbon imports are largely from West Asia.

Russia is India's most important arms supplier and both work on settling mutual payments in national currencies.

- According to Stockholm International Peace Research Institute, India's arms imports during 2010-20 from Russia was $ 22.6 billion, around 63% of our total arms imports. Lessening this dependence has to be priority. India's fiscal policies should manage price pressure without weakening economic growth.

**Relevant Thought:** As Russian forces unleash their assault, we are resolved to continue imposing massive costs on Russia that will further isolate it from our economies.

**- Unsula Von Dev Leyen**

## Evacuate Indians from Ukraine (Dt: 01.03.2022)

- GOI announced 4 ministers, Jyotiraditya Scindia Hardeep Puri, Kiren Rijiju and VK Singh will initiate the western border countries to evacuate Indian nationals GOI efforts are focused on borders between Ukraine and neighbours Poland, Romania, Slovakia, Hungary and Moldova by airlifting from these countries.
- Around 20000 Indians including students were in Ukraine. Following GOI advisories about 4000 nationals left Ukraine. after launch of the evacuation, named 'operation Ganga' 1156 have been flown back to India Now there is no paucity of flights to bring them back out of war zone. Foreign ministry has dispatched officers with knowledge of Russian to Kyiv.
- Students are pursuing medicine in Ukraine as it is cheaper than private Indian medical colleges. The demand for flights out of Ukraine resulted in fares surging up to Rs.1 Lakh, making them unaffordable.
- It is a serious problem in Indian education system that shows that Ukraine with a per capita GDP about 2 times that of India can offer more affordable medical education. This should be a wake-up call to GOI and states.

**Relevant Thought:** A man's mind will very gradually refuse to make itself up until it is driven and compelled by emergency.

**- Anthony Trollope**

## Sanctions Can Wreck Russian Economy (Dt: 02.03.2022)

- Even if Russia achieves victory in Ukraine, its economy will be severally damaged. Its balance sheet around $640 billion in foreign exchange reserves and gold are based on key assumption according to a break up by the institute of International Finance (IIF). The weakness is this assumption is that any Russian action that invite a forceful combined response of US, EU, UK, Japan put almost 70% of this balance sheet at risk.
- Russia response to US sanctions after annexation Crimea in 2014 has been to partially switch its US dollar holdings to gold and renminbi (Chinese Yuan).
- The worst unfolded on 28 Feb, 2022 when U.S. and allies immobilized a large part of Bank of Russia's assets. Western response is working to destabalise the financial system through Russian Central Bank's balance sheets. Collapse of rubble required Russia to compel Russian enterprises to sell 80% of their export revenues. Russian economy has on largely to rely on domestic savings raised at abnormal interest rates as households hold 21% of their deposits in currently inaccessible foreign currency. Russia's hydrocarbon fields may be deprived of critical investment. Hence Russians victory may be pyrrhic.

**Relevant Thought:** Wars springs from unseen and generally insignificant causes, the first outbreak being often but an explosion of danger.

**-Thucydides**

## India's Diplomacy with Change Of Time (Dt: 03.03.2022)

- War in Ukraine is severe and civilian deaths are mounting. Putin is not pulling back and has warned with World War III with the nuclear weapons.
- Countries previously in favour of Russia are now changing their positions. Neutral Switzerland has frozen Russia assets. Non-aligned Finland is sending weapons to the Ukraine resistance. Turkey has limited access to Russian Warships to the Black Sea. Russian energy dependent Germany is already planning for scenarios where Moscow weaponries the supply of gas. At UN, criticism against Russia is growing.
- Despite Russia's current actions, its increasing isolation and dangerous gambles of putting nuclear weapon on alert; can India maintain a 'neutral' position and hold 'abstain' position in UN indefinitely?
- The clearest and best test in geopolitics is cold calculations of national interest.
- Putin's continued belligerence is based on comfort from Chin Beijing can extract much from resource rich but weakened Russia seeking its help. China is India's biggest threat. India needs US to counter China as a QUAD partner. Times have changed, hence should be Indian diplomacy.

**Relevant Thought**: Anyone who thinks must think of the next war as they would of suicide.

**-Eleanor Roosevelt**

## Inflation Tax collection to Go up (Date-04.03.2022)

- Outcome of Ukraine War available economic fallout. Immediate impact will be on energy and commodity prices. Duet to boycotts of Russian logistic network, global supply chain will be affected. Specific to India; will be loss of supply of sunflower cooking oil from Ukraine and Russia. Combined impact of these will be upward inflation.

- India basket of crude was $111.9/barrel on March-2 about 49% higher than the price at beginning of year commodity prices particularly aluminum and nickel where Russia is an important producer are rising. RBU forecast in February for retail inflation 2022-23 to be 4.5 % will have to be rewarded due to changed environment.
- Potential private investment will be shelved. Higher inflation will push up nominal GDP which in Taru will result in tax collection exceeding budget targets.
- For FY 2022-23 nominal GDP is likely to be higher than the budget estimate of 11.1% growth. This will give GOI the space to exceed its FY 2022-23 forecast of a mere 4.6% nominal growth in budget expenditure, without jeopardizing debt sustainability.

**Relevant Thought**: Many markets work best with little or no outside interference. But others – especially those subject to big 'externalities' – need a helping hand. - Eric Maskin

**Estimate for 2022-23** (America Economist and 2007 Nobel Laureate)

**GDP:** Government. has estimated a normal GDP growth rate of 11.1% in 2022-23 9 i.e. real growth plus inflation)

**Expenditure:** Government. proposes to spend Rs. 39,44,909 cr in 2022023 which is an increase of 4.6% over the revise.

## Ukraine Returned MBBS Students (Date-05.03.2022)

- Ukraine returned Indian MBBS students have anxieties how to continue their interrupted education.
- Demands grow upon the Government. to intervene in this Relaxation of NMC (National Medical Commission) rule that blocks migration from one college to other should be expedited.
- 16 lakh students take NEET, some 8 Lakh quality and then only 90,000 are the seats . So 20,000 students had gone to Ukraine cannot have spare seats there.
- There is the issue of whether returnees who paid lower fees, should get discounts in Indian private colleges – a complicated question.

- For Indian students and for Indian health, there is need to expand medical education. New medical colleges with quality education, qualitative faculty, hospital linkages and other high quality resources should be approved and established.
- There is good news on 4th March that NMC allows Ukraine-returned Indian MBBS students to complete Internship in India.
- Even then, decades of official neglect would mean that Indian students will look for options abroad.

**Relevant Thought**: Waste of plenty is the resource of scarcity

**–Thomas Love Peacock**

## 5 States Assembly Election Getting Over (Dt: 07.03.2022)

- Voters are talking about desperation over present economic scenario. Pandemic and Russian invasion of Ukraine have aggravated the conditions. Fuel price after election will have sharp rise unless centre cuts taxes. Inflation is the new worry.
- UP with 20 crore population and 80 Lok Sabha seats is most important in politics. As per Niti Aayog, nearly 38% of the state's populations are languished in "multidimensional" poverty.
- UP produces 16 lakh graduates, postgraduates and diplomats every year. The clamour among youngsters preparing competitive and skilled employment is rising.
- Punjab has waived off electricity and water dues Goa's loss of mining revenues is a challenge. Uttarakhand's frustration at unrealized tourism potential is the challenge to preserve both ecology and development. After 20 years of stable Government Manipur is the turn its back on AFSPA during next Government like Tripura.
- In these elections, cast census, Hindu-Muslim divides, populist handouts, welfarism and unlocking Government jobs are the dominant rhetoric's. Needs of the private sector for jobs, growth and wealth found scarce mention.

**Relevant Thought:** If you present good government, then elections look after themselves.

**– Jay Weatherill**

## Sharp Increase In Oil Fuel Price (Dt: 09.03.2022)

- Price of Indian basket of crude reached $ 126/barrel. The pump prices of petrol and diesel may now have sharp increase. But this should be avoided by GOI by making the increase gradual.
- At this stage any sharp oil price increase will lead to a demand shock and undo some last year's economic recovery. GOI should absorb some of the uncovered costs of oil refiners now. This will help avoid a demand shock while protecting the companies.
- GOI should cut central fuel taxes. Central duties on a litre of petrol in 2014 were Rs. 9.50. Currently, they are about Rs. 27.90 per litre. Reduction in fuel tax revenue will be offset by a likely increase in tax collections – as an increase in inflation will help GOI overshoot its target of 9.6% growth in tax revenue in 2022-23.
- Crowding in private investments in increasing public spending may take longer than expected. Given that economic uncertainty coupled with higher inflation will act as a drag on private consumptions. Revenue spending should not be contradictory in inflation adjusted terms.

**Relevant Thought:** Since imports exceeds exports, largely because of commodity imports net contribution of trade to domestic demand is negative.

**– Ashima Goyal**

## Bihar Alcohol Ban Impact (Dt: 10.03.2022)

- Ill-advised 2016 Bihar Prohibition and Excise Act creates trouble for administration as thousands has been arrested for drinking and then jailed i.e., 3.8 lakh cases, 4 lakh arrests under law 20,000 bail applications pending disposal in Patna HC and trial courts.
- On 8 March 2022 SC threatened to release all accused persons on bail. CJI criticized the laws design, than a chastened Bihar cabinet approved amendments that will let of first time drinkers with a reasonable penalty and will confiscate suppliers property. These changes may not solve the problem.

- As the original 2016 Act punished drinkers with 5-7 years jail terms and Rs.1-10lakh fines facing flack a 2018 amendment-imposed fines not less than Rs.50,000 or 3 months imprisonment for first time offenders and jail terms of 1.5 years and fine upto Rs.1 lakh for report offenders.
- Bihar's annual per capital income is Rs.46,000. If imprisonment is to be avoided, the new penalty should be lower. But if penalties are very small, disincentive against breaking. The laws will also be very small. That is the problem with prohibition-bad law.
- As confiscation of property of liquor suppliers; supply typically happens via gangs, not individuals. So, it is likely a frontman will get penalized while the big guys walk away.
- NCRB found 16lakh (25%) of 66lakh cognizable offences filled in 2020 were violations of covid social-distancing. Energy spent on these detracts from prosecuting pending heinous offences.

**Relevant Thought:** We implemented prohibition sincerely but failed as no such, law is prevailing in neighbouring states. I am not ashamed to admit that prohibition is impractical.

## Five States March 10 Poll Verdict (Dt: 11.03.2022)

- Incumbent BJP beat history in UP and Uttarakhand and won. In Manipur and Goa, BJP improved its tallies and won. In Punjab voters gained massive mandate rejecting so-called big names. Many stars lost their seats, Nehru-Gandhi brand faded fast across states, see the irrelevance of Mayavati in UP failure of Akhilesh Yadav, unable to extend his SP's social base. Yogi Adityanath is now a worthy politician with potential of transcending state boundaries. Arvind Kejriwal is now in opposition leader with best potential to take fight to BJP.
- Narendra-Modi, the brightest star of this show, whose popular appeal is most important reason of BJP spectacular win in UP, Uttarakhand, Manipur and Goa. Kejriwal earned trust on welfare delivery and will replace congress as main challenger in Hindi-heartland.

- Congress is a lesson for other family-led parties as in SP. If a family party does not deliver and you have no culture of encouraging new talents, you can't imagine a future. Today's BJP is formidable only because in 2014, it made Modi its national face against many then opposition national leaders. Our growth and job requirement will be reached via smart policies of sustainable political economic formula.

**Relevant Thought:** The problem with socialism is that you eventually run out of other people' money.

**-Marget Thacher**

## Congress Failing Under Gandhis (Dt: 12.03.2022)

- In the five states poll results, death of congress is clearly visible. But the party even with all its debacles, has around 700 MLAs nationally, compared to BJP's 1300 plus. This shows congress has the footprint. It does not have a political identity or leaders to make the presence.
- Nehru-Gandhis have entirely lost their power to pull in votes. But some of congress cadre still value the family. It may be because if Nehru-Gandhis no longer lead congress, it may disintegrate. The family's biggest contribution currently is probably being the glue that holds together prone to savage.
- So, either Nehru-Gandhis lead congress to likely further humiliations or minus them congress will splinter. Even if a non-Nehru-Gandhi were to emerge and the party does not implode/collapse; it is unlikely that he or she will be able to command respect or loyalty from congress state leaders. G-23 offers no hope at all as must members of that group are not relevant electorally in meaningful sense.
- Some view congress to have hard secularism against BJP's 'Hindutva'. But India's political system right now is defined by versions of emotive 'Hindu-ness' and clever politician like Arvind Kejriwal have recognised this. Opposing this will have divisiveness without annoying the majority.

- Everyone is cautious about reforms. BJP and AAP has stolen congress's welfarist clothes. Congress has no governance left. It carries the baggage of corruption with it.

**Relevant Thought:** I have taken my time. I have thought about it; I havc consulted, and I have decided that we are going to create a new political movement.

**-Emanuel Macron**

## Accidental Lunch of IAF Brahmos (Dt: 14.03.2022)

- Accidental launch of an IAF Brahmos supersonic cruise missile that landed 124 km inside Pakistan is an accident, which should not happen. The missile was inadvertently launched during a training and maintenance exercise.
- Either the mechanical and electronic locks were accidentally bypassed by operators during the training exercise or there was a serious technical malfunction. Both are extremely worrying.
- The operational command and control procedures must be reviewed. A technical glitch may create doubts over the weapon system, especially when India is now ready to export Brahmos to countries like Philippines, A court of enquiry has been ordered.
- Other important point is India and Pakistan do not have robust risk-reduction protocols or mechanism to deal with such mishaps. Both countries must look into now.
- In 1983, during cold war period Soviet Union reported the launch of intercontinental ballistic missiles form the US. Luckily, World War III was prevented because Soviet Officer Stanislav Petrov rightly judged the warning to be false due to malfunctioning detection system.
- It is high time, India and Pakistan work out protocols to prevent accident or false alarm.

**Relevant Thought:** War is the unfolding of miscalculations.

**- Barbara Tuchman**

## Lowest Interest On EPF (Dt: 15.03.2022)

- Trustees of EPF last week recommended interest of 8.1% on 2021-22 funds, the lowest since 1977-78, when a rate of 8% was notified.
- EPFO had 46.2 million contributing members by 2020-21. Its legal mandate covers 3 separate schemes of which EPF and Pension Scheme are most important. These 2 schemes are intertwined as PF deductions and employer's contribution are spread across them. Returns on EPF are linked to investment performance. But, the pension Scheme is hybrid – there is a partial Government guarantee built to it. Most accumulated funds are directed into debt instruments over Rs 14 lakh crore at the end of FY 21. About 50% of this is invested in GOI and state Government. debt. Interest rates have tended downwards over last 3 yrs and return on EPF followed suit. In 2020-21, the yield on debt investment was just 6.8%.
- How EPFO returns declare over 8%?
- Extra return comes from investment upto 15% of annual inflows to Fin-Instruments linked to equities. Inadequate Info: On what happens to this retirement saving scheme, which grows fast because of EPF's mandatory nature and GOI subsidies to formalize jobs. Publicly available data on EPFO;s investments is scanty. Hence lowering returns is a great concern when retail inflation is firming up. EPFO needs to be move transparent about details of its investments. Pension Scheme needs timely actuarial assessments as there is sovereign guarantee involved.

**Relevant Thought:** For many people, being asked to solve their own retirement savings problems is like being asked to build their own cars.

**– Richard Thaler**

## Hijab Judgment By Karnataka HC (Dt: 16.03.2022)

- Karnataka High Court gave judgment that Hijab is not an essential religious practice in Islam and declared that educational institutions enforcing a uniform is not violative of fundamental rights. State Government's order of Feb. 5, 2022 has not violated individual rights and collective of the community.

- By Hijab Bans whether religious freedom as guaranteed by Article 25 of the constitution was violated by institutions? Here the court rested its argument on the primacy of institutional norms and goals over a practice that is not deemed essential for ensuring religious freedom. The court observed that a critical purpose of school uniforms is to "promote harmony", and 'transcending religious or sectional diversities".

- The court said, young minds can't develop "so long as any propositions such as wearing of Hijab or Bhagwa are regarded as religiously sacrosanct and therefore, not open to question". Description of schools as "qualified public spaces", where certain sensible rules, if applied to everyone equally, can't be deemed as discriminatory to anyone. a school uniform is a universal requirement, and therefore not sectarian.

- On a broader point issue for greater import confront India's young such as: quality of education employability of students, employment opportunities and low women's workforce participation etc. should in these all

**Relevant Thought:** We should not give up and we should not allow the problem to defeat us.

**-APJ Abdul Kalam**

## India's Deal For Russian Oil (Dt: 17.03.2022)

- India is dealing with Russia for buying 3.5 million barrels of its crude at discounts. It has divided opinion in the West.

- Us indicated that without violating American sanctions against Russia, India may go ahead with the purchase.

- After all, despite Ukraine war, European nations are continuing to buy energy from Russia. For this the US did not go for a complete ban on Russian oil exports and chose instead to just bar Russian energy imports to US.

- In fact, the EU recently discussed new sanctions against Russian oil majors, but clarified to continue buying oil from them. Hence there is no ground to question India in case it goes ahead with Russian oil deal. Besides 3.5 million barrels is not big volume for India as its daily consumption is 4.5 million barrels and Russian oil only accounts 2% of total Indian imports. It is more as symbolic in nature and will be test case of Delhi-Moscow trade.

- Payment by rupee-rubble arrangement is under consideration since Russian banking is under sanction, payment would have to be routed through Indian banks not having business in West.
- Now due to sanctions there is impetus to review dollar as a reserve and primary currency of global trade. Saudi Arabia is talking to China for oil sales in Yuan. Riyadh recently rebuffed US to produce more oil for US ban on Russian imports. Thus, India is compelled to internationalise the rupee.

**Relevant Thought:** The essence of strategy is choosing what not to do.

– **Michael E Porter**

## Renewed Surge in Covid (Dt: 18.03.2022)

- Fresh covid rebound across Europe, East Asia and Australia are likely driven by Omicrons sub-variant, BA.2. GOI should have greater disease surveillance and genomic sequencing.
- After Dec-Jan 2022, the new wave has spread in weeks in UK, Germany and Australia. India's covid trajectory is not alarming at present as 2500 infections detected on 16 March and the weekly positively rate is a low 0.4%.
- Plentiful booster doses were admitted in these countries, such as 63% in South Korea, 57% UK, 57% Germany, 48% Australia whereas India 1.4% doses only.
- GOI decision to remove 'Comorbidity' precondition for 60+ age group to avail precautionary doses is welcome. Allowing over 45 age any adult with comorbidities to avail booster dose is next logical step.
- Adults received 2nd doses over 6 months. Waning of immunity amid infection surges abroad and resumption of normal international air travel from 27 March are uncomfortable prospects.

- CMC Vellore's mix-match study of Covaxin administered to 2 doses of Covishield as booster is under whelming / disappointing.
- Bhart Biotech's intranasal vaccine SII's Covovax and Biological E's Corbevax will offer greater clarity.
- GOI should reveal timeline for the booster program.

**Relevant Thought:** It history repeats itself, and the unexpected always happens how incapable must Man be of learning from experience.

**– George Benard Shaw**

## Promoting English (Global) and Local Language (Dt: 21.03.2022)

- Both English the global language and Indian Local Languages are indispensable for India.
- 'English' opens the door to rapidly expanding universe of knowledge, which is a global product.
- English medium enrolment is growing fast from the UDISE Report of 2019-20 data on 265 million school children. About 26% of children are English medium school, next 42% in Hindi medium. The trend shows English medium is set to be dominant in future.
- Over a 5-year period Haryana and Telangana witnessed the sharpest increase of children enrolled in English medium school. At least 7 states have already seen English medium school's enrolment exceed the medium of instruction in the local language.
- National Education policy 2020 observed that Indian languages have suffered inadequacy of learning materials, shortage of skilled instructors. Hence, English Medium is driven by aspiration and offers Indian children to tap vast pool of knowledge and easily fits into global commerce. Many countries like Japan and China are promoting English to equip their students to thrive in a knowledge economy.
- Government should accept shortcoming of Indian language in pedagogical material. A lot more research should be done by GOI. English medium instruction is an advantage to needs to be built on.

**Relevant Thought:** I can't understand how there can be any version of our constitution in any Indian language without our having to coin new words.

**-KM Manshi**

## Politics for EVS in India (Dt: 22.03.2022)

- Suzuki motor corporation on date 19.3.22 signed as MOV with Gujrat to invest about Rs10,440 crore over year period to manufacture electric vehicles (EVs) and related batteries. Almost 70% of the investment will be spent in battery manufacturing.
- International combustion engine ICE being replaced by EVs is a great shift globally in the backdrop of anxiety over climate change.
- In 2020, electric cars were 4.6% of total car sale globally. By 2030 EU aims to ensure 60% of new sales comprise EVs. India is moving with a goal of 30% of new vehicle sale by 2030 are EVs. Nit Aayog estimates investment of Rs. 19.7lakh crore over the next 8 years.
- There has been policy action by both GOI and states for these goals. There are demand side incentives for potential customers. Equally are the supply side measures to encourage investment and manufacturing.
- Batteries may be 40% of total value. Japan, South Korea and China dominate this segment. China is measure in lithium-ion cell supply. India should have best possible supply side incentive through GOI's and states' the Production-linked Incentive Scheme.
- EVs present India a great opportunity. To capitalize on it, our policies need be move outward looking.

  **Rely Thought:** Globally, firms that that both import and export compromise 15% of all firms but they capture 80% of total trade.

  -GVC Report 2021-(Global value chain are evolving for technological development as Robotics Big Data and IOT, AI etc.)

## Common University Entrance Test (CUET) (Dt: 23.03.2022)

- In education reform CUET is to extend to all central universities and affiliated colleges. Undergraduate admissions will be on the basis of students' CUET scores from coming session. It was launched in 2010, but National Education Policy 2020 and pandemic firmed up the resolve around it. Admissions of students would now be an efficient process.
- It will a radical departure from admission exclusively by board exam marks and these marks will have zero weightage UGC notice date 21.03.2022 said CUET UG from 2022-23 session in all UGC funded Central Universities will be conducted in 13 languages.
- Many class XII feel the rules keep getting changed on them randomly and stressfully. CUET applications will open in 1st week of April with the test taking place in 1st week July. The time window adjusting the new entrance system is very narrow.
- CUET is expected to be more credible and fairer. Also, instead of hundreds of universities own entrance modules the new system will be more efficient in entire education system. Now 45 Central Universities are mandated for CUET. For state, private and deemed universities this is optional.
- CUET had wide choice of subjects but before they make a choice, colleges have to finalize which subjects are required for which courses. Finally, CUET is aiming to provide fairer access to quality education, it does not change the quantity.

  **Relevant Thought:** Education is what remains after one has forgotten what one has learned in school.

  **-Albert Einstein**

## India's Diplomatic Leverage with Russia (Dt: 24.03.2022)

- Russia relies hugely on exports of oil and arms. India trades with Russia mainly by arms and crude oil primarily from West Asia.

- Due to Western sanctions Russia's 8 million barrels/day exports of oil and petroleum products (world's largest) way come down to 5 million barrels/day. Therefore Russia needs arms exports even more.
- During 2017-21, Russia was world's 2[nd] largest arms exporter behind the US with market share of 19%. Its largest customer was India, the recipient of 28% Russian arms exports.
- During 2012-16, Russia had a global market share of 24% which fell by 5% (i.e. 19%) mainly because India began to diversity its sources. In 2017-21, India and Saudi Arabia were the largest arms importers in the world.
- Trade ties are harder to shift than diplomatic positions. If India needs Russian ammunitions, it is also true that Russia needs India to buy them more than before given the economic hit it is facing. India has diplomatic Leverage against Russia, which should be used.

**Relevant Thought:** Although our intellect always longs for clarity and certainty, our nature often finds certainty fascinating.

**-Carl Von Clausewitz**

## Lessons from India's Covid Response (Dt: 25.03.2022)

- Lessons must be learnt from India's major success and big failures in Covid response.
- Disaster Management Act invoked by GOI 2 years ago for Covid response will not be used beginning from April as the level of threat has diminished. There were 43 million infections and around 5.2 lakh deaths. Both are likely underestimated as proxy data by sera survey.
- With hindsight, the intensity and duration of first nationwide lockdown was excessive (after suffering crucial in first 15 months). A sudden shutdown led to both human suffering and severe economic dislocation. India was unprepared for Delta wave between April and June, 2021.
- Success story has been India's vaccination drive, which has now crossed 1.82 billion doses. By Feb 8, about 73% aged 15 and above had been administered 2 doses.

- Its cost Rs. 27,945 crore is less than 1% of total expenses in 2021-22 Union Budget. Vaccines would have been pre-ordered in larger quantities in 2020 as Serum Institute had capacity.
- India lagged in follow-up research on mix-and-match doses as well as boosters. We relied on studies done overseas.
- Two year's takeaways are (a) Data collection to improve and be shared (b) should upgrade epidemiological science and research (c) Economic disruption must be little and (d) India needs sound public health architecture.

**Relevant Thought:** We all want to move on from the pandemic. But no matter how much we wish it away, this pandemic is not over.

**– Tedros Adhanom Ghebreyesus**

## India Russia Stance On National Interest (Dt: 26.03.2022)

- India's repeated abstentions in UN resolutions will answer whether cost of continued neutrality on Russia's aggression is outweighing benefits purely by national interest calculations.
- National interest means Russian supply of arms to India. This dependence works both ways. As largest buyer of Russian arms, New Delhi too has leverage over Russia. It is unlikely that Russia will retaliate by making arms supply difficult. After all, despite EU rations sanctioning Russia and actively aiding Ukraine. They continue buying Russian energy and Russia is happy to supply it. Russia needs arms exports even more for balancing cost of sanctions on its economy. This bargain shall have ot be used by India diplomatically.
- The geopolitical implications concern India by 2 points (i) If Russian plan changes to offensive in awful ways to crush Ukraine, will India lake a cautious position and will sit out another UN resolution? (ii) However, the Ukraine invasion ends, if Putin is increasingly shunned by most of democratic world, what might be the implications for India as geopolitical stances harden all around?
- Keeping eye on Russia, USA and China, India may change its mind.

**Relevant Thought:** Ukraine is a geopolitical pivot because its very existence as an independent country helps to transform Russia.

**-Zbigniew Brzezinskz**

## Households Savings In Equities (Dt: 28.03.2022)

- In 2021-22FPIs (foreign Portfolio Investors) have been net sellers of equity. The net outflow was huge $ 18.5 billion. In same period, BSE Sensex have risen 10% equity prices struggling off such huge FPI outflow, a watershed. It indicates the rise of domestic investors growing of savings in financial assets.
- Households are India's main savings. Traditionally, they used to allocate greater share in physical assets and a smaller percentage to financial avenue as bank deposits. Allocation to physical assets declined and were rerouted to financial savings. Year 2020-21 was a milestone, net financial savings exceeded physical assets of Rs. 43.9 lakh crore household saving, and 52.4% is net financial savings. Lockdown of FY 21 affected this.
- Household savings flow into equities through EPF, NPS, Mutual Funds, Insurance and direct investments. In 2021-22, Rs. 1.12 lakh crore was raised compared to Rs. 43,921 core 5 years back. NSDL data showed 25.3 million active demat accounts of residents at end of February; up 68% over a 5-year period. Jefferies estimated that 4.8% of the household balance sheet is in equities. Increase in financial savings and drop in physical assets will influence. Shift of household savings from bank deposits to equities, is a risk-return equation that investors should be aware of.

**Relevant Thought:** Risk comes from not knowing what you are doing.

**–Warren Buffett**

## Parliamentary Committee Recruiting IAS (Dt: 29.03.2022)

- Parliamentary Standing Committee report says vacancies in IAS affect both central and State governments.

- GOI had amended service rule to ensure more officers for central deputation by making states comment immaterial. GOI was unhappy that officers an central deputation reserve had reduced by 27%. Parliamentary committee has revealed that over 1500 sanctioned IAS officer posts (22%) at state level are lying vacant.
- This is in spite of conferring IAS on state civil service officers or temporary appointment of other central or state cadre officers to posts reserved for IAS. The committee remarked that a panel constituted to increase the intake to fill sanctioned posts. But bureaucracy is battling a crisis of quality along with quantity.
- GOI initiatives like Mission Karma yogi and Capacity Building Commission must lead to a performance management system that can reward the best and the brightest. Currently talented officers are sandwiched between mediocrity and officer scarcity are heavily overworked.
- Unlike pyramidal hierarchies, IAS and IPS have "cylindrical" structures because of assured promotions. Lateral entrants face the outsider tag despite the grassroots experience they may possess.
- Officers in non-essential departments, commissions, corporations and possess should be reviewed to cut governance flab.

**Relevant Thought:** If you have a reputation as a big stiff bureaucracy, you are stuck.

**– Jack Welch**

## India's Crime-fighting Laws (Dt: 30.03.2022)

- Criminal Procedure (Identification) Bill authorization collection, storage, analysis of biological samples, biometrics, and physical measurements of convicts, arrested persons and persons in preventive detention has bad drafting. This bill seeks to replace "The Identification of Prisoners Act, 1920: but restricts itself to finger/foot prints of arrested persons and their storage only for convicted persons, needed an upgrade. Even FBI (Federal Bureau of Investigation) have moved on to advanced biometrics and that has crime-fighting uses.

- Arrested persons of less than 7 years imprisonment or not facing sexual crimes against women or children can refuse to give samples, but actual policing in India rarely gives such leeway to ordinary citizens to withhold their consent. Process to mandate police officers to secure a magistrate's order to collect samples should be a better legislative design.
- Persons in preventive detention even before committing any criminality are held on apprehension with convicts and those arrested for major offences. State Governments use police to hound opponents. Bill lakhs checks and balances to prevent abuse by police to harass or implicate innocent persons, on unauthorized access to stored data thro hacking and on misuse of data by police.
- Narew-analysis, prone-to-abuse facial recognition, allow for any other examination, other tests etc. need reformation by correct wordings
- India has few forensic science lab, Governments should have more forensic facilities.

**Relevant Thought:** It is not possible to make a bad law. If it is bad, it is not a law.

**– Carrie Nation**

**(American activist, member of temperance movement used a hatchet to demolish barrooms, supporter of women's suffrage women's rights)**

## Liberal Compensation for Accident Victims (Dt: 31.03.2022)

- SC counseled judges to take liberal view in awarding compensation to those grappling with 100% disabilities. SC awarded Rs. 1 crore to a 17 year boy left bed ridden after 2010 accident. But 12 yrs have lapsed in dispute with the insurer to reach closure.
- In 2020, about 1.30 lakh deaths in Road accident, has happened whereas 3.75 lakh accidental deaths happened; caused by fires, electrocution, drowning, structural collapse factory accidents etc.
- Legal architecture and infrastructure require upgrades.

- In new rules the, detail police investigation of all accident is mandatory form April 1, 2022 with a 90-day timeline. The police is expected to guide MACTs (Motor Accident Claim Tribunals). But MACTs are backlogged with 9 lakh petitions, a third pending over 3 years.
- Fixing liability on public and private authorities can achieve deterrence against negligent conduct. SC's paltry Rs. 750 crore award to Bhopal gas tragedy victims from Union Carbide was a missed opportunity to settle the law. Chantel's Paradise collapse in NCR and Vaishno Devi stampede must be prosecuted for fixing civil liabilities compensating victims and building laws.
- Consumer Protection Act 2019 allowed to approach consumer forums for compensation has made a tepid start.

**Relevant Thought:** A society that has more justice is a society that needs less charity.

**-Ralph Nader**

## AFSPA Curtailed In 3 NE States (Dt: 01.04.2022)

- GOI has decided to reduce the Area under AFSPA in the states of Assam, Manipur and Nagaland. The law gives armed forces extraordinary powers to search arrest and shoot on suspicion has been 'commended by' civil society for undermining democratic rights. AFSPA continues in NE due to violent insurgency. Killing of 14 people by security forces in Nagaland last year, intensifies the demand of repeal of AFSPA throughout NE.
- Centre has decided to remove 'Disturbed Area' tag for operation of AFSPA from 23 completely and partially from other in Assam. In Manipur, AFSPA will not apply to 15 police station areas of 6 districts In Nagaland 15 police stations across 7 districts will be exempted. All these changes are respective from1/4/22. Relatively small areas are being exempted in Manipur and Nagaland.
- Around 7000 militants in NE have surrendered, plus 2020 Bodo Accord, 2021 Karbi-Anglong pact have addressed the root causes of regional insurgencies. Normalisation in NE and facilitating economic

development is best antidote to insurgencies. Centre should continue the work to repeal AFSPA across all NE.

**Rely Thought:** A reputation once broken may possibly be repaired, but he world will always keep their eye on the spot where the crack was.

**-Joseph Hall**

## Relaxed Covid Restriction (Dt: 02.04.2022)

- Covid related restrictions have been largely relaxed in India's states, Maharashtra, Delhi and Telengana. Fines have been removed on de-masking in public places.
- Watering down vaccination masking in public are unwise decisions; as there is no clear signal that the threat of transmission has gone. It also ignores the available research by epidemiologists on the likely trajectory of the pandemic.
- WHO has laid out 3 scenarios of pandemic in 2022 (i) Virus will continue to evolve (ii) The severity will diminish (iii) A more virulent variant can emerge, which can undermine the efficiency of vaccination.
- Currently in Germany, 3062 cases per million records daily, compared to barely 1 case of India. This has happened despite Germany fully vaccinating 75% of population and providing boosters for 58 of every 100 people. In India 60% fully vaccinated and less than 2 for every 100 been boosted.
- India needs to implement masking mandates and supplements on expanding vaccination coverage. India did well to provide 1.84 billion cumulative, doses but states have 156 million doses lying unutilized. ICMR chief has said, everyone needs the booster. Centre and state must get on.

**Relevant Thought:** We can prevent transmission with masks, distancing, hand hygiene and ventilation

**.-Tedros Adhanom Ghebreyesus**

## Pakistan Politics (Dt: 04.04.2022)

- Imran Khan's National Assembly dissolution and calling for polls could not succeed. Pakistan's Supreme Court decision can dramatically change the dynamics.
- The Army Generals will have their own calculations.
- Imran has shown ability to mobilize street protests and may not follow the decision of the court and the army. He has already become the first Pak-PM to out-maneuver an army backed de facto coup.
- The hearing of SC was adjourned today will resume tomorrow (Tuesday) and is expected to determine whether no-confidence motion can take place.
- Imran has claimed that opposition acting in concert with US to oust him. He has proposed Farmer Chief Jushio Gulzar Ahmad for office of caretaker PM.
- Whoever may be PM, but 2 things won't change: (i) Terror will continue as Pak policy against India, (ii) Pak's economic crisis will deepen. Consumer price inflation is over 12%, Pak rupee lost 50% value in 5 years and may go in bankrupt and dept burdened.
- With QUAD becoming more cohesive and China's big focus on Indo-Pacific and its rivalry with US; Utility of Pakistan as India-baiter may be less valued.

**Rely Thought:** Chaos was the law of nature; order was the dream of man.

**-Henry Adans**

## Challenges for Banking (Dt: 05.04.2022)

- Merger of HDFC and HDFC Bank will create private sector banking large and powerful. It will result a balance sheet of Rs.18lakh crore with emphasis on mortgages and retail loans.
- Indian banking and speedy growth between year 2000 to 2010 Bank credits as propagation of GDP increased from 24% to 50%. In the next decade the credit to GDP ratio stagnated at 50%. The slow process of first accountants for bad loans and then clean up were the

reasons for this last decade. To aid the process, IBC (Insolvency and Bankruptcy Code) was introduced in 2016 as a far-reaching measure.

- Three trends are observed: (i) PSU banks were worse hit by NPA and have lost market share over last decade. (ii) Risk aversion of NPA's caused by exposure during pandemic. Industry and service sector trailed in loan recovery whereas agriculture and retail segments led the recovery. (iii) Level of gross NPA's to total advances has trended downwards to 6.9% at the end of Sep,2021.
- Before Omicron and Ukraine conflict, RBI stated that NPA may rise to 8.1% by Sep,2022.
- India's banking sector remains vulnerable. Despite IBC and private asset reconstruction companies; a state backed Bad Bank had to be created last year.
- There is need to upgrade skills in upper echelon of banking; and privatization of PSU banks.

**Relevant Thought:** There is no other major country which imposes what is called burden of financial repression, on this scale and intensity.

**-VV Reddy, 2018**

## Nuclear Energy for Future (Dt: 06.04.2022)

- Energy sector contributes largely to global warming. India's pledge to have zero carbon emission by 2070 requires overhaul of both logistics and electricity sectors to reduce reliance on fossil fuels.
- Within reliable, solar energy won't be enough to meet the targets. Anil Kakodkar former Chairman of Atomic Energy Commission has started that India can't meet its net zero commitment with nuclear power. Today India's nuclear power contributes mere 3% of total electricity generated and has a capacity of 6780MW.
- After India-US civil nuclear deal in 2008, progress has been disappointing and opened a pathway to stable supply of Uranium from Kazakhstan and Canada. The design of bill of civil liability for nuclear damage killed the participation of Western firms. India's main partner today is Russia. It is challenging to depend on just Russians.

- Recent progress on creating SMRs (Small Modular Reactors) upto 300 MW will make rapid state-up.

**Relevant Thought:** Nuclear Power is well suited to decarbonizing both electricity and heat production, and it can also produce low carbon hydroxide.

**-IAEA**

**Focus On Vaccination (Dt: 07.04.2022)**

- In some countries Covid has peculiar turns and new variant XE mutant has also surfaced. India should focus on complete vaccination. GOI must motivate the laggards in vaccination the North East (minus Assam) and Jharkhand. States like Bihar, Punjab, and Maharashtra and Tamil Nadu trail significantly in double-dose vaccination. Double dosed in North East are 58% and in Jharkhand 57% nearly 20crore in 15+ age population are yet to get both doses.
- In double dosed 60+ citizens, 1.23crore out of 11.5crore have taken boosters. In remote places without hospital facilities; the risk of serious illness has to be conveyed and taken care. NIV started that all adults need boosters, NTAGI must take immediate decision.
- CMC, Vellore declared that a Covishield dose after 2 Covaxin doses is safe with 6 time rise in antibodies. SII can accelerate production of Covishield for this. SII Covovax was approved for 12+ age group, but bulk order is not yet placed for this vaccine. In UK mix-match trials as a booster; Covovax was administered following 2 doses of Astra Zeneca/Covishield which should high antibody and neutralizing response. Covovax has dual utility for child and booster vaccination.
- Government can make personal medicines like flu shots to allow all adults double dosed over 6 months ago to take booster. On India's vaccination program more clarity will be appreciated.

**Relevant Thought:** Nothing happens quit by chance. It is a question of accretion of information and experience.

**-Jonas Sahl**

## CAG's UIDAI Audit (Dt: 08.04.2022)

- Around 1.3billion residents including 99.9% of adults have been assigned Aadhar. It is single most important database in India and is de facto yardstick for all other databases.
- CAG presented this week its performance audit of Aadhar's regulator, Unique Identification Authority of India (UIDAI). The audit covered its mature phase from 2014 to 2019. By this time, it had generated about 800 million Aadhar numbers. CAG's audit pot rays an unsatisfactory picture of the systems and processes in UIDAI. The main result is the laxity in the organization which is worrying for the laxity in the organization which is worrying for the risk.
- UIDAI operates Aadhar through a layer of subcontractors. When an applicant's biometrics are uploaded to central Identities Data Repository, it is executed by a 3rd layer of subcontractors. Similar system is in place when financial intermediary seeks to authenticate the identity of a customer by using Aadhar database. UIDAI is unable to identify the cause for authentication failures; for which it forces people to pay to update their biometrics. In 2018-19 there were 30 million biometric updates out of which 73% were voluntary updates. CAG observed they were mostly on account of authentication failures.

**Relevant Thought:** You can delegate authority but you cannot delegate responsibility,

**-Byron Dorian**

## Boosters needed at Government Vax centers (Dt: 09.04.2022)

- GOI declared adults above 18 yrs who received their 2nd doses over 9 months should get 'precaution doses' at private vax centers.
- a booster is both protection and peace of mind with dilution of mask mandates. Uncontrolled European and east Asian have surges are the warnings. Indian adults with covnorbidities are catching adults younger. Boosters should be extended to Government vax centers with greater reach.

- single-shot booster in vaccine market is cheaper. Hence GOI should make bulk purchases at even lower prices requiring not even 0.5% of this year's budgetary outlay. Economic and health setback of virus rebound would hit GDP harder.
- Different booster increases protection for those double dosed with viral vector and inactivated vaccine Covaxin - Covishield trials on boosting with biological E's Corbevax and Bharat biotech's intranasal vaccine went ahead only by January and with Covovax is march. CMC, Vellore study should enable Covaxin recipients to get Covishield booster. using Covovax to boost Covishield recipients are available. A potential mRNA vaccine, mix and match boosters are the way to go.

**Relevant thought-** some of our important choices have as timeline. if we delay a decision, the opportunity is gone forever. – James E Faust

## Exit of Pak PM Imran Khan (Dt: 11.04.2022)

- Imran Khan the first PM of Pakistan lost no trust vote after the National Assy adjured multiple times. No-confidence motion was taken up by the ruling of Pakistan Supreme Court.
- Imaran never had numbers. Intra-party dissensions, parties that are traditionally ro-military had long sealed his fate. The final no trust vote-174 out of 342 voted in favour of the motion.
- Imran is the first creation and victim of Pakistan's 'Hybrid Regime', where the Pakistan army remains at the centre of power but wraps itself with cover of institutional propriety.
- The model is a weak PM being brought to power by the military and then made to dance to Palters tune. Imran's time saw, media heavily censored, civil rights curbed with extremist outfits activists hounded and systemic corruption n military-ISI complex.
- Pakistan is with highest debt burden, lowest level of currency ever, the 3rd highest level of inflation in the world and relations with India is quite poor.

- Pak Parliament meets today to elect new PM with leader of opposition Shehbaz Sharif. It would signify the continuation of dynastic rule, but hybrid rule is successful for the generals.

**Relevant Thought:** History will remember Imran Khan as a sham character who violated the constitution again and again. Is his ego bigger than the whole country?

**– Shehbaz Sharif**

## 'Long Covid' Efforts (Dt: 12.04.2022)

- 'Long Covid' – is a spectrum of long term health damaging condition that affect many who recover from Covid and even, those who were asymptomatic.
- US will prepare in 4 months an exhaustive public report on 'Long Covid' with plans to support financial and healthcare needs of patients and co-ordinate national research. India must begin such efforts.
- A comprehensive national study can document the full spectrum of ailments form life-threatening blood clots to fatigue, breath lessens, anxiety attacks, muscular pain, brain fog etc. and estimate the no of afflicted, their healthcare and financial needs, initiate sharing of medical-now how between doctors and kick-off research.
- In UK, 1.7 million people, 3% of entire population reported Long Covid symptoms last month; 45% had the infection over a year ago. In India, a Max hospital survey of 990 Covid positive persons found around 10% of them having Long Covid symptom a year later. Even 1% of India's adult have Long Covid, afflicted will be 10 million.
- National clinical Registry to drack Covid patients began in Sep 2020 but have not released enough data to establish India's 'Long Covid' challenge. To collaborate on the long covid by deviate research across India is GOI's great challenge.

**Relevant Thought:** People are still getting Covid right now and people are starting to get symptoms of 'Long Covid' right now. It is not over.

**– Lindsey Port**

## Virtual Meeting of PM India and President US (Dt: 13.04.2022)

- Indian PM Narendra Modi an US President Joe Biden had virtual meeting on 11.04.2022 (Monday)
- While US insists that it is not India's interest to increase energy imports from Russia; India has stuck to its strategic autonomy of divorcing the politics around the conflict.
- Modi raised the Bucha Killings and condemn them without blaming any side.
- India's abstention on the UNGA vote to expel Russia from UNHRC has favoured the US resolution. India has dispatched humanitarian aid to Ukraine and prepares to do more on Kyiv's request.
- India's tie with Russia is akin to Europe's energy dependence on Russia despite several EU nations promising a drawdown.
- India and US will have to work together, as Russia will be China's junior partner for foreseeable future. China is biggest threat to international order and India's territorial sovereignty. China's diplomatic support for Russia at UN will be to use Russia fox its agenda in India-Pacific after Ukraine crisis is over.
- US secy of state, Blinken - crucially said that US had not made a determination to apply CAATSA sanctions on India for purchase of Russian arms.
- The 2 sides have now signed a bilateral space situational awareness arrangement and are deepening co-operation in cyberspace. Thus, world's 2 largest democracies ought to be natural partners in upholding the global order.

**Relevant Thought:** It is important that democracies stand together and speak with one voice to defend the values that we share.

**– Antony Blinken**

## Bulldozing Alleged House, Shops (Dt: 14.04.2022)

- MP Government's demolition of houses and shops of alleged rioters is a violation of due process and procedure. Government claims it was acting against those rioters squatting on Government land.
- But this act mandates Dist. Magistrate or officers to first approach a Claim Tribunal. Even demolition for encirclement requires notice period.
- Inversion of due process and procedure by razing houses/shops of alleged suspects also victimizes entire families, who may have nothing to do with riots. Meanwhile accountability of police and admin in preventing riots goes unmentioned.
- Anyone's life, livelihood and property are at risk when arbitrariness becomes the norm
- US secretary of State Antony Blinken's remarks on the US monitoring "rise in human rights abuses by some Government, police and prison officials" are an indication that world attention on due process in India is not going to fade away.

**Relevant Thought:** Design of purely arbitrary nature cannot be expected to last long. – Kenzo Tange

## Excess Deaths of 7th May Linked with Coved. (Dt: 15.04.2022)

- Global excess mortality of Covid is 14.9 million more than twice reported deaths.
- In India WHO has estimated excess mortality to be 4.7 million almost 10 times the reported deaths. GOI disagrees with methodology of WHO's statistical model. Even developed western countries did not fare well when excess mortality is adjusted according to population.
- India's statistical system needs much improvement Timely reliable data including CRS and SRS records will help in policy making.
- India's household consumptions data which is basis of statistical estimates has not been updated in a decade.
- India's data collection exercise has to improve.

**Relevant Thought:** Nothing should be taken for granted even if everybody believes it.

**-Yuval Nooh Harari**

## Strategic Understanding of China (Dt: 16.04.2022)

- The Indian Army are trying to address capability voids in Mandarin and boost specialization on Chinese issues.
- Mandarin training for soldiers, both within the force and through MOUs with universities offering Chinese language courses.
- India's defence and strategic establishments need decoding China.
- This is what the US has done over decades.
- It would be helpful to boost Mandarin education and China studies co-operation with Taiwan, as Taiwan knows China best.
- Thus, GOI must look it having more Taiwan Education Centres in Indian Universities and even fostering Mandarin language cooperation between Indian armed forces and Taiwanese Universities.

**Relevant Thought:** If you know the enemy and know yourself, you need not fear the result of a hundred battles.

**– Sun Tzu**

## Covid Cases In Delhi-NCR Warning (Dt: 18.04.2022)

- Rise of Covid cases in Delhi – NCR cities in Haryana and UP is warning that Covid is not over.
- Only 59 Covid hospitalizations in Delhi was until Saturday, but transmissibility of virus remains. Strategies like genomic sequencing, testing masking vaccination and sero-surveys are highly relevant.
- Global spread of the XE sub variant believed to be more transmissible than parent omicron strain. There should be prompt genomic sequencing of all positive samples.

- Home testing kits, comparatively mild Covid symptoms since rise of Omicron explain the low demand for tests nationally, but Governments can offset this by random testing in public places. A national serosurvey is long overdue which would give clarity on antibody prevalence in the general population.
- Relaxation of mask by Maharashtra and Delhi after 3rd wave was hugely premature, must be enforced again.
- India has slow progress on administering booster doses and also child vaccination henceforth should stay masked. Just 1.5 lakh precaution doses have been administered a week into booster for 18-59 age group. Twenty crore doses are lying unused with states. Reducing gap for booster from 9 months to 6 months is absolutely essential.
- Vaccination for 12 – 14 year group is slow complacency should be avoided by Government.

**Relevant Thought:** One is not exposed to danger who even when in safety is always on their guard.

– **Publilius Syrus**

## Ukraine War's Economic Fallout (Dt: 19.04.2022)

- Russia-Ukraine war has been longer than expected. The economic fallout into global economy has 3 channels. It has pushed up fuel prices, other commodity prices and logistic costs. Finally it weakens the global demand.
- Impact on India is unlikely to be severe. India has already faced core inflation excluding fuel and food which are sticky and higher than pre-covid period. RBI expects crude oil price average $100 a barrel which is over 30% of budget's assumption.
- Retail inflation is likely to hover around 6% RBI's upper limit of tolerance. RBI forecasts that economic growth in FY23 will be 7.2% lower than expected before the war and it has signaled a tighter monetary policy.
- Fiscal policy has to take over the role of boosting growth. In this India is not badly placed. Inflation has provided a boost to tax revenues. In

FY 22, GOI's tax revenue overshot the budget target to exceed Rs. 27 lakh crore. It grew twice as fast as nominal GDP and was 11.7% of GDP, a 2-decade high.

- GOI has space to slash fuel taxes and push ahead with its infrastructure spending and private investments.

**Relevant Thought:** Many of the economic challenges we face today stem from the neglect of supply side policies over the past decade or move.

**– Agustin Carstens**

## Permission for Processions (Dt: 20.04.2022)

- UP CM Adityanath's directives to state police is to have prior permissions for processions. Violent incidents were reported from Delhi, MP, Gujarat, Uttarakhand, Karnataka, Maharashtra and Andhra Pradesh. He has asked local cops to seek mandatory affidavits from procession organizers pledging to maintain peace and harmony and initiate dialogue with influential local citizens and religious leaders.
- Hanuman Jayanti at Jahangir Puri had riot and had no permission of police. The police further went on to bring in ammunitions to the procession, which aggravated the riot.
- Police forces in India are understaffed and overworked require better training and are in need to structural reforms. Truth about communal riots in India is that they are allowed to happen.
- Adityanath directs police to give permission to only traditional processions and reject new/unnecessary events.

**Relevant Thought:** The nose of a mob is its imagination. By this at any time, it can be quietly led.

**– Edgar Allan Poe**

## Southwest Monsoon Forecast for 2022 (Dt: 21.04.2022)

- Southwest monsoon is the mainstay of India's agricultural cycle and through it the entire economy. The forecast for 2022 of a normal monsoon is reassuring.
- This year's monsoon will be against 3 important developments. One is Russia-Ukraine war as the two countries jointly account for 30% of global wheat exports. Hence India which exported Rs. 74,491 crore of cereals in FY 21 will have an outsized impact on global market this year. Two, is escalating annual mean land surface temperature. Three, is water stress in northwest India, which will have impact on India agriculture.
- India's yields on most essential crops have improved over the last decade. Even though agricultural land has shrunk marginally, both cereal and vegetable output have increased.
- A good development is that the area under vegetables cultivation has increased by 10% over the last 5 years. Patient reform in logistic chain of this this environmentally sound trend should intensity.

**Relevant Thought:** Cereal crops will be ready for harvest in June. Whether farmers in Ukraine would be able to harvest them and deliver to the market is unclear.

**- Qu Dongyu**

## HC Sandwiched Between SC and Lower Courts (Dt: 22.04.2022)

- This week, Supreme Court found serious fault with HCs failing to uphold judicial discipline while pronouncing order. Rajasthan HC granted bail to a history sheeter accused of raping his minor niece without specifying reasons. An Allahabad HC ordered acquittal in a murder case, but gave the reasoned judgment 5 months later. In 2020 SC had spotted 9 months gap by Bombay HC and a 10 months gap by Delhi HC between the operative order and reasoned judgment.
- Rajasthan HC ignored the alleged rapist facing 20 criminal cases Allahabad HC's failure of a prompt reasoned order forced SC to order fresh heaving consequently, the case lodged in 2009, convicted

by trial court in 2012 and acquitted in 2019 must be heard by Allahabad HC.

- Propels like All India Judicial Services OR a national district judges recruitment examination has made no headway. Collegiums are struggling to attract good candidates to HCs amid power struggle with GOI and unrealistic low retirement age of 62.
- Despite absence of relevant data-many bad orders are going un appealed. Dysfunctionality in the rule of law affects all aspects or governance.

**Relevant Thought:** Judges are the weakest link in our system of justice and they are also the most protected.

– **Alan Derhowitz**

## Flagging Vaccine Demand Vs Free Boosters (Dt: 23.04.2022)

- CD SCO recommended EAU for Corbevax to 5-11 years old is important toward vaccinating school going Youngers.
- Covid case rise in Delhi is due to easing of Covid restrictions like masking. Hospitalization is low but sporadic infections increased among school goers. The 5-11 age group has 16 crore children. Besides Corbevax, Covaxin and inoculating this age group.
- Flagging vaccine demand is becoming a key problem. Vaccination for 12-14 and 15-17 age groups has slowed. Precaution doses are in slow off take among adults. Against 3.15 crore in 45-59 age group eligible for precaution dosed; just 2.13 lakh (0.6%) have taken the job. But of 3.25 crore in 60+ age group eligible for precaution doses with a 9 months gap, 42% of those eligible have been jabbed.
- Bihar and Delhi Governments decided to offer free precaution doses at Government vaccination centre to all adults.
- If the gap between 2nd and 3rd dose is reduced from 9 to 6 months, another 3 crore senior citizens would be eligible for precaution doses immediately. Compulsion masking and aggressive vaccination will help us live safety with Covid.

**Relevant Thought:** In skating over thin ice our safety is in our speed.

– **Ralph Walolo Emerson**

## Thermal Power Plants Grappling With Coal (Dt: 25.04.2022)

- India's Power sector suffers with over dues on cash trapped electricity distribution companies in the range of Rs 1 lakh crore by end Feb, 2022.
- To this perennial problem, new challenges of grappling with coal inventory have been added. GOI owned coal mining and logistics through railways reflect poorly on its official management.
- Tamil Nadu Government wrote to PM, India seeking adequate railway rake to transport enough coal
- On April 1, Central electricity regulator capped the price on energy exchange at Rs. 12 /Kwh to insulate from high rates. On April 21, 62% of plants were classified by CEA had 25% of normative stock. Many plants indicated inadequacy of railway rakes are reason for low stock.
- Weak distribution companies cannot import coal as Australia's price has more than doubled in a year to an average of $197 per ton in January-March.
- Distribution should be efficient in price system as overdue mounts. The primary logistics provider the railways need to step us.

**Relevant Thought:** Risk comes from not knowing what you are doing.

– **Warrren Buffett**

## GOI's Airport Monetization Plan (Dt: 26.04.2022)

- 25 Airports has been identified by AAI for action over next 3 years. 4 international airports are located in Tamil Nadu need to be studied with TN Government industry policy 2022-23 to realign incentives between 2 Governments.
- If the state transfers land free to GOI, the state should be entitled to a share of the gains. Revenue from infrastructure flows to Governments through 2 streams. One, through taxes which are split between GOI and states on the Finance commission recommendations and GST council's decision. Two, through subsequent monetization of an asset.

- Land is obtained by invoking legislation to forcibly take over private property to serve a public purpose. This extracts political cost that is born entirely by state Government. This risk can be mitigated by giving states a share of the upside arising out of monetization. There is need to re-evaluate mechanisms of awarding compensation when land is acquired.
- Amendments in laws allowing acquisition can help mitigate resistance to acquisition. The doctrine needs to be balanced with fairness.

**Relevant Thought:** To win without risk is to triumph without glory. - **Pierre Corneille**

## Food Inflation Predating Ukraine Conflict (Dt: 27.04.2022)

- In procurement exercise of GOI, Punjab and Haryana have tightened their agricultural markets. Crop arrivals in the market are tapering.
- FAO cereal and vegetable oil price hit high in March22.
- It explains why Punjab's links of agro-chain are holding back stocks. The upward agricultural prices, however predates the Ukraine conflict. Drought in North America and South America has constrained supply of grains and soyabean. India's food inflation too hit before the conflict.
- Since September 2021, food inflation has steady increase. Consumer food price index won 7.68% in March, 2022, higher than Sep, 2021. The combined pressure on price lead to inflation of 6.95% in March, 2022 above RBI's inflation upper limit target of 6%.
- Unlike oil, domestic control over food basket is significant. GOI and states are in a position to mitigate food inflation. India's stock of food grains needed to be released regularly to control cereal prices. States should refrain from bans on movement of agricultural products as this impact the international trade. Controlling food inflation will make for smoother transition to a tighter monetary policy.

**Relevant Thought:** Inflation is an emotive matter and it gives rise, understandably, to popular resentment.

**-Kaushik Basu**

## Scrapping Of Sedition Provision (Dt: 28.04.2022)

- Sedition provision in IPC, a colonial era is a major threat to political and personal freedoms. Section 124A IPC punishes words or actions that attempt to incite 'Hatred', 'contempt' and 'Disaffection' towards Government so with 3 yrs to life imprisonment. Hundreds of dissenters over the years have paid heavy price being falsely accused of 'Deshdroh', British imperialists used to jail freedom fighters for long periods for their writings and utterances against the Crown. Today's Governments are guilty of same tactics.
- In 1962 Kedar Nath Singh judgment had attempted to narrow sedition to offences betraying an 'intention' and 'tendency' to cause public disorder or endanger state security. Hence 6 decades, it has had no influence on police or Governments. SC and HCs have emphasized that criticism of Governments is not sedition, but the message does not percolate. To fix political opponents, the continuing existence of criminalizing the act of sedition in the IPC sedition is often used as a tool to inflict charges of harassment.
- Not only sedition cognizable and non-boilable, it does not require on actual crime to have been committed and lends to criminalizing any political expression. Growing trend of private complaints of sedition where any motivated individual can lodge sedition complaint and make life hell for people not even remotely connected to complainant.
- Britain which gifted sedition to India has extirpated it in 2009. SC should scrap the sedition provision.

**Relevant Thought:** In a free and democratic society, defaming the Government is the right of every citizen.

**– Geoffrey Palmer**

## Fuel Tax Reduction (Dt: 29.04.2022)

- GOI and states independently tax petrol and diesel. GOI's taxes are to be shared with states according to a formula recommended by finance commission. But Article 270 allows GOI to completely retain taxes, classified access and surcharges. GOI has power over classification to decide how much it will share with states.
- During lockdown of pandemic, oil prices collapsed, but GOI increased its taxes on petrol and diesel. Between Mar 14, 2020 and May 6, 2020 control excise on petrol and diesel increased by 44% and 69% respectively. This has collected in the forms of cess, which meant, it was not shared with states. Even as crude oil price fell from $65/barrel in Jan 2020 to $20 in April 2020, the pump price of diesel increased form Rs. 67.96/litre in Delhi to Rs 69.39 in May.
- India's GDP contracted by 6.6% in 2020-21. GOI's fuel taxes were the exception to this trend. GOI's revenue form petroleum sector for 2020-21 was Rs 4.5 lack Cr, an annual increase of 36%. But states revenue for 2020-21 shrank by 1.5% to Rs 2.2 lakh cr. About 68% of Rs 6.72 lakh crore of revenue generated by petroleum sector in FY 21 went to GOI.
- Crude price rose in 2021, public pressure for tax relief mounted. In Aug. 2021, Tamil Nadu Lowered tax on petrol. In Nov, GOI cut taxes on both petrol and diesel which catalyzed reduction by 20 states. Taxes remain high GOI should cut fuel tax. This will put pressure on states to follow suit.

**Relevant Thought:** Governments are political institutions and hence fiscal policy both represents and measures the role of these political institutions in the economy.

**– Rathin Roy**

## IRS Failure On Planning and Forecast (Dt: 30.04.2022)

- IR will cancel 670 trips of passenger trains till May 24 to focus on moving coat to thermal power plants.

- Shortage of railway rakes for transporting coal is an account of poor planning. Coal transportation is 18% of its goods traffic and is most important of IR freight operation.
- On Feb 1, 2021, IR estimated, it would move 118,750 million NTK in FY 2020-21. A year later, the revised estimate forecast 143,462 million NTK.
- In FY 2015-16, IR moved 196,136 million NTK. IR over last few years has increased investment with rolling stock taking up the largest chunk of capital expenditure.
- IR has fallen short on planning and forecasts.
- This situation shows that different arms of GOI are working in sides, which is not correct.

**Relevant Thought:** We can only see a short distance ahead but we can see plenty there that needs to be done.

**- Alan Turing**

## Reducing Government Litigation (Dt: 02.05.2022)

- With PM and CMs in attendance, CJI: NV Ramana laid down a manifesto on good governance to mitigate judiciary's pendency crisis. Government is the largest litigant. From Panchayats and civic bodies to Tehsildars, Revenue officials, Policing at Thanas to service laws that trigger disputes over postings transfers; signal how nonperformance kicks off copious litigations.
- Hasty enactment of laws by legislatures without discussion, litigation by Government departments, Government inactions, transferring the burden of decision making to courts, slow process of judicial appointment and log in judicial infrastructure are the list of lapses.
- Judges can only interpret law, everything pertains to governance. CJI remarked that land disputes account for 66% of pendency, offers Governments a focus area to clearer policies which can solve these disputes.

- Government must address the fear of prosecution that haunts officers and decision making at all levels. That is the reason administrators find it safer to go to court than settle a dispute.
- If Government depts can ensure justice to citizens by following due process, courts would not be overburdened and would not fail in their watchdog duties.

**Relevant Thought:** We win justice quickest by rendering justice to the other party.

**- Mahatma Gandhi**

## India For Renewable Supply Chain (Dt: 04.05.2022)

- PM Narendra Modi had 3 nation European tour on the developmental aspects of India with bilateral talks on climate and energy having green and sustainable development partnership. Germany will support India's green growth plans with development assistance of $10 billion by 2030 and both countries will create Green Hydrogen Task Force.
- IPCC's report in 2021 says global temp was 1.09$^0$C higher in 2011-20 than 1850-1900 baseline. India has contributed only 4% cumulative greenhouse gas emissions between 1850 and 2017.
- Midi declared last year that a net-zero commitment by India will be by 2070. India is to reduce carbon emission by 1 billion ton and 50% of the energy are to be soured through renewables.
- EU has set a net-zero target by 2050 and is in transition to sourcing most its energies form renewables. Denmark has already sourced 32% of its energy in 2020 from renewables. In EU, wind and water provide most of renewable electricity. This is being complemented by solar. India has to be a part of the EU's renewable supply chain with access to technology.

**Renewable thought:** Climate change knows no border … the whole of the international community here has to shoulder a responsibility to bring about sustainable development.

**-Angela Merkel**

## Inflation A Big Challenge (Dt: 05.05.2022)

- RBI MPC voted to hold policy repo rate at 4% and changed course, increased to 4.4%. RBI will increase case reserve ratio by banks to 4.5%. This is expected to suck out Rs 87,000 crore of liquidity.
- There is elevated inflation and uncertainty around its trajectory. There is surge in prices of many commodities. Retail inflation in March was 6.95% led by jump in food prices.
- MPC fears 2$^{nd}$ round impact of high commodity and food prices which occurs when firms raise sales prices and employees seek higher salaries. Hence, aim of increase in repo rate is to head off 2$^{nd}$ round effects and preserve macro-financial stability Borrowing costs on personal and home loans will rise. For savers in FD, the rates are set to increase.
- Return of inflation is an important macroeconomic challenge. Both GOI and states are to adjust fiscal policy to adapt to the emerging situation. Taxes on pump prices of petrol and diesel need to be lowered to ease price pressure. Agricultural policies need adjustments to ensure that food prices do not rise too high. The right fiscal policy will insulate the economy from a demand shock.

**Relevant Thought:** It is not what happens to you, but how you react to it that matters.

**- Epictetus**

# TURN OF NOTABLE EVENTS (Contd.)

## Managing Food Inflation (Dt: 06.05.2022)

- World Bank's commodity markets Outlook has forecast that wheat prices this year will increase over 40%. India despite its large stock of wheat expects to procure about 19.5 million tons of wheat, less than half of what initially forecast. This dip is also large as wheat production is expected to fall 6% this year.
- Global wheat prices are surging for draught in North America and Russia-Ukraine conflict. India's market wheat price this year is reversed i.e. more than MSP due to drop in procurement as traders are offering farmers the rates higher than MSP in anticipation of wheat price rise in future. GOI will switch to extra rice in place of wheat in cereal allocation to states.
- The risk is the wheat price trend will spill over to other crops, such as edible oil in response to price signals. Farmers may reallocate land from other crops to wheat which will put upward pressure on the price of those crops.
- Given dominance of wheat in the rabi land use even small shifts can have a big price effect on other crops. A well-judged release of GOI's wheat stockpile must play an important role in dampening food inflation this year against the above backdrops.

**Relevant Thought:** Anticipate the difficult by managing the easy.

**– Lao Tzu**

## GOI On Larger Bend for Sedition Law (Dt: 09.05.2022)

- SC's decision was to hear pleas on sedition that concerns enormous power of misuse. But GOI has argued the 1962 Kedar Nath judgment is a good law needs no reconsideration and remedy for any abuse lies in preventing it on a case-to-case basis.
- Between 2016 and 2019, number of cases filed under section 124A rose by 160% even as the rate of conviction dropped to 3%.
- GOI argued that the challenge to the 1962 constitution bench's verdict should be decided by a larger bench.

- Petitioner says that there has been a sea change in jurisprudence since 1962. The sedition law whose language invites arbitrary and frequently motivated application, which is expedient for police or the state but oppressive for many citizens, needs reconsideration by effective debates, and discussions.

**Relevant Thought:** What do you despise? By this are you truly known.

**– Prank Herbert**

## Financial Adjustments in Rise of Inflation (Dt: 10.05.2022)

- RBI's MPC increased repo rate forecasts a declining financial trajectory. Both savings and investments will influence the household response Bank personal loans are on a par with industrial lending.
- There is a tilt towards saving in the form of gold. Net financial household savings were 32% of total savings in the high inflation phase, rose to around 40% when inflation fell.
- Investing in equity shares has emerged an important avenue for household savings. There are also 2 options that will attract more personal saver attention – Bank FD's and Insurance Policies.
- Household financial behavior will see big adjustments as inflation rises.

**Relevant Thought:** we may be on the cusp of a new inflationary era. The forces behind high inflation could persist for some time.

**– Augustine Carstens**

## Japan needs People and India needs Jobs, Skills and Quality Education (Dt: 11.05.2022)

- There is existential threat for Japan where the death rate has outstripped the birth rate which is the lowest in the world. Fewer working age citizens depresses consumption overall and increases social security burden on the available workforce. Unlike US, Canada, Germany, and Australia bolstered by immigrants, Japan has waffled. A plan to let half million blue collar workers by 2025 was stalled by pandemic.

- India's birth rates are falling too. NRHS-5 survey reveals that total fertility rate or average children born to each woman has declined below replacement levels to 2.0 from 2.2 in 2015—16. But India is still in midst of demographic boom that is swelling young people in teen, 20s and 30s. Policy should be able to create jobs; skilled citizens provide quality education for matching the technological needs of 4th industrial revolution.
- Reformed education with 5G, AI, automation, robotics, nanomaterials and biosciences are required to impart and develop the youths of present and future generations.

**Relevant Thought:** India needs jobs. Germany needs people, and collaboration is crucial to

meet the demographic needs of both countries.

**- Angela Merkel**

## Sedition Law to be Reviewed (Dt: 12.05.2022)

- GOI has agreed that sedition law need re-examination and SC has restrained all authorities for filing cases under IPC Section 124 A till review is complete.
- However sincere intent of SC and GOI to guard against misuse of reformed law, there is doubt that it will be misused. State and local authorities will always find a way to use it as a blunt instrument.
- The 1962 Kedar Nath Singh judgment by SC attempted to narrow sedition application betraying an "intention" and tendency to cause public disorder or endanger the security of the stat. But words like "hatred," "contempt" "disaffection" which were in colonial era law and are still present in provisions and "intention" and "tendency" lend to broad and subjective interpretations. Also 1995 Balwant Singh judgment by SC too had little effect.
- UAPA is another law that needs relook. Terrorism is citied as a justification for UAPA.

**Relevant Thought:** Even when laws have been written down, they ought not always to remain unaltered.

**- Aristotle**

## Congress must think about (Dt: 13.05.2022)

- Congress leaders are congregating in Udaipur to think they are likely to think on leadership of party. In past BJP was humiliated in 1984, 2004, 2009 etc. Each time it changed its leadership, ultimately in 2014 it chose Narendra Modi.
- In UK and US also, similar changes have happened. In UK, Changes have ushered like Margaret thatcher, and Tony Blain. In US, Bill Clinton, Barack Obama and Donald Trump, in France Emmanuel Macron.
- Regional parties in India didn't change leadership. SP and BJP, Akalis, Shiv Sena, DMK want change leadership. But congress is facing oblivion, so its incentive should be far greater.
- Congress needs to think the unthinkable.

**Relevant Thought:** Everyone's job is important, but no one is indispensable.

**– Chuck Holl**

## Prolonged Inflation Now a Global Phenomenon (Dt: 14.05.2022)

- Finland and Sweden will soon apply for NATO membership. Thus, Finland will be a 6$^{th}$ treaty member to share border with Russia, Norway, Estonia Latvia, Poland, and Lithuania. Russia has warned of consequence, the economic disruption caused by tension will be prolonged.
- India will face eco fallout through commodity prices and financial market. Most central bank have started aggressive monetary lightening. Fluctuation in rupees exchange rates against major currencies will be challenge to RBIs efforts in reining inflation.

- India has dealt earlier with such high inflation and market volatility. RBI's cushion of $ 532 billion foreign currency asset should be adequate to smoothen the adjustment.
- Both firms and individuals will have to adapt to these situations.

**Relevant thought:** Nothing happen to any man that he is not formed by nature to bear.

**Mareus Aurelius**

## No Reforms for Empowering Economically (Dt: 16.05.2022)

- In post 1991, India had economic growth, job creation and systemic improvement that has pulled millions out of poverty. These reforms have lost impact and India needs greater liberalization. Instead, political talks are largely on welfarism, freebies and caste politics in the name of social justice.
- What parties are talking today will not improve productivity, faster competitive markets or generate new jobs. Indira Gandhi's 'Garibi Hatao' slogan facilitated protectionism, rent-seeking, not poverty elevation. Even BJP is a hesitant reformer today. It lost its mojo after Rahul Gandhi's "Suit Boot Ki Sarkar" jibe on key land acquisition amendments. And it lost again after anti farm reform protests by a vocal minority of farmers. This a vast majority is denied better prospects.
- The current political timidity extends to whetting voter appetite for had policies like freebies. These cut expenditure for schools, hospitals, other public works Domicile and Caste quotas in private sector are injurious. Reforms in land, labour and agriculture laws are crucial. Without reform in land and labour, manufacturing will be stuck-up. It will not power an 8% growth witch India needs for 10 years to come close to China.

**Relevant Thought:** Capital is not scarce; vision is.

**- Sam Walton**

## Analysis For Ideological Fight (Dt: 17.05.2022)

- Congress assertion that only Congress and not regional parties can lead fight against BJP and RSS is not appropriate in the face of their track record. Sincc their 3 state victories in 2018, congress lost successive contests with the BJP. In the same period regional parties like TMC, DMK, AAP and BJD have checked BJP's advance. Further, Congress failed to tap anti-incumbency against BJP in Assam, UK, Goa, and Manipur. Neither could it win over CPM in Kerala.
- GOP Congress have better, success playing 2nd Biddle to JMM in Jharkhand, DMK in Tamil Nadu and Shiv Sena-NCP in Maharashtra. Regional parties no longer consider congress their spearhead and are not obsessing overly with Rahul's ideology. They are betting on welfare policies, organizational strength and popular connect.
- Personality cults, nepotism and indiscipline are weakness for most regional parties that BJP is poised to exploit.
- Poll survey has revealed that most important issue for voters is economy and good governance. BJP's adeptness at filling political vacuums, identifying under-represented castes, wooing talents from other parties and keeping Netas on their toes is a lesson for both congress and regional parties.

**Relevant Thought:** What we all want is public safety. We do not want rhetoric that is framed through ideology.

**- Kamala Harris**

## SC on Gyanvapi Mosque (Dt: 18.05.2022)

- Sc has interim order on Gyanvapi Mosque; that removes restrictions on Muslims offering namaz, but protecting the spot where Shivling has been found-seems to make neither side unhappy.
- It is to be seen whether Places of Worship Act 1991 should be upheld?
- Following Varanasi Court ruling, there are now demands on surveying and examining the religious character of Mathura's Shahi

Idgah Masjid including Taj Mahal, Qutub Minar and Jamia Masjid at Srirangapatna in Karnataka. The 1991 Act prohibits conversion of religious places and maintains their religious character as it existed on 15 Aug, 1947. The law had exempted Ram Janmabhoomi Babri Masjid title dispute which was of pre-1947 vintage. All other suits filed after independence should not be entertained by any court of law.

- All eyes are on SC's verdict. There is apprehension of relitigating history, rise of communal flashpoint and disputes may move from courts to streets or alternatively must follow the 1991 act rigorously.

**Relevant Thought:** Human history becomes more and more a race between education and catastrophe.

**- HG Wells**

## SC Justice to Rajiv Gandhi Assassination convict (Dt: 19.05.2022)

- AG Perarivalan, a 51 years life convict serving 31 years in jail for his involvement in assassination of former PM, Rajiv Gandhi was set at liberty by Supreme Court.
- Successive state governments in Tamil Nadu belted for his release while GOI resisted it every time, and made state governors to defeat the possibility.
- Madras HC had stayed their execution of hanging (along with 2 others) scheduled on 9 Sept, 2011.
- TN cabinet on 9 Sep. 2018 recommended release of Perarivalan and requested the governor to approve it under Article 161 of the constitution. But the governor kept pending for 2½ years and referred to the President.
- SC faulted TN governor's interpretation of constitution on 4 main grounds. (i) State cabinet's advice is binding on governor in exercising remission under Article 161. (ii) Governor not exercising or causing inexplicable delay is subject to judicial review. (iii) Governor's reference of cabinet recommendation later is without constitutional backing. (iv) The reference to the President was

incorrect as no power is conferred on GOI by constitution to supersede state government's Article 161 powers in IPC 302 cases.

- It is a win-win for all. Spotlight is now on remaining 6 convicts.

**Relevant Thought:** A nation should not be judged by how it treats its highest citizens but its lowest ones.

**- Nelson Mandela**

## SC's GST Council Ruling (Dt: 20.05.2022)

- Three Judge SC verdicts overturned the remit of GST Council. In 5 yrs, the GST council chaired by the Union finance Minister and preventatives of all states has been the decision-making body on key matters like tax rates. Division is of the Council are put to vote and binding on both GOI and States. SC's verdict now says the Council's decision is merely recommendatory.
- It introduces a level of uncertainty and is bound to undermine confidence. This will act as a drag on economic activity.
- Gujarat HC in Jan 2020 had ruled against GOI on domestic industries challenge of tax leveed by GOI on imported coal. GOI subsequently brought the matter to SC where GOI stated that GST council's decisions are binding on both legislature and the executive. This won rejected by SC. This verdict will defeat to create a common market in India by dismantling fiscal barriers between stats.
- As this verdict seems to be judicial overreach and intrudes into domain of legislature; GOI should file review petition in SC.

**Relevant Thought:** Judicial judgment must take deep account of the day before yesterday in order that yesterday may not paralyses today.

**- Felix Frankfurter**

## SC shifted Gyanvapi Suit to Varanasi Dist. Judge (Dt: 21.05.2022)

- SC has shifted Gyanvapi Suit from a civil judge to the Varanasi District Judge and said he is "senior and experienced"

- The Places of Worship Act, 1991 prohibits conversion of religions places and maintains their religious character as it existed on 15 Aug, 1947.
- SC's oral observation is that the 1991 Act only bars change in religious character but not ascertainment of religious character.
- SC could have ended the Gyanvapi Matter

**Relevant Thought:** There is purpose underlying the enactment of the Places of Worship Act. The law speaks to our history and to the future of the nation.

**– Supreme Court**

## Centre's Fuel Tax cuts (Dt: 23.05.2022)

- On 21 May, Saturday, GOI lowered excise duties on petrol and diesel, as well as offered a subsidy for LPG cylinders. States must follow now. Kerala Government has announced a reduction in state fuel levies.
- This time in the backdrop of 5 years of economic weakness, pandemic shock and during slow growth, the spell of inflation is happening; which requires different approach in finding the right mix between fiscal and monetary policies.
- Excise duty reduction of GOI takes us back to the level that prevailed in March 2020. Since then, we have experienced annual contraction in GDP.
- Rise in inflation has helped governments to buoyant tax collections. The growth of nominal GDP is more than the interest on government borrowings. Hence there is no threat to the sustainability of government debt.
- Net tax revenue of GOI and states between April 2021 and February 2022 was much higher than what was collected 2 years ago in a pre-pandemic year.
- There is room for using fiscal policy as the primary tool to find balance between check on inflation while protecting private consumption and economic growth.

**Relevant Thought:** Government supply side action can also reduce future rate rises, output sacrifice and borrowing costs.

**– Ashima Goyal**

## Freedom of Expression (Dt: 24.05.2022)

- Delhi University Hindu College Associate Professor Ratan Lal was arrested over an allegedly objectionable social media (Facebook) post about the claims of a shivling being discovered inside Gyanvapi mosque.
- Chief Metropolitan Magistrate Siddhartha Malik granted bail to Lal noting that this post was speculative in nature about the structure symbol which as of now is not accessible in public domain.
- The court agreed that the accused did an act which was avoidable considering the sensibilities of persons around the accused and public at large and the post though reprehensible, does not indicate an attempt to promote hatred between communities.
- He was not a criminal or a habitual offender. He is a professor in a reputed college. He could have been served a notice, waited for a reply, and then arrested. Lal's lawyers argued that his arrest was in violation of SC guidelines in the Arnesh Kumar judgment and that he did not incite anyone through his social media post. Where is the criminal offence in any of this?
- Obviously, there is motivation to please political masters. The police's job is to do due diligence. CMM said courts must "adopt higher standards" before jailing a citizen.

**Relevant Thought:** What is freedom of expression? Without the freedom to offend, it ceases to exist.

**– Salman Rushdie**

## Indo Pacific Economic Forum (Dt: 25.05.2022)

- IPEF (Indo-pacific Economic Framework of prosperity) is a platform for economic negotiations among members (now 13 countries), who contribute 40% of global GDP, and whose common anxiety is about China's aggressive positioning.

- IPEF need to be juxtaposed to 2 critical FTAs; CPTPP and RCEP. RCEP came to force in January includes China and is world's largest FTA spamming 30% of global GDP. China has also applied to join CPTPP which is gold standard for free trade agreement. Many IPEF members chose tighter trade integration with China despite security concerns.
- Barring the US and India, other key members have moved towards greater harmonization of their trade with China. China will remain a part of supply value chains which run through these economics.
- IPEF represents a useful platform for India as it has chosen to opt out of RCEP. India should not shy away from real trade agreements spreading across the Indo-Pacific.

**Relevant Thought:** Contemporary trade agreements go much beyond traditional trade restrictions at the border.

**- Dani Rodrik**

## China-Russia: its exercise near Japan (Dt: 26.05.2022)

- Russia and China conducted air force exercise close to Japan's airspace. It forced Japan which was holding QUAD summit – to scramble own jets response.
- Russia is in no mood to end the Ukraine war as its defence minister said his military operation will continue Russia and China is forming a close strategic military compact to take on Western hegemony. For collapse of Soviet Union; Putin is reactive and China sees it as 100 years of humiliation between 19th and 20th centuries and restore the glory of Middle Kingdom.
- Now there is serious possibility that Beijing will use Moscow for its strategic security aims in the Indo-Pacific. It puts India in military ties to Russia and confrontation with China.

- Delhi has maintained non-aligned position, refusing to condemn Russia but geopolitical situation now demands to be alone with the West.

- A good mode here is Vietnam. It has relation with Beijing, but staunchly defends its maritime territorial claims in South China Sea against Chinese belligerence and has joined Japan-led CPTPP and the recently launched US-led IPEF. Vietnam has also historic ties with Russia as Soviet Union strongly aided it during Vietnam War. But communist Vietnam can take such nimble position, India may do so.

**Relevant Thought:** Success in foreign policy, as in carpentry, requires the right tools for the job.

**– Richand N Haass**

## Target Killings in J and K (Dt: 27.05.2022)

- Special NIA court in Delhi gave life term to JKLF Chief Yasin Malik for funding terror in J and K. Amreena Bhat, a Kashmiri TV artist was shot dead one day before it, an off-duty constable Saifullah Qadri was shot dead in front of his home in Srinagar. These are all latest target Killings in Kashmir.

- The militants have targeted Kashmir Muslims, Pandits, non-Kashmiri Hindu and Muslims and security persons to show fear, disrupt life since nullification of Article 370 in Aug, 2019.

- Over last 2 yrs, joint security in J and K has been successful in neutralizing cross border terrorists. Targeted Killings use hit and run tactics by local agents may not be on security radar.

- The main challenge is to curb extremist network that have proliferated aiding terror organizations in recruiting locals. About 40 cases of local recruitment have been reported this year.

- This can be countered by strengthening J and K civil society which can happen after democratic process established by assembly polls soon. The number of stakeholders for peace in J and K many increase when the legislative executive structure is rebuilt.

**Relevant Thought:** Our only security is our ability to change.

**– John Lilly**

## International Booker Prize for "Tomb of Sand" (Dt: 28.05.2022)

- On 26 May 2022, International Bookers Prize was announced on book Tomb of Sand. It was awarded on Geetanjali Shree and Daisy Rockwell, respectively the Hindi Book 'Ret Samadhi's author and the English translator. Tomb of Sand is the first book written in an Indian language to have won the honour. It is the first novel translated from Hindi to be recognised by award.
- These days, English publishing houses are keen to have a foothold in other languages and literature festivals are competing to be more multilingual.
- Frank Wynne, the Chair Person, Judge Panel said: "We were captivated by the power, the poignancy and the playfulness of Tomb of Sand, Geetanjali Shree's polyphonic novel of identity and belonging, in Daisy Rockwell's exuberant coruscating translation. This is a luminous novel of India and partition, but one whose spellbinding brio and fierce compassion weaves youth and age male and female, family, and nation into a Kaleidoscopic hole. It is a joyous cacophony and an irresistible novel."
- Within the country, English remains the commonest target language and hence the main bridge across our richly diverse linguistic landscape.

**Relevant Thought:** It is not enough to find words that match: if images in the translated text are unclear, then the thoughts and feelings of the author are lost.

**– Haruki Murakami.**

## Urban Employment Guarantee Plan (Dt: 30.05.2022)

- PMEAC (Prime Minister Economic Advisory Council) recommended roll out of Urban Employment Guarantee Programme. Kerala and Rajasthan have launched their version of scheme

Parliamentary Standing Committee on Labour recommended it to gain momentum at union level. Beside Kerala, Tamil Nadu, Odisha, HP have shorter experience in this.

- CMIE jobs data shows monthly unemployment has fluctuated between 6.56% and 11.84% over a year, with urban employment exceeding rural in 10 of those months.
- State level initiatives are limited and at nascent level. It is important to gauss how useful they are for workers from UP, Bihar, Rajasthan, and West Bengal where more than 60% of the 11.4 million migrant workers were returning during 1st lockdown.
- Like GOI's health insurance scheme synchronized with state level initiatives, it is possible to have national UEGP.
- The latest GOI annual budget is pegged at Rs 39.4 lakh Cr. It is prudent to take DUET (Decentralized Urban Employment and Training). It envisages to use public institutions to introduce the scheme. It will allow GOI to observe its working in smaller setting.
- Urban Employment Guarantee Plan (UEGDP) will help those most hit by recent economic shocks. It will be NREG for cities.

**NREG** = At least 100 days guaranteed wage employment in every fin-year to every household whose adult members volunteer to do unskilled manual work.

**Relevant Thought:** To reach a port, we must sail-sail, not tie at anchor – sail, not drift.

**Franklin D Roosevelt**

## UIDAI Advisory Warning withdrawn (Dt: 31.05.2022)

- UIDAI had given warning for misuse of Aadhar card photocopies and e-copies by unlicensed entities. GOI now withdrew the note and asked to exercise "normal prudence" while sharing Aadhar number. Many private agencies demand and collect Aadhar photocopies even when they are not licensed to do online authentication. Digital tools can manipulate images and text on Aadhar copies and it is a fraud.

- UIDAI allows OVSE which is not accredited to scan the QR code on Aadhar cards to check identity and demographic information f a person. Aadhar Act 2016 Section SE (4) stipulates that no OVSE shall "collect use or store" Aadhar numbers or biometric information of any individual. Recognizing the unauthorized storage; UIDAI had mandated in Feb that any organization seeking identifies offline should scan the QR code on Aadhar cards, verify authority's digital signature and tally identity. Such digital identity scanning should replace collection of photocopies.
- GOI should strongly regulate biometric and Aadhar data collection by private entities. SC had barred commercial entities from demanding Aadhar. Restrictions should be put in for entities demanding and storing Aadhar.

**Relevant Thought:** We live in a time when if you make it easy for someone to steal from you, someone will.

**- Frank Abagnale**

## Murder after withdrawal of Security Covex (Dt: 01.06.2022)

- Punjab Government (AAP) has withdrawn security cover from 28-year singer congress politician young Sidhu Moosewala one day after that he was shot dead.
- It needs investigation whether security was scaled down to rationalize VIP security.
- Security covers are often political favours bestowed on those close to power and gun-toting caps are another status symbol. Real assessment of threat is not done while granting a security cover and similarly it is not done while withdrawing the cover.
- More than 66000 police were providing protection to more than 19000 ministers, MPs, MLAs, Judges Bureaucrats, and others in 2019 in the centre and states as per data from Bureau of Police R and D.

- Bengal had more than 3000 VIPs under protection, Punjab more than 2500, but Maoist hit Chhattisgarh had only 315 people under security cover although it had heavy massacre Jhiram Ghati in 2013.
- India has 156.78 police per lakh population against the UN recommended standard of 222 cops per lakh. Many parts of non-urban India are seriously under-policed.

**Relevant Thought:** I do not want to be a VIP. I want to be an LIP, a less important person.

**- Mamata Banerjee**

## BJP's Strategy on 2022 Gujrat Assembly Election (Dt: 02.06.2022)

- Hardik Patel crossed over from Congress to BJP.
- Regular sojourns by PM, Narendra Modi and scheduling Gujarat visits by foreign notables like Boris Johnson UK's PM and Tedros Ghebreyesus DG, WHO.
- Back-pedaling on Par-Tapi-Narmada interlinking project due to protests by tribals against it.
- Managing the unrest of Patidars and congress desertions like death of Ahmad Patel and defection of other leaders form Congress.
- Receding of issues like-job quotas, GST, and low cotton prices.
- Higher cotton and groundnut prices this year will make agricultural labourers happier.
- The state has 19 lakh factory workers. 61 lakh employees in MSMEs are affected by rising input costs and household consumption costs. This is where Gujarat's low state taxes on fuel may benefit BJP.
- The ruthless sacking of Vijaya Rupani has mitigated Government's Covid-related anti-incumbency. Further, Patel Government accepted compensation claims for over 80,000 Covid deaths by February; despite just over 10,000 official deaths.
- AAP is still a new kid in Gujarat, it may end up snatching some congress votes, giving BJP a help.

**Relevant Thought:** Seize the day, and put the least possible trust in tomorrow.

**– Horace**

## Western Sanctions against Russia (Dt: 03.06.2022)

- Western sanctions continue against Russia for its invasion of Ukraine. It is now harder for EU to keep own flock together to cripple Russian energy. Although EU leaders agreed to stop imports of Russian crude by end of 2022, however they were forced to grant Hungary an exemption, even Bulgaria is likely to extend and for Russian gas there is no deadline.
- In case Iron, US sanctions from 1979, could not change and conversation is still about changing Iron's behavior.
- Sanctions are intended to limit the economic potential of victim, but evidence shows that it does not achieve.
- Sanctions do not work because both sovereign nations and private firms have powerful economic incentive to bypass them. Iran's secret finance system is straddling the globe.
- IEA data showed, Russia remained the OPEC + group's 2nd largest crude oil supplier (9 million barrel/day). Russia is source of 55% of Germany's natural gas which is harder to substitute. Immediate halt of Russian energy imports will shrink Germa's economy by 2%. Moreover, Germany's current inflation is over 7%.
- India rightly has said that Western lectures on buying Russian oil do not square with Western purchase of Russian gas.

**Relevant Thought:** Sanctions are a bad idea.

**– Mohamed ElBaradei**

## Special Security and Bar Closing (Dt: 04.06.2022)

- Providing special security and bar closing time these decision should be taken by executives.

- An opposition leader in Punjab raised petition in Punjab and Haryana High Court on security cover withdrawals (e.g. death of Sidhu Moose Wala). Punjab Government Claimed the operation Blue Star anniversary temporarily required extra personnel as the excuse.
- Meanwhile, Delhi HC is examining Delhi Government's decision to allow rest bars to open till 3 am.
- Based on threat perceptions, the granting and withdrawal of security are executive decisions.
- States do grant undeserving people security cover based on political preferences.
- HCs have 59 lakh pending cases, hence must be selective about what they hear.
- Delhi bar matters: In Gurgaon resto bars can be open till 8 pm, in Noida till 4 pm. In Delhi the closing time extension to 3 AM from 1 AM faced police objections; but that is between Delhi police Delhi Government. Courts should not play arbiter.

**Relevant Thought:** Judges are like umpires. They make sure everybody plays by the rules. But it is a limited role. Nobody ever went a ballgame to see the umpire.

**– John Roberts**

## First Heterologous Booster-Approved (Dt: 06.06.2022)

- Biological E's Corbevax, a protein subunit recombinant vaccine is approved by drug regulator DCGI as the first heterologous booster for adults.
- Next step will be to recommend it for induction into precaution dose programme by NTAGI although the health ministry has skipped this process while approving Corbevax for 12–14-year-olds.
- Corbevax phase 3 mix-and-match trials showed increase in neutralizing antibody titers against the Omicron variant. Hence GOI should make Corbevax the choice in administering precaution dose.

- It remains to be seen if 6-month gap for administering Corbevax after 2nd dose of Covishield or Covaxin (as per DCGI) will be echoed by NTAGI too.
- The 9-month gap between homologous boosting must also be reviewed.
- Bio-E and GOI must pursue WHO emergency we listing for Covovax with greater vigor and export of vaccine. Bharat Biotech's intranasal vaccine and Covovax are in race to become heterologous boosters.
- GOI must offer free precaution doses for all adults.

**Relevant Thought:** Science is the highest personification of the nation because that nation will remain the first which carries the furthest the works of thought and intelligence.

**– Louis Psteux**

## Action Against Spokesperson Nupur and Naveen (Dt: 07.06.2022)

- BJP had to take diplomatic censure from important Gulf Countries so that it acted suspension against its two spokespersons, Nupur Sharma and Naveen Jindal.
- Nupur and Jindal's appalling comments on TV and Twitter as political discourse coarsened so much that the MEA had to describe these well-known BJP figures as fringe elements.
- Divisive rhetoric, state/police actions and responses have become much frequent. Relentless aggressiveness of religion-rights turns to nasty remarks. Lack of intervention and green light for official agencies lose the pretense of neutrality. Bulldozing houses, sedition charges evicting hawkers selling non-reg foods, controversies on kind of meat, venues of prayers, mosque-temple petitions have been encouraging TV and Twitter loudmouths. Nupur Sharma and Naveen Jindal's comments are products of this ecosystem; Course correction can have firm signals from the top. There is a limit to rabble-rousing.
- Government's electoral successes depend now on (a) cast politics and (b) welfare politics. Some government like Bengal is good

on welfare and caste does not quite work, and some other are vice versa. Costs of these can outweigh benefits both domestically and internationally.

**Relevant Thought:** Ours is a multi-religious country, a multilingual country we have many different modes of worship. We believe in peaceful and harmonious coexistence.

**-Atal Bihari Vajpayee**

## India's Environment and Carbon Footprint (Dt: 08.06.2022)

- EPI(Environmental Performance Index), 2022 released its cross country ranking of 180 countries. India ranks last. The ranking does not accurately reflect India's performance. India's $CO_2$ emissions till 2019 were only 3% against 47% of US and EU combined. In this context, India fares quite well in per capita terms.
- GHG (Green House Gases) intensity of growth rate is a measure of progress in decoupling emissions form economic growth. India ranks 34, while US and Germany are at 44 and 48 respectively.
- In terms of per capita GHG emission, India is at 53 and ahead of Norway. EPI data shows, India's economic rise has come with a smaller environmental footprint.
- India's per capita energy consumption in 2019 was 25% of world average of 272 KWh.
- EPI shows that India's performance on air quality is abysmal. Pollution Control Board data shows that poor air quality is on account of post-harvest practices like stubble burning and natural causes of dust. Their solutions lie within. Marketing of stubbles and need of public transport are indispensable.

**Relevant Thought:** What is the use a house if you have not got a tolerable planet to put it on?

**- Henry David Thoreau**

## EC's Move on Remote Voting (Dt: 09.06.2022)

- Election Commission (EC)'s pilot project of remote voting for migrant workers is a big plus. Nearly 300 million citizens out of total 910 million electors did not cast their votes in 2019 is election.
- Internal migrants now are estimated to be 600 million. Short-term migrants rarely acquire a vote in their place of work. This category will benefit from ECs more.
- Logistics will be complicated. Migrants will be mapped, and then enrolled for remote voting. Verifying voter identities and ensuring the vote cast on the EVM should be channeled to the correct booth and constituency. Also, those listed for remote voting but turning up physically at domicile polling booths due to personal or other emergencies like lockdown etc. – must be accommodated.
- With institutional and political will difficulties can be overcome. EC should also start the process of identifying migrant voter clusters. Gujarat is a migrant worker hub. Let the pilot happen there and EC should aim for 2014 full rollout.

**Relevant Thought:** Migration is as natural as breathing, as eating as sleeping. It is part of life, part of nature. So, we must find a way of establishing a proper scenario for modern migration.

**-Goel Garcia Bernal**

## Election of President of India (Dt: 10.06.2022)

- Election Commissioner announced the schedule for electing India's next president on July 18, 2022. BJP led NDA is short of 50% electoral college (all MLAs, MPs vote and each vote has a value with bigger states, all MPs votes have equal values). This time J and K having no assembly the Electoral College will be marginally smaller. If BJD and YSR congress votes with NDA, the Centre's nominee can be elected.

- In 2017, Ram Nath Kovid was a Dalit outreach. Now there are social groups and regions that need BJP's attention. Interesting is whether NDA allies, JD(U) and AIADMK will need cosseting and BJD and YSR congress will become targets of opposition wooing?
- Weakened congress may not be able to pick combined opposition candidates. KCR, Mamata, Pawar, Stalin and Kejriwal are leading opposition is may turn out with efforts.
- President will be potentially interesting when he comes from a stable political party different from the governing party.

**Relevant Thought:** I personally believe that the office of the President of India is not to be sought. It is to be offered.

**-Pranab Mukherjee**

## RS Poll Fights (Dt: 11.06.2022)

- There were hard poll fights in 4 holly contested seats. Congress in Rajasthan Haryana and Karnataka and Shiv Sena in Maharashtra put up a determined fight against BJP.
- BJP kept its rank and file in constant battle readiness by fighting every election form Panchayats to Parliament with utmost zeal. No opposition party except TMC has matched up. Congress, SP and RJD learned this the hard way.
- BJP has excelled in key department like disseminating narratives, mobilizing cadre, and wooing voters. Winning direct election is to assemblies and Lok Sabha involving crore of voters is a big task. After RS polls settle down, the recent debacles in UP, Uttarakhand, Manipur and Goa and the disarray in Gujarat and Himachal Pradesh should give the opposition much food for thought.
- There is lesson for BJP too: bearing down too hard on rivals can scale up the opposition unity.

**Relevant Thought:** Power without principle is barren, but principle without power is futile. This is a party of government and I will lead it as a party of government.

- **Tony Blair**

## Nagaland Tragedy and Army Action (Dt: 13.06.2022)

- Nagaland Police SIT filed charge sheet against 30 Special Forces personnel with charges of murder and criminal conspiracy that killed 6 civilians in Nagaland Mon district.
- The onus is on GOI and the army for further legal and disciplinary action. Parallel, the army's Court of Inquiry probe has given distinct judicial pathway for authorities to proceed. Army act gives the commanding officer discretion to decide whether accused's will be court martialed or be subjected to civilian law.
- Mob violence after the tragedy had taken 7 more civilian lives and one paratrooper. Civil society denounced AFSPA, which empowers armed forces to fire on people. Standard operating protocols by Supreme Court to check misuse of AFSPA have failed, as these get fouled by officers during crisis.
- GOI's piecemeal AFSPA withdrawals a big win for Northeast is the conclusion in of the Naga peace accord. Security forces are not confident to curb illicit activities of insurgents in Nagaland and Manipur without AFSPA. Only political problems like extortion, gun violence, narcotic smuggling.

**Relevant Thought:** The strengthening of our statehood is, at times deliberately interpreted as authoritarianism.

- **Vladimir Putin**

## As Bulldozers Roll On (Dt: 14.06.2022)

- Bulldozers go on demolishing illegal encroachments at MP, Delhi, UP etc. A rule for demolition varies across states, but low requires proper notice in all cases.
- In Khargone (MP), Jahangirpuri (Delhi), Gujarat Pragyaraj (UP), Tripura and Assam, etc. such demolitions have been carried out. Status no has been maintained at Delhi as per SC orders and next hearing is in August.

- A petition was filed in Allahabad HC against Pragyaraj House demolition. It is said that bulldozers are posing challenge to constitutional rights, but higher courts are not responding.
- Reasons against bulldozing illegal encroachments

  a) 'Guilt' can be established in law court only

  b) Relatives of accused are innocent cannot be punished.

  c) Government cannot behave like a criminal as it is mandated to uphold the law.

  d) Which law covers bulldozing citizens' property?

**Relevant Thought:** An ounce of prudence is worth a pound of cleverness.

**– Baltasar Gracian**

## Agnipath Scheme with Agniveers (Dt: 15.06.2022)

- GOI declared 'Agnipath Scheme' for recruitment of 'Agniveers' in 3 branches of Indian defence in this 'Agniveers' will be recruited for 44 yrs; and out of this 25% will be taken in permanent cadre. Salary will be Rs 30,000 in 1st yrs then 33000 in 2nd yrs, 36,500 in 3rd yrs and Rs 40,000 per month in 4th yrs. Age limit is 17 yrs to 21 yrs and every year 40 to 45000 will be recruited.
- In the US, about 80% of service personnel retire without pension. China over last 8 yrs pruned 50% of its land-based Army while boosting Navy and Air Force. PLA retrenched 3 lakh troops. By these metrics, India's recruitment reform is not radical.
- Retired army generals have questioned that it will strain existing training resources and produce quality problem. Lt Genl, J S Sandhu argues that if unit commanders can manage solders morale, the new recruitment scheme will not affect Army's fighting spirit. GOI will look on how the change is affecting ground realities.
- What will thousand young Indians released annually after 4 yrs of army service do? Partly contributory severance package for Agniveers is just over Rs 11 lakhs. This will be a good cushion to

start life in Civvies Street, provided there will be scope for plenty of employment.

**Relevant Thought:** The soldier is the Army. No army is better than its soldiers.

**Geoge S Patton**

## Unemployment in India (Dt: 16.06.2022)

- GOI's PLFS puts joblessness at 4.6% for June 2021. GOI announced 1 million recruitments over next 18 months CMIE's April 2022 data says the rate is 7.4%.
- GOI's unemployment 2020-21 data for 15-24 age group is 12.9% while CMIE's April 2022 data shows 42% for the 20-24 age group and 12.7% for 25-29 cohort.
- GOI's recruitment of 1 million over 18 months is a small help when 5 million annually join the labour force which is 430 million strong.
- There are big youth unemployment's, increased unpaid works, non-white collar jobs' quality declining, choice of self-employment for low-income earners goes up and real wages have been falling.
- Azim Premji University study shows that over last decade, the total employment for every 1% increase in GDP has been just 0.1%.
- World Bank showed that most countries, the share of manufacturing in total employment dropped between 1994 and 2011.
- There must be joint Centre-state policy making. Ob-stack to creating low-skill manufacturing jobs need to be removed. This combined effort should also generate high-skilled young India.

**Relevant Thought:** It is one thing to desire, another to be in capacity fit for what we desire.

**Thomas Hobbes**

## Violent Protests against Agnipath Scheme (Dt: 17.06.2022)

- In parts of India's Hindi speaking belt, violent protests erupted against GOI's military recruitment scheme. Frustrated youth set drains on fire.
- CMIE April 2022 data: 15-19 age unemployment 50%, 20-24 age unemployment 38.7%. In Bihar for 15-19 age unemployment 76% lasing long term job is big blow to youth.
- The military has a pension problem. There are 3.2 million defense pensioners, with about 55000 added annually. In 2020-21, pension total was 19% of total defense expenditures. In November 2015, OROP was introduced. By 2020-21, pension outgo rose to 26% of defense expenditure.
- The US in 2018, set aside 10% of defense expenditure towards pension. In the UK, in 2019 pension was 14% of total defence pending. IN Indian military budget, approach should be to prune intake and raise quality standards.
- Job preference in paramilitary or police or bank loans for entrepreneurship are inadequate and the youth see the military as a career that meets aspirations.
- US keeps pension costs down. It takes 20 yrs of service to be eligible for a pension. It is possible because America is more effective in employing former soldiers.
- GOI needs to quickly design a more effective package.

**Relevant Thought:** For some reason, which we have not yet been able to understand, men like to watch other men hit balls.

**- A Global Sports Channel Head**

## Agnipath Firestorm continued (Dt: 18.06.2022)

- Defence of India is not a job creation scheme as many rioters seem to believe. India urgently needs to modernize its military capacity focusing on high tech areas such as cyber warfare, drones, missiles, and space weapons. A thorough overhaul of human resources is imperative.

- OROP reforms have made defence spending on pension more than spending on military hardware. Agnipath will reduce the pension bill gradually but substantially. Money saved can be redirected to high-tech staff and equipment. India will have more skilled fewer better equipped armed forces.
- 46,000 Agniveers will be hired, every year. 34000 will leave service after 4 years with lump some benefits of Rs 11 lakhs. The aim is to have regular soldiers and Agniveers in 50:50 ratio. This will reduce their average age from 32 years to 26 years, a huge improvement since younger soldiers are fitter and tougher.
- They will be recruited in following various organization of requirements of GOI

  i)1.2 million Armed Services

  ii) 1 million in 10 Para military (iii) Civilian Security Forces (iv) CRPF of 350000 persons (v) CISF of 1,50,000 persons (vi) PSUs (vii) RPF of 75000 persons (viii) Assam Rifles (ix) BSF (x) ITBP (xi) Sashatra Seema Bal

**Relevant Thought:** Sweat saves blood, blood saves lives, but brains save both.

**Erwin Rommel**

## Monsoon and Government Policy on Agriculture (Dt: 19.06.2022)

- In 1st half of June S-W monsoon was deficient by 30% In north-western India rainfall deficiency was 77%. The update for 2022 monsoon is expected to be normal
- India is a water stressed country and it supports about 17% of world's population with 4% of freshwater. About half of India's gross cropped area is irrigated. Two crops: paddy and sugarcane receive almost 60% of irrigation water. Adding to wheat, it covers about 80% of the irrigation. A sizeable proportion of output of paddy and sugarcane comes from regions unsuitable for cultivation.

- A study carried out jointly by NABARD and ICRIER on the water productivity mapping of major crops concluded that there is significant misalignment between cropping patterns and available water resources.

- Indian farmers like any other economic agent responds to price incentives. Individual farmers cannot ignore prevailing price dynamics and act on consequences of current water usage pattern. Government policy must enable rational cropping patterns through price mechanism. Sensible policies need to constantly adjust incentives t dynamics of relative prices and crop risks.

**Relevant Thought:** When the well is dry, we know the worth of water.

**– Benjamin Franklin**

## Burning Trains easy for Arsonists (Dt: 21.06.2022)

- Over 500 trains were cancelled following arson and willful destruction of railway property. Indian Railway (IR) is of vital importance e.g. it carried 22 million passengers a day in pre-pandemic period. Railway rakes transport 3.3 million tons of freight daily, mainly coal. Senseless destruction, disruption, cancellation not only great inconvenience to millions, but it drastically affects our economy.

- IR's security is Railway Protection Force (RPF). State Governments also come into picture as trains crisscross states. Government Railway Police (GRP), funded by IR and states equally but under the administrative control of the local Government and local police assist in safe guarding railway assets and passengers.

- IR's security is unsatisfactory because of gaps in coordination with state police. GRP and the state police handle security of trains, tracks, and railway premises, while RPF protects properties and consignments. Performance of local policing is influenced by state government is political signaling. Consequently, agitators get leeway and impact on IR assets.

- CAG audit report on IR's security reveal that a unified overseeing arrangement between RPF and state police is missing and there are coordination problems. People dependent on train travel will suffer. RPF headed by a police officer on deputation may be needed to strengthen coordination. Trains should not be easy targets for arsonists.

**Relevant Thought:** If your train is on the wrong track, every station you come to is the wrong station.

**- Bernard Malamud**

## Fiscal Policy on Growth (Dt: 24.06.2022)

- RBI's MPC (Monetary Policy Committee) in the June meeting hinted the impact on GDP following the 0.9% points increase in repo rate since May. RBI estimates GDP to grow 7.2% in 2022-23, and possibility of average GDP growth rate of 6.7% till and March 2024.
- The inflation is not because of excessive demand; as the per-capita private consumption in 2021-22 was Rs 61215 a level below pre-pandemic year. Source of inflation is therefore, supply side; which has the remedy only in Fiscal Policy. Readjustment of fiscal policy can control inflation and counter growth slowdown. It can be done without threatening debt; as inflation will push up nominal GDP growth and help both GOI and state governments overshoot budgetary tax estimates.
- Governments are needed to carefully time the removal of post pandemic welfare and fulfill capital expenditure commitments; which will crowd in new investments by private firms. Disinflation can be brought without affecting growth. India needs average growth rates above 7% in the medium term.

**Relevant Thought:** In the real world, information processing in costly, and confusion engendered by inflation can be a serious cost.

**– R Agarwal and M Kimball**

## Ban on Right to Abortion in USA (Dt: 25.06.2022)

- US Supreme Court overruled the 1975 Roe Vs Wade decision and eliminated constitutional right to abortion. It will have great impact on US healthcare. It is a big setback for Biden's presidency and affirmation of Trump's.

- 50 yrs back, women of US had won the right to abortion. It is a serious setback for women's bodily autonomy and she can make decision about herself. Before 50 yrs; only 20% are without child. Only 11% of 25–44-year-old women had a college degree as compared to 41% today. Only 17% of management jobs for aged 16-44 were held by women compared to 45% today.
- In months to come US may see legislative feedback against this decision. However, in all other countries, the trend of liberalizing abortion laws will not be impacted.

**Relevant Thought:** No woman can call herself free until she can choose consciously whether she will or will not be a mother.

**- Margaret Sanger**

## Power Sector's Main Problem (Dt: 27.06.2022)

- Electricity Regulator of Kerala on 25th June 2022 raised average consumer tariff by 6.6%, the 1st hike in 3 years where as state Discom sought an average increase of 18% in total.
- Discom losses are huge it was Rs 5 lakh crore in 2019-20.
- Root cause of Power Sector Problems is the approach of state governments and not the performance of regulators. Electricity Act allows states to subsidize customers on the condition that they pay subsidy amount to their Discoms in advance. But it never happens consequently Discoms delay payment to power generation companies. At the beginning of June, 2022 over Rs 1 Lakh crore is the aggregate Discom overdue.
- GOI tried for 2 decades, but had negligible success is solving the problem. Two critical benchmarks are never met.

  a) Uday scheme to eliminate deficit between electricity cost and revenue by 2018-19.

  b) Lower the transmission and commercial loss to 15%.

GOIs efforts on finance and incentives are not effective.

- Currently GOI is in another effort: Regulators are to act on existing low to adjust tariffs in a way that brings them within 20% of average cost of supply.
- Pilot projects of DBT for electricity subsidy carried by Kerala and HP need to be debated. DTT is only durable solution.

**Relevant Thought:** Because a thing seems difficult for you, do not think it impossible for anyone to accomplish.

**- Marcus Aurelius**

## IPC's Criminal Deformation (Dt: 28.06.2022)

- Nagpur branch of Bombay High Court has ruled against misuse of IPC's criminal defamation provision. It said newspaper fairly reporting information in the public domain without insinuation or innuendo cannot attract defamation charges.
- The Nagpur bench concluded that registration of crimes, filing court cases, investigations and arrest of persons constitute "news events which public has right to know." Bench noted that a newspaper is not to investigate FIR's contents and verify its truthfulness; but to report facts connately.
- Criminal defamation allows complainants to claim the accused had intention to harm reputation. Tamil Nadu's AIDMK governments were infamous for lodging criminal defamation cases indiscriminately against journalists.
- With Public Prosecutors appearing in courts, magistrates often take cognizance of frivolous matters, prompting a dash to HCs for relief.
- The British has decriminalised defamation in 2009. India should shed criminal defamation from IPC, and get an effective civil libel low.

**Relevant Thought:** A tolerant society is one in which we criminalise an activity only as a last resort.

**- John Gummer**

## G7 on Limiting Price of Russian Oil (Dt: 29.06.2022)

- G7 nations now try to limit the price of Russian oil, but sanctions and embargoes imposed by EU, US and their allies and little impact on Russia's War ability against Ukraine. On the contrary, squeeze on Russian oil has elevated global crude prices, helping Russia earn more. Elevated price has aided inflation and pushed up cost of living.
- Reports indicate lifting sanctions on insurance for cargo ships transporting Russian oil in return for a price deal. London based Protection and Indemnity clubs insures 95% of world's cargo shipment. The group may face sanctions if it ensures Russian Oil cargo above the to be determined price. Some countries like China are unlikely to go along with G7 on this.
- Better is French idea of getting Iran and Venezuela back to the oil suppliers' fold. But Iran nuclear deal with US is inconsistent and conflicting. Venezuela has political challenges for Biden administration.
- The West wants to weaken Russia even if it damages the global economy including Western ones. Every new plan to punish Russia hurts the global economy.

**Relevant Thought:** Sanctions always hurt the poor, the weak, the children.

**- Brian May**

## Horrific Act of Terrorism at Udaipur (Dt: 30.06.2022)

- The gruesome murder, beheading Kanhaiya Lal in Udaipur on 2806.2022 is an act of terrorism. GOI on 29/06.2022 directed the NIA (Nat Investigation Agency) to undertake the probe. CM of Rajasthan, Ashok Gehlot said the murder was to spread terror and the information indicated the 2 perpetrators have contacts overseas.
- Two terrorists Md Riyaz Akhtari and Gaus Mohammed belong to groups that believe that the "punishment for blasphemy must be death." They did videography of ISIS style brutality which required multilevel and multi-agency response quickly.

- Quality of local policing is in question. The victim Lal had a formal complaint to police about threat to his life. The state has suspended an Asst Sub. Inspector in Udaipur for negligence. The state should implement basic police reforms. Political parties must keep watch on groups and individuals who can do things that may aggravate the volatile situation.

**Relevant Thought:** In time we hate that which we often fear.

**- Shakespeare**

## Tactical Move in Maharashtra (Dt: 01.07.2022)

- BJP demonstrated its tactical intelligence by making Eknath Shinde CM of Maharashtra and Devendra Fadnavis as Dy CM, which should have been the vice versa as per logic of majority.
- By this Shiv Sena's bigger faction re-enters NDA with respectful accommodation. CM Shinde stands a better chance to woo Uddhav Camp followers. In 2024 election, BJP will have a dominant and happy Sena faction against Uddhav Sena, NCP, and congress.
- Shinde's MLAs are from geographically diverse areas while Uddhav has Mumbai legislators. A race to corner the Sena party name, symbol, offices, elected representatives and workers has started. The next battle ground will be BMC, Thane and other urban civic polls. The most non-urban Sena MLAs switched to Shinde indicates about dangers facing Thackerays.

**Relevant Thought:** Next to knowing when to seize an opportunity, the most important thing in life is to know when to forgo an advantage.

**-Benjamin Disraeli**

## Anti-Defection Law in focus (Dt: 02.07.2022)

- The Shiv Sena rebellion issue has brought the Anti-Defection law into focus. Disqualification of members on their defection from a political party was mentioned in $10^{th}$ schedule of Indian constitution by its $52^{nd}$ amendment in 1985 and was further inserted in 2003 by $91^{st}$ amendment.

a) The law's provisions give no time frame for taking decision.

b) Speakers and Governors are not neutral umpires

c) Courts have muddled waters with differing interpretations

- In Maharashtra 16 random Sena rebel MLAs received disqualification notices although the Shinde fraction had crossed the 2/3rd threshold to evade disqualification. (As per 10th Sch 1/3rd members communicating merger with other cannot be disqualified) It was a clear attempt to break legitimate rebellion by reducing member.

- In 2019 Karnataka Speaker disqualified 17 Congress – JD(s) MLAs despite resigning their house membership and barred them for assembly's tenure which the constitution does not prescribe.

- Above is example of quick punishment. Now the other is a slow punishment e.g. AIADMK rebels in TN and Congress defectors in Manipur and MP.

- In 2016 SC gave judgment that restored a Congress Government in Arunachal Pradesh, although rebels of 2/3rd threshold had crossed over to Peoples Party of Arunachal under Kalikho Pul. Sometimes verdicts are delayed defanging the law. Tenth schedule's bar on defections must be honoured by Parliament president officers and courts with more elegant versions.

**Relevant Thought:** Power attracts the worst and corrupts the best.

## Electricity and Petroleum in GST (Dt: 04.07.2022)

- June 30, 2022 GOI levied indirect tax in the form of cess on domestic crude production sold at import parity prices, and on export of petrol, diesel, aviation turbine fuel which will accrue entirely to GOI.

- GST council had last week approved reform of indirect tax by closing some exemptions and correcting inverted duties, which is a welcome move.

- Aim of GST is to improve India's economic competitiveness by removing cascading impact of taxes. Keeping Petroleum and Electricity inside GST will help to realize this goal.

- States are reluctant to include thee into GST as they feel GOI has eaten into pool f taxes by cess and surcharge. They refer to the share and surcharge in gross tax revenue increased 10.4% in 2011-12 to 15.3% in 2018-19.
- The forward way should be: GOI, by avoiding frequent recourse to cess and surcharge, persuade states to bring petrol, electricity, and all real estate into GST. Its direct impact will be on India's competitiveness.

**Relevant Thought:** Cooperative federalism is in the rapture of a repeated game between the two entities.

**- V Kelkar and A Ranade**

## Poll Battle in Telangana (Dt: 05.07.2022)

- Keeping poll target in 2023 Telangana; BJP had organized national executive meet at Hyderabad.
- Both BJP and TRS faced fines by GHMC for unauthorized banners and posters which is a publicity for poll battle.
- GHMC elections in 2020 and 2 by poll victories signaled BJP surge in Telangana.
- Factors in BJP favour is:

  i) By KCR's decimating Congress in 2 assemblies has helped BJP.

  ii) BJP's strategy of alleging TRS-AIMIM alliance in GHMC polls has tasted success. Slogans like renaming Hyderabad and flying saffron flag on "Golla Konda" fort and Despotic Nizam rule are further strategies.

  iii) Highlights on KCR family's over-dominance and inadequate backward class representation and promoting OBC leaders are next strategies.

  iv) PM Modi is a key vote-catcher recalls to 2019 LS polls defeating even KCR's daughter.
- BJP's wary (a) TRS is led by veteran politician KCR with complete control of party who is cleverly playing the native Vs outsider game.

(b) KCR has a formidable welfare delivery record.

(c) Alleged unwillingness of Centre over procuring state's parboiled rice.

(d) BJP lacks formidable state leader to take on KCR.

**Relevant Thought:** Ah, but it is nice to be in the opposition, nice to be a bone in somebody's throat.

**-Jack Levine**

## NGT-Vital for Environment Regulation (Dt: 06.07.2022)

- NTT (National Green Tribunal) is vital for environment regulation in India. But its orders are being appealed in SC and HCs. Recently SC critiqued NGT for mechanical and pre-drafted orders which was not heard before a penalty of Rs 40 crore was imposed on the firm.
- NGT's tendency to set up expert committee was frowned by another SC bench nothing that its adjudicatory functions cannot be delegated.
- NGT is expected to quickly settle growing numbers of environmental matters, as it is an adjudicatory body staffed with judicial and technical experts having significant powers. No of NGT rulings held the field are- deregistering 10 yrs old diesel vehicles, ban on firecrackers, RO water purifiers and sand mining – had minimal impact in absence of political support. NGT has ended up as casualty of "Development vs Environment."
- NGT now lacks staffs. It has presently 7 judicial and 6 expert members against its mandate to have 10-20 judicial and expert members each. In 2019 these members were 4 and 2 respectively. Due to fewer members, 2 extreme scenarios have cropped up: backlogs and hasty disposals. Routinely stays are secured from SC and HCs against NGT orders clearing or blocking projects.
- These erode credibility of NGT. It must get support from GOI.

**Relevant Thought:** At the end of the day, is Singapore society better or worse off? That is the test.

**- Lee Kuan Yew**

## Air Accidents and DGCA Actions (Dt: 07.07.2022)

- DGCA, India's civil aviation regulator has issued show cause notice to Spice Jet after series of accidents reported from Apr 1. DGCA concludes that the airline had poor internal safety oversight and inadequate maintenance. There have been 7 in stances since May and worst was on July 5, when there were 3 instances.
- The auditor raised doubts about company's ability to continue as going concern. Statutory dues such as PF and GST had not been regularly deposited. DGCA conducted financial assessment in Sep, 2021. The finding showed that suppliers are not being paid regularly which has led to a shortage of spares.
- The findings of infestations by GOI in March into 49 air accidents since 2016 showed the reasons for accidents were: failure of cockpit crew to stick to standard operating procedures, technical defects and inclement weather and ATC.
- In 2013-14 US federal Aviation Authority (USFAA) decided to degrade Indian Civil Aviation from category I to category II after an audit brought out shortcomings in safety and maintenance sine then matters have improved and recent USFAA audit went off well.
- A key international safety will be carried out by ICAO a specialized UN agency. DGCA's primary responsibility is to take timely action to guarantee safely standards.

**Relevant Thought:** An ounce of action is worth a ton of theory.

**-Ralph Waldo Emerson**

## RBI Foreign Exchange Inflows (Dt: 08.07.2022)

- On 06.07.2022, RBI took measures to encourage Foreign Exchange inflows.

  a) Incremental deposits raised till Nov through FCNR

  b) NRE do not have to meet regulatory requirements such as CRR which is more attractive for banks

  c) Attract FPI (Foreign Portfolio Investment) into debt.

d) Conditions by Indian firms to raise debt abroad are eased.

- India's Foreign Exch Reserve is comfortable at $ 593 billion. But we run a current a/c deficit for the most part; hence accumulated reserves are relatively less stable.
- Uncertain global economic condition can lead to sudden outflow, a currency depreciation and adverse inflation as we are a net commodity importer. Adequate F Exch Reserves act as a shock absorber and allow RBI to smoothen currency depreciation.
- Russia-Ukraine conflict is root cause of global volatility and surge in commodity prices. Indian crude basket is 10% lower ($104/ barrel) than price of few weeks ago. Similarly, Urea, Copper, Aluminum and Sunflower oil prices declined.
- Food and fuel prices are 55% of consumer price index and are not under RBI control. A surge in these prices leads to effects and consequent increase in interest rates. RBI should encourage capital inflows when India's macroeconomics are not in red.

**Relevant Thought:** As inflation rises, price increases come into sharper focus, and move out of the zone of "rational inattention."

**-Agustin Carstens**

## Tribute To former Japanese PM Shinzo Abe (Dt: 09.07.2022)

- Former Japanese PM Shinzo Abe was assassinated on 08.07.2022 during an election campaign. He was Japanese globally best-known leader in long time and has tried to free Japan from its conservative cover with a foreign policy reorientation and economic reforms dubbed as "Abenomics."
- He had grasped the implications of the rise of and aggressive China and was original visualizer of free and open Indo-Pacific region. He was a key driving force behind resurrection of QUAD realizing Japan's important security role in Asia to counter balance China. He believed in India's rise and ability to deliver for Asia.
- Abe was resolute in pursuing the civil nuclear agreement with India. He has offered most generous terms for High-Speed Rail in India.

His contribution to India-Japan relations was richly recognised by India's conferment upon him the prestigious 'Padma Vibhushan' in 2021.

- Ave had deep insight into complex and multiple transitions in world the vision to be ahead of time in politics, society, economy and international relations, wisdom to know the choices, capacity to make clear and bold decisions and ability to carry his people and the world with him. The world will always be indebted for his foresight in recognizing the changing tides and gathering storm of our time and his leadership in responding to it. He was energetic, captivating charismatic and witty.

**Relevant Thought:** Politicians should be humble in the face of history. And whenever history is a matter of debate, it should be left in the hands of historians and experts.

**-Shinzo Abe**

## Sri Lanka Economic Crisis and Unrest (Dt: 11.07.2022)

- Sri Lanka public stormed residence of President, Gotabaya Rajapaksa driven by anger and frustration due to inflation and shortage of food and fuel. Sri Lanka needs a functional Government to act together, conduct negotiation with IMF, with major nations and restructure viable economy.
- PM Rani P Wickremesinghe's private home was set on fire as Lankan people have lost patience and want results immediately. July 9 protests and May 9 violence are warning to political parties to be united and brainstorm for course of action and fresh elections.
- China accounts 15% of Sri Lanka's external debt. Inflation has topped 50% and Sri Lanka rupee is 350 for a dollar.
- It has strategic location in Indian Ocean with international busy shipping route passing by it. It must stir other nation is to offer more aid to the country.
- Sri Lanka was South Asia's brightest spot with high human development indices. Now, the economic mismanagement threatens

regression with schools shutting and hospitals running out of medicines and supplies. A chunk of shipping business is shifting to Indian ports.

- The course left for Sri Lanka is belt tightening and a peaceful transfer of power to a credible government which will struggle to attract tourism, trade, and foreign investment as it has been doing.

**Relevant Thought:** Civilization begins with order, grows with liberty, and dies with chaos.

**-Will Durant**

## Control of AIADMK By EPS and OPS (Dt: 12.07.2022)

- AIADMK party was jointly run by 2 leaders EK Palanisami and O Panneerselvam, duo EPS and OPS. In 2017, EPS as Tamil Nadu CM and Party CO-convener, OPS as Dy CM-cum AIDMK convener, joined hands to oust an imprisoned VK Sasikala who was party leader following Jayalalitha's death in 2016, but a 4-year jail commencing in Feb, 2017 slipped veins from her hands.

- Both EPS and OPS were one time favourite of Sasikala OPS for CM was first choice of Jayalalitha, but EPS a dark horse ousted Sasikala and strengthened his control over the government and marginalized OPS.

- The game of thrones for AIADMK's top post continues Executive committee and 2000 strong general council comprising leaders and office beavers have spoken, but OPS can still test his strength among the cadre.

- In 1989, after post-MGR AIADMK split, with most of the then seniors siding with MGR's widow, Janaki; still Jayalalitha clawed back. Hence the cadre similarly could still be restive that the party lacks a leader with a cult.

- In this situation, new caste or regional divides could emerge. OPS joining with Sasikala both being Thevars may dent AIDMK's social base which may suit DMK. EPS, the leader of opposition is an effective administrator may storm back and match up.

**Relevant Thought:** I would rather be first in a village than second at Rome.

**-Julius Caesar**

## SC Suggested Progressive Bail Reform (Dt: 13.07.2022)

- Supreme Court (SC) has suggested that India needs comprehensive bail legislation on the lines of UK Bail Act. About 70% of prisoners are under trials, mostly poor and unable to secure monetary bail. Poor and poorly educated citizens are unable to take advantage of legal system unlike the educated, affluent, and influential persons. Therefore, a progressive bail reform can check this inequity.
- Now, arrests and interrogations, warrants and summons, bonds and sureties, powers of police and courts are dispersed across Cr PC and binding SC guidelines.
- SC wondered; judges adopt negative attitude towards bail for low rate of conviction.
- SC now has directed that bail applications should be disposed of within 2 weeks in normal course. It is reasonable. Sometimes bail applications are kept pending for months. Appeals by convicted are pending for decades in some HCs. They deserve bail if appeals are delayed for no fault of theirs.
- SC has reiterated that arrests to be used sparingly are a draconian measure. SC's skepticism over compliance with its 2014 Arnesh Kumar judgment reveals that well intentioned verdicts are being subverted. The judgment had directed cops to record specific reasons necessitating arrest and magistrates to grant bail if the reasons do not make a persuasive case. But quick bail is a good corrective against unnecessary arrests.

**Relevant Thought:** When it comes to revamping our bail laws, we cannot rely on judicial discretion alone.

**-Eric Adams**

## Cardinal Error, Anxiety and Panic in CUET (Dt: 14.07.2022)

- Common Univ. Entrance Test (CUET) is set to go on live in 90 universities on 15.07.2022 by 15 lakh registrations with release of its schedule on 18.07.2022. It has caused anxiety and panics due to new unaware pattern of examination errors in admit cards and scheduling of exam.
- Much of this could have been averted, had the NTA (National Testing Agency), UGC and the Education Ministry undertaken better public communication on these ahead of the release of schedule.
- Students are experiencing injustice and fear, if they have been allotted an early test date compared to their peers. A student's score card will carry percentile score and his relative performance vis-a-vis students appear in same test on July will matter. Those who take the test in August will be scored as a separate cohort.
- There is distress about students being told to test for multiple subjects on the same day.
- Because of poor communication by authorities a smart admission-reform, CUET that originated in the commendable goal of reducing student stress is producing the opposite effect.
- NTA must now accommodate student requests for shifting test centre fixing admit card errors and address all glitches.

**Relevant Thought:** Our age of anxiety is, in great part the result of trying to do today's job with yesterday's tools and yesterday's concepts.

**Marshall Melham**

## RBI's Measures for Rupee Settlement (Dt: 15.07.2022)

- RBI has initiated measures this week to allow rape settlement of cross-border trade deals. Indian banks will be custodians of funds in international transactions settled in rupees. These measures are to cope with developments in foreign currency market to cope with developments in foreign currency market and gradual shift in currency composition of global foreign exchange reserves.

- In addition to market intervention, RBI adopted other measures to cope with the rupee depreciation. It has liberalized forex inflows. Now it has provided a window to settle trades in rupees.
- This window helps India to grab opportunities such as discounts on Russian oil. India imported $ 1.3 billion of Russian crude in April, making it the 4th longest source. A year ago, there was no import of crude from Russia.
- Rupee settlement allows Indian firms circumvent Western sanctions that bite their dominance over global financial system.
- In long term, there will be opportunities to internationalize the rupee on account of shift in composition of global FE reserves. The US dollar's hold is slowly receding, it is about 59% now from a level of 70% two decades ago.
- India needs to learn from Bank of Israel which pans to reallocate part of its US dollar holdings to currencies of Australia, Canada, China and Japan.

**Relevant Thought:** Victory comes from finding opportunities in problems.

**-Sun Tzu**

## US CAATSA Waiver for India (Dt: 16.07.2022)

- The Countering America's Adversaries through Sanctions Act (CAATSA) is a US federal legislation (law) that imposed sanctions on Iran, North Korea, and Russia. The Bill was passed by the senate on 27 July 2017 after it passed the House.
- On 14 July 22 US House of Representatives drew bipartisan support to pass amendment that urged Joe Biden administration to extend India a waiver from CAATSA sanctions on purchase of Russian S-400 air defence system. The S-400 transaction was in 2018 i.e. after 2017-CAATSA.
- The amendment pointed out that S-400 is needed to deter China and India is only QUAD member burdening China. US thus took step to India's pivot away reliance on Russia.

- Our bilateral strategic relations with US started in 2008. Prior to 2008 US defence contracts with India was just $500 million. Since 2008 it added up to $20 billion. In 2016, US recognised India as a major defence partner.
- Russia's dependence on China has increased significantly following invasion of Ukraine. China next only to India as the 2nd largest recipient of Russia's arms exports. Looking to India's long-standing border dispute with China, dependence on Russian arms is unwise. Hence, US response by House of Representatives should be positive.

**Relevant Thought:** You must remember, something is legally right are not morally right.

**- Abraham Lincoln**

## Freebies undermines Economic Development (Dt: 18.07.2022)

- Now India has political culture of canvassing for votes by promising "freebies." Freebies are shorthand for substandard monetary/economic choice by governments. It is an area where all major political parties are blameworthy. By promising free or subsidized goods and services they canvas votes. Political parties are unable to bring environment to create decent jobs which is inclusive indicator of economic development. India cannot afford to continue this road.
- If freebies are fiscal choices, we need a widely accepted understanding of kind of choices that forced this termism.
- Tamil Nadu is synonymous by Dravidian political parties with freebies for last 55 years. Yet the state has the 4th lowest poverty ratio in India as per Niti Aayog. It has highest no of operating factories in the formal sector. But the recent fiscal slippages catalyzed the state government last year to present a white paper on public finances.
- To forge consensus on freebies; reliable data is essential. GOI should go by finance commissions and establish an independent fiscal council. It should be backed by law to access all accounts of both states and GOI. A debate with data with help politicians to make fiscal choices.

**Relevant Thought:** Sometimes one pays most for the things one gets for nothing.

**- Albert Einstein**

## India's Vaccination Crossed 2 billion Doses (Dt: 19.07.2022)

- Cumulative covid vaccination coverage in India crossed the 2 billion doses mark on 18.07.2022. GOI announced free jobs beginning July 15, which resulted in a surge in daily uptake now. India's vaccination coverage has crossed 66% of population for full protocol of 2 doses.
- Overall cost of vaccination has been modest. The total cost of vaccination coverage by Feb 7 is less than 1% of union budget expenditure for 2021-22. Key reason for rapid ramp up of vaccination in 2$^{nd}$ half of 2021 was its free admission in government centres.
- There are 2 reasons for rapid ramp-up. i) Overall health spending out of packet in India is 65%, a relatively high level. ii) For job losses Covid extracted an economic cost. Free vaccination in addition is critical in expanding its coverage fast.
- Boosters were initially not free for adults. Some states like Bihar in last week of April made booster free for everyone over 18 years and uptake increased considerably after that. GOI's free booster resulted in an immediate uptick and it contributed to 80% of the total jobs on 18 July.
- Missteps in Booster Policy: i) Local trial on booster was belated. ii) When the rollout started; India avoided heterologous boosting (with different Vax). CMC Vellore trial showed that heterologous boosting provides enhanced immunity.

**Relevant Thought:** Protection delayed is protection denied for senior citizens and at rise groups.

**-T Jacob John**

## DGCA Order to Airlines (Dt: 20.07.2022)

- DGCA, India's Civil Aviation Regulator on 18.07.2022 issued order to airlines that increased instances of engineering related occurrences had triggered spot checks by the regulator. The findings pointed to maintenance issues that the identification of reported defects has been improper and there is shortage of trained staff. Airlines have been asked to comply with safety protocols and report back to DGCA by July 28. A day after this order was issued; 2 more instances of snags were reported.

- Latest information red flags deficient maintenance and conclude that large numbers of failure incidents occur due to component failure.
- DGCA's safety audits are ongoing feature and are reported in an annual surveillance plan. There is constant communication between airlines and the regulator on the subject.
- Aviation policy was tweaked to help airlines overcome covid shock and prepare for the future. For example, even as seating restrictions have been removed, a price band continues. BST on domestic maintenance, repair and overhaul has been lowered from 18% to 10.5%.
- There are questions on performance of both the regulator (DGCA) and GOI. DGCA needs to strictly implement its safety protocol.

**Relevant Thought:** The safety of the people shall be the highest law.

**– Marcus Tullius Cicero**

## Sri Lanka President and Bailout Negotiation (Dt: 21.07.2022)

- Sri Lanka parliament chose Ranil Wickremesinghe as the new president. Protesters for last few weeks had wanted him to step down as PM and did not want him to secure the presidency as he does not have the people's mandate for presidency.
- Wickremesinghe has been in politics for 4 decades and represents the old guard quality of bankrupting the country. Protesters aim to usher in wholesale systematic change, including a new constitution.
- His time in public office has seen him well-acquainted with foreign governments and international institutions; hence he is a good bet as a rescue negotiator. When Mahindra Rajapaksa stepped down and he was appointed PM, there have been some signs of economic relief,

like reduced power cuts, fertilizer to farmers and improvement in gas supply etc.

- Wickremesinghe's prime job will be to form a cabinet and conclude bailout talks with IMF. He must also win over the trust of protesters and set the ball rolling on constitutional reforms.
- India has stood by Sri Lanka through this crisis and has emerged as chief lender should provide support to Wickramasinghe.

**Relevant Thought:** For past 28 years he was leader of one party who could never become president. Country is in a situation out of which only, Ranil Wickremesinghe can take us out.

**- Harin Fernando**

## India Elected its First Adivasi President (Dt: 22.07.2022)

- India elected 15th President a first Adivasi Lady, Draupadi Murmu, as a tribute in democratizing diversity in political representation BJP deserves this credit by nominating a strong deserving tribal woman for India's top ceremonial constitutional post.
- Her journey to Rastrapati Bhavan (Rai Rangpur to Raisina) is an inspirational story of overcoming adverse circumstances and personal setbacks.
- She was born on 20 June, 1958 at Rai Rangpur District, Mayur Bhanj in Odisha. She completed high school education and graduation 1979 at Bhubaneswar. She had worked as Junior Asst in Irrigation and Power Odisha Government in 1979. She was teacher at Sri Aurobindo Integral Education and Reach Centre, Rai Rangpur (1994). She joined BJP in 1997 and become councilor of Rai Rangpur NAC. In 2000, she became MLA, Rai Rangpur.
- BJP ticket. IN 2000 till 2004 she served as commerce and transport minister and later fishery and Animal Resources Development minister. In 2004 reelected as MLA and got Best MLA award in 2007, she served as BJP Odisha Sch Tribe Morcha President in 2006-2009 and in 2013-2015 became Mayurbhanj District President of BJP. From 2015-2021 she served as Governor of Jharkhand.

- She had lost her both sons and husband in quick succession (Sr=9% of population) lowest wealth: 71% Adivasi, 49% Dalit, 36% OBC.

**Relevant thought:** Every successful individual knows that his on her achievement depends on a community of persons working together.

**-Paul Ryan**

## SC's Ruling on saving Aravali Hills (Dt: 23.07.2022)

- Aravali range is one of the oldest mountain blocks in the world. SC's Aravalli ruling was to save the Hills. The verdict was that all land in Haryana covered under Punjab Land Preservation Act will be treated as forest land. This verdict is in harmony with the tone of 3 decades of jurisprudence on Aravalli range a key feature of NCR.
- Three states of NCR – Haryana, Rajasthan and UP have forest cover significantly lower than National Average of 21.7% Haryana is the lowest at 3.5% Development Vs Environment. – They are intertwined and need to be nurtured together for progress. The destruction of Aravalli has extracted a large economic and health cost in the NCR.
- World Bank estimated in 2013 that annual cost of India's economic degradation amounted to $ 80 billion or 5.7% of GDP.
- Hopefully by this SC ruling; the Aravalli will have a chance of survival.

**Relevant Thought:** What's the use of a fine house if you have not got a tolerable planet to put it on?

**-Henry David Thoreau**

## Monkey Pox – A Global Health Emergency (Dt: 25.07.2022)

- WHO has declared Monkeypox a global health emergency. Nearly 18,000 cases have been detected worldwide. India with lessons of Covid pandemic is in a better position to implement prevention and treatment strategies for Monkeypox.

- Monkeypox is less transmissible and the infection starts only after appearance of symptoms. Community disease surveillance is a must and should be increased. There is possibility of Monkeypox being overlooked as chickenpox. Healthcare workers must get reports of patients manifesting chickenpox-like symptoms.
- Heightened surveillance coupled with prompt quarantining individuals will prevent major outbreak. Smallpox vaccination to medical workers as a protection against Monkeypox should start early. India must start a massive vaccine manufacturing infrastructure and incentivize vaccine companies to scale up production.
- US has ordered 7 million Jynneous vaccine for delivery in 2022 and 2023 and many US states are reporting its shortages. It is a warning for India which must short getting a manufacturing license. Monkeypox a battle for India to win.

**Relevant Thought:** When a prevention campaign works, nothing happens.

**-Norman Swan**

## India needs a Joint Commands and CDS (Dt: 26.07.2022)

- Defence Minister Rajnath Singh re-emphasized that joint theatre commands are a defence reform priority, but a little headway has been made so far. Warfare is changing and modern response is joint commands with resources of 3 services. Converting the currently existing 17 single-service commands into joint theatre commands would be a radical change in culture of armed forces.
- The thematization model will have 4 new integrated commands 2 land-centric commands and 1 air defence command, and 1 maritime command. Air force had expressed reservations about splitting assets as those have dual offensive and defensive roles.
- Centre had mode 8-member panel under Chief of Defence Staff Late Gen Bipin Rawat in June 202, for report by April, 2022. Due to Rawat's death, it had sellback. India's security challenges have

become complex with rise of China Pakistan axis. China has radically transformed its military and PLA established 5 theatre commands.

- GOI has moved on the first step through Agnipath. It must new quickly appoint next CDS and more thematization.

**Relevant Thought:** We are determined to innovate and indigenize; we are determined to fight Indian wars with Indian solutions.

**– General (Late) Bipin Rawat**

## FIR Against Ranbir Singh for Obscenity (Dt: 27.07.2022)

- The actor poses nude for a magazine photo-shoot A6 is inevitable with social media, some people say they are offended. Ranveer Singh the actor is now booked by Mumbai police for "obscenity." He has been booked under Section 292 of IPC which includes anything that is "Lascivious, appeals to prurient interest or tends to deprive or corrupt persons likely to read, see or hear the matter." In Indian law, it is defined in such ridiculously loose and vague manner of which cops and lower courts get opportunity to harass.
- Shilpa Shetty for 15 years is still fighting obscenity case filed in 2007. Because someone felt offended by American actor Richard Gere Kissing Shelfy, police in Alwar, Rajasthan filed and FIR.
- Madhu Sapre and Milind Soman had to wait 14 years before their acquittal in 2009 in obscenity case of 1995, Tuff shoes advertisement. When the police do not file FIRs, they use Section 292 as an instrument of extortion. Section 292 of IPC is out of sync with modern democratic society. Police has discretion to not register FIRs if the complaint is frivolous. Magistrate courts should quickly discharge to discourage police. High Courts should quash FIRs and impose penalties on complainants.

**Relevant Thought:** Obscenity is whatever happens to shock some elderly and ignorant magistrate.

**- Bertrand Russell**

## Census – 2021 Must Begin (Dt: 28.07.2022)

- GOI had notified to start work on Census 2021 on March 28, 2019. This week it informed in Parliament that on account of Covid the census has been put off. Social or economic activities are now completed, multiple assembly elections have been held since 2020, yet field work on census got postponed. It is not good to defend this by extrapolating key indicators from census 2011.
- India's first census got postponed. It is not good to defend this by extrapolating key indicators from Census 2011.
- India's first census year was 1872. A census enumerates population and spans critical data of a demographic, social and economic profile of population, its postponement reasons are not quite convincing.
- GOI recently addressed that census data will not be used to create not's Register of Citizens (NRC) as the statutory law governing census operations restricts it to the use of aggregated data.
- An innovation feature in Census 2021 is self-enumeration, whose details are not in public domain.
- May political parties have raised to use Census 2021 to enumerate population based on castes.
- Census data is for public good, GOI should not put field work on Census 2021 any longer.

**Relevant Thought:** The Indian census is often billed as the largest peacetime mobilisation in the world.

**- Census India**

## Spectrum of Political Corruption (Dt: 29.07.2022)

- Partha Chatterjee, Min of Industry, commerce and Enterprise of West Bengal had hoardings of ill-gotten cash stored in apartments. Chief Min Mamata Banerjee sacked him form her cabinet and from party posts.

- How the CM remained unaware of his rampant corruption? Corruption scandal coming to light ae higher now than before. Chatterjee's case was brought to limelight by central agencies.
- In another case at Karnataka, a victim went to public. A contractor's complaint and subsequent suicide opened the lid of Karnataka's rampant "Commission" system for clearing government projects. Rural development minister KS Eshwarappa had to quit.
- In Maharashtra's pot boiler MVA politics, evidence of financial dodginess has been apparent.
- There are shameful use of vital services and infrastructure to extract money. Selling of teacher's posts is a widespread practice. Haryana politicians hit headlines for this some years back.

**Relevant Thought:** It is not the young people that degenerate; they are not spoiled till those of mature age are already sunk into corruption.

**- Montesquieu**

## NCR Pollution and Uttarakhand Heat Waves (Dt: 30.07.2022)

- To curb stable burning, Delhi Government proposed Rs 2500 per acre cash incentive to paddy farmers; will require centres handholding.
- AAP Government in Punjab and Delhi is willing to contribute Rs 500 each and expect GOI to fund the rest.
- But Haryana another farm fire contributor must be roped in too. UP-cities like Noida and Ghaziabad, Delhi, Haryana-cities like Gurgaon and Faridabad, all NCR are affected by air quality dips due to stable burning.
- Various straw management machines and bio-decomposer jointly developed by IcAR-IARI and pesticide company UPL must be prioritized alongside the cash incentive. Time is limited; stubble burning peaks in October. Farmers pocketing the SOP must be penalized if they still burn stable.
- Another threat is fast-changing Himalayan ecology. Uttarakhand recorded most heat wave days this year. High temperatures are triggering more forest fires and depleting glaciers. High pilgrims and

tourists aggravate solid waste management problem. Solid waste burning or burying is unsustainable. GOI must take up this on emergency and spend money to preserve it.

**Relevant Thought:** We could have saved the Earth but we were too damned cheap.

**-Kurt Vonnegut**

## Poor Payment of Power to DISCOMS (Dt: 01.08.2022)

- On 30.07.2022, PM Modi drew attention to poor payment habits of Power DISCOMS. It results in financial problems that plague the electricity supply system.
- Electricity Generating Cos are in huge loss states have arrears of Rs 1.2 Lac Crore to pay to electricity generating companies. Government Departments and local Nikay (Nagar Nigam etc.) have Rs 60,000 Crore arrears to pay to Gen Cos. States subsidy of Rs. 75,000 crores are arrears to be paid by states to Gen Coms. Total 2.5 Lakh Crore (1.134 + 75,000 Crore + 60,000Crore) are over dues to be paid to Electricity Generation Cos.
- GOI's 2016 tariff policy allows 'cross subsidies' if tariffs are within a 20% band around the average cost of supply.
- Electricity Act allows states to subsidies consumers provided they meet one essential condition: Discoms need to receive the subsidy in advance. If the law is followed, there will be no over dues.
- Tamil Nadu, Maharashtra, Telangana, UP and J and K are (among states) and UTs (Union Territories) with large over dues.
- PM Modi's call for a joint effort at finding solution must be viewed.
- There's a statutory law to notify a road map to bring tariffs within 20% of the average cost of supply. Regulators need to follow the law all states need to follow the examples of Kerala and HP, among others, which are trying a switch to direct transfer of electricity subsidy to the consumer. DBT can end a regime of cross-subsidy that leads to delayed payments. Discom reforms need to start right away.

**Relevant Thought:** The only thing that will redeem mankind is cooperation.

**– Bertrand Russell**

## India's Narrow Tax Base (Dt: 02.08.2022)

- Before GOI's deadline on July 31, only 6.7 million income tax returns had been filed. There are 617 million individuals with a PAN of whom 467 million have linked it with their Aadhar India's potential tax base seems unusually large. From practical revenue raised, it is despairingly narrow.
- In 2018-19, half of 58.7 million returns filed among all taxpayers showed no income. Hence, the potential tax base that yields revenue is small.
- GOI's budget showed corporate tax base of 9.17 lakh firms in 2019-20. Of this, a mere 0.2% or 1.843 companies contributed 69% of the corporate tax. That means, the budget's performance is influenced by less than 2,000 firms. A key reason for narrow base is the tax exemption window; as indirect subsidy to preferred taxpayers.
- As an example, firms with a pre-tax profit above Rs 500 crore had 58% share in the total profits open to taxation. The firms had an effective tax rate of 20.19% in 2019-20 when the average statutory rate was 34.58%.
- India's direct taxes contribute a little over 50% of the total tax revenue. It needs to be more for an economy with a per capita income of around $3,000.
- Greater use of AI and a legal architecture can widen the tax base.

**Relevant Thought:** The hardest thing to understand in the world is the income tax.

**– Albert Einstein**

## Spectrum Auction for 5G (Dt: 03.08.2022)

- Auction of spectrum for 5G concluded on 1st Aug, 2022. Major 71% spectrum was sold for Rs. 1.5 lakh Cr which can be paid over 20 annual in statements. Three features stood out i) GOI helped by diluting the cost of acquisition payment in installment was introduced. (ii) Bank Guarantees were waived off. (iii) Spectrum usage charges are eliminated.
- Auction was in 3 bands: 700 MHz, 3300MHz and 26 GHz. All 4 bidders picked up spectrum in 26GHz. The 700 MHz and 26MHz bands will see different 5G rollout. The farmer, a low frequency band can cover wide areas with fewer base stations but with slow download speed. The 26 GHz are fast speed of 3Gbps but limited range for signals. This will be for captive networks among business.
- 3300 MHz midband of most revenue generation. About 54% of total spent were in bids of this band. Three telecom firms competed for it and 76% spectrum was sold. Incumbents can continue to augment their 4G capacity. This band also offers to upgrade later as the market evolves.
- Just 17% of spectrum in 900 MHz, the mainstay of voice calls, got sold.
- Spectrum is a finite resource, when sold it is a precious economic resource. GOI's pragmatism must extend to reserve price.

**Relevant Thought:** Dream in a pragmatic way.

**-Aldous Huxley**

## Nancy Pelosi's visit to Taiwan (Dt: 04.08.2022)

- Speaker of US House of Representatives, Nancy Pelosi along with 5 democratic members of the House visited Taiwan (Republic of China) on 2 Aug, 2022. She is the highest-ranking US leader and a vocal critic of the Chinese Communist Party. As XI Jinping is hoping to secure 3rd term in the 20th Chinese Community Party Congress coming up in the year; Pelosi's Taipei trip is a direct challenge to his leadership authority.

- Beijing has announced 4 days of extensive live-fire military drills encircling Taiwan and completely blocking off surrounding airspace and waterways. This shows China is refraining from escalating military tensions with US. But the costs of Taiwan could go up in days ahead, if China decides to move against Taiwan controlled outlying islands like Kinmen and Matsu.
- China would be wary of attacking Taiwan, given how Russian invasion of Ukraine has happened. Plus, Taiwan's best defence today is cutting-edge semiconductor industry. Any attack on Taiwan would cause global disruption across industries, turn global opinion against China and support for Taiwan.
- India has headroom for two-way trade with Taiwan. From collaboration in semiconductors, green techs, building smart cities, to furthering AI, R and D, etc. are incentives to scale up. The two democracies, India and Taiwan should explore such relations.

**Relevant Thought:** They (China) did not say anything when the men came.

**-Nancy Pelosi**

## Matters For Adjudication by Courts (Dt: 05.08.2022)

- Supreme Court (SC) has decided to get rid of India politics of the freebie culture, which is outside its remit (area of activity). It has many pressing matters to attend.
- There can be debates about using state resources to offer SOPs. Some subsidies are necessary, some should be temporary and some are just bribery. Some should be temporary and some are just bribery. It is true that cost of such polices show up tower spend on social and economic infrastructure and in overall government deficits. But none of this is a matter for courts. These are promises made by elected politicians. Legislators can debate them, voters, tax payers can assess and accept or reject them.
- SC's job is to speed up hearings on crucial matters, like Article 370 nullification electoral bond, IT Act rules, demand to reassess PMLA ruling etc.

- After SC\s quashing of NJAC, judicial appointments are mired in controversies and delays: 40% cases in lower courts and 60% in higher courts are pending for over 3 years. SC has 342 five judge bench matters, 15 seven judges and 135 nine judger matters pending. There is 70% of under-trial prisoners. Which subverts the innocent until proven guilty. These are priority areas where judiciary has to be hard at work.

**Relevant Thought:** You can always find a distraction if you are looking for me

**– Tom Kite**

## Forensic Labs need Government Help (Dt: 06.08.2022)

- Forensic Science Labs (FSL) has pendency of 20,000 forensic tests catering to Delhi police with backlogs of 4-5 years. Forensics-chiefly cyber, biological/DNA, chemistry and ballistics are core of modern criminal investigations.
- There is severe under-staffing of FSLs. In Delhi, 40% posts are vacant in Karnataka and Haryana it is 64%. In Odisha (India's 2nd lowest conviction rate) 70% scientific officers and 40% Asst SO posts were vacant.
- Charge sheets are often filled without forensic reports because of long delay in getting results. Trials are delayed because of long delay in getting results. Trials are delayed and under-trial prisoners are incarcerated longer. The Police look good in NCRB reports thanks to high charge-sheeting rate, courts, hampered by lack of evidence preside pendency rates 90% in rape and other serious offences.
- FSLs are not uniformly distributed. UP and West Bengal had four and two functional regional FSLs respectively, while smaller AP and Telangana had 5 each in 2021. For mobile labs in practice and crime scene expertise; many more persons are needed. National Forensic sciences University can help tide over shortage of experts. Government should allocate more funds to forensic depts for upgrading technologies and filling vacancies.

**Relevant Thought:** Nothing matters but the facts. Without them, the science of criminal investigation is nothing more than a guessing game.
**- Blake Edwards**

## New Vice President and Opposition (Dt: 08.08.2022)

- Commanding victory of Vice President Jagdeep Dhankhar shows BJP's being competitor in states with BJD and YSRCP, these 2 neutral parties preferred to vote for BJP. In both President and Vice President elections they did not align with dispirited opposition parties.
- Monsoon session of Parliament was near washout. RS chairperson Dhankhar and LS Speaker on Birla should rethink how to have smooth functions. Suspensions of MPS in Parliament are not helping. Good debates on issues like Inflation Jobs China, Agnipath and Finances can help policy formulation.
- There is no semblance of opposition Unity that is needed to challenge BJP. CM, West Bengal Mamata Banerjee had abstained in BP polls. The sole national big party Congress has successive defeats in state election and Rahul Gandhi's approach does not enthuse other parties.
- Opposition must ponder how it can battle BJP.

**Relevant Thought:** The test of courage comes when we are in the minority. The test of tolerance comes when we are in the majority.

**Ralph W Sockman**

## CWG 2022 Medals by India (Dt: 09.08.2022)

- In the 2022 Common Wealth Game Birmingham, India has bagged 61 medals of 22 gold, 16 Silver and 23 Bronze. Most Indians had never heard Lawn Bowls, in which for the first time, our women's team delivered a gold and men's team a silver. This became India's best CWG performance.
- Next year, China will host Asian Games, which will be much tougher for India. It is important to analyze the CWG performance and address the letdowns. The investment in foreign exposure trips has

surely proved in delivering medals. For example, Avinash Sable CWG silver medalist in 3000 meters steeple chase and the nine-time national record holder credit his training in the US with enormous impact on his development.

- Lack of confidence seems to have sapped our women's cricket team as well as men's hockey team demanding special attention.
- A malaise the saga of Tejaswin Shankar India's first ever men's high jump bronze medal winner is an eye-opener as he took the Athletics Federation of India to court and then could get selected in 2022 CWG.
- Last Olympics made Indians interested in Javelin. Like that CWG success will inspire in track events. India sport still underperforms and underplays.

**Relevant Thought:** I had a feeling that athletics was my way to financial safety.

**Eldhose Paur, Tripple Jumpev**

## New Alignment in Bihar Politics (Dt: 10.08.2022)

- Bihar CM, Nitish Kumar stepped down as CM of NDA ministry and then joining alliance with RJD and congress took oath as CM of Mahagathbandhan.
- The breakup gives the opposition a better shot at Bihar's 40 Lok Sabha seats for 2024. Notionally the realignment boosts opposition unity.
- Governance reset is the direct need of Bihar. Since 1991 economic reforms, all big states have widened their lead over Bihar in per capita income. The state remains as a net exporter of low-skilled migrant labour. Niti Aayog's analysis depicts that 51% of Bihar's population remain poor and the state logs in education, healthcare and nutrition.
- JDU and RJD should learn from their records of poor governance and frequent ego classes. BJP-JD(U) affair has also no better. JD(U) and RJD may have their cast edifice; which will put BJP in struggle. The Bihar-youth are growing fiercely impatient

looking for employment and it is evident from Bihar's violent Agnipath protests that happened in recent past.

**Relevant Thought:** Every man is guilty of all the good he did not do.

**- Voltaire**

## Opposition And their Prospects (Dt: 11.08.2022)

- There is a breakthrough in position at Bihar as Nitish Kumar and Tejaswi Yadav assumed office again. BJP has won elections in UP, UK Manipur, Goa, and topped Maharashtra's MVA by engineering Shiv Sena's split and dominated the President and Vice President elections. Congress got defeated in 5 states including Punjab and trying by "Chintan Shivir" and "Nationwide Padayatra" etc.
- Mamata Banerjee has now dimmed. Arvind Kejriwal and AAP have long way to go. Sharad Pawar and K Chandrashekhar Rao are gagged down in battle with BJP. State-level politics is now proving harder to accomplish. Congress being unable to be credible alternative to BJP, Now battle ground has shifted to state capitals.
- For 2024, if the opposition is serious the starting must be unity and a common national manifesto. Opposition also needs a suitable political face nationally. Mamata's venture outside Bengal have massively flopped. Nitish brings useful OBC and Hindi heartland identity. NDA is raring to take its national dominance to states during coming assembly elections. Opposition should harness their prospects in states into credible national campaign.

**Relevant Thought:** Geography has made us neighbours. History has made us friends. Economics has made us partners and necessity has made us allies.

**-John F Kennedy**

## SC Bail To UAPA Accused (Dt: 12.8.2022)

- Supreme Court granted permanent medical bail to Varavara Rao, a UAPA accused, raises questions for justice system. SC made it clear that restrictions against bail in UAPA don't hinder courts from protecting fundamental rights.

- Varavara Rao, a poet, teacher, and writer from Telangana is an accused in 2018 Bhima Koregaon Violence and has been arrested under non-bailable UAPA, Rao was arrested on charge of plotting to assassinate Indian PM. He was released in Aug, 2022 on bail by C, granted on technical grounds, medical condition advanced age adherence to bail conditions, delay in framing charges.
- Many people, not been proven guilty are in jail. Bail is defeated by laws like UAPA that require judges to deny bail if they believe police cases to be true.
- Despite multiple SC ruling on prompt hearing and disposal of bail applications, Stan Swamy died in judicial custody waiting Bombay high court to decide on bail on medical grounds.
- Long process delays give credence to custody as punishment. The problem of under trial prisoners must take top priority under trials have been increasing and are 76% now. SC bench reiterated that courts must decide bail applications within 2 weeks and investigators must set down reason for arrest.

**Relevant Thought:** People should not be imprisoned without having the ability to challenge the legality of that imprisonment.

**- Jeff Bingaman**

## CUET NEET -JEE Interaction (Dt: 13.08.2022)

- CUET-Common University Entrance, NEET – National Eligibility Entrance Test (for MBBS and BDS), JEE- National Entrance Examination for engineering. Higher education regulator is working on a proposal to integrate engineering and medical entrance exams into undergraduate CUET.
- Higher education institutions that will be impacted by CUET-NEET-JEE integration include some of India's most cherished centre of excellence. NTA should be able to arrive at robust alternative testing through consultation with them as well as with other key

stakeholders. Both NEET and JEE test class XI as well as class XII syllabi while CUET quizzes only the class XII syllabus. NTA will reinvent ground work for reconciling these divergent needs.

- South Korea, a quality education exampler channels all university intakes through a single day 5 sessions exam.
- Processes have to be developed to work across our own diverse local contexts. CUET-NEET-JEE integration will be looking at 43 lakh applicants compared to 5 lakhs for South Korea's CSAT (Civil Service Aptitude Test).

**Relevant Thought:** India has exam system, not education system. When all young people stop taking exams and do something worthwhile?

**-CNR Rao**

## Reform of Institutions (Dt: 15.08.2022)

- Independent India gave every individual the right to vote and created one institution the election Commission for this purpose. But most Indians were denied the right to conduct their economic affairs freely and many in situations were created with expanding remits. Socialism and economic perversions took deep roots which are difficult to remove. That the world's largest democracy and world's fastest growing major economy is merely a lower middle-income country on its 75th birthday. It is because India went wrong with the Institutions. Extreme poverty once was of India has vanished. The once small middle class has vastly expanded.
- Examples of badly run institutions are an under staffed Judiciary that has become constraint to economic growth, and an under-staffed but barely accountable Bureaucracy, which rules over an empire of 'permissions' and 'clearances'
- The political system is incapable of correcting these two wrongs because politics is focusing on collectives, not individuals. Votes are sought invoking castes languages via rhetoric or rewards; neither individuals nor institutions need be priority areas. Politicians get away by spending too little to provide quality education and healthcare to individuals.

- We should fix the institutions, remove unnecessary restrictions, then 8% economic growth annually over next decade powered mainly by industrial manufacturing will take India into different league.

**Relevant Thought:** We are Indians firstly and lastly.

**BR Ambedkar**

## India: A Developed Country By 2047 (Dt: 16.08.2022)

- Independence Day speech of PM Modi has set ambitions target of India become a developed country by 204. Income and per capita income are criterion with nonfarm employment must be more than farm employment from beginning of Industrial Revolution in Britain in 1760 it has proved that farming goes down and jobs in manufacturing and services do multiply in every developed country.
- In India around 41% labour are in agriculture in 2018-19 and manufacturing employed only 12.1%. Farming should be reformed to move out labourers faster and manufacturing should flourish. Centre-state joint manufacturing should flourish. Centre-state joint effort should clear projects faster and the centre should stop hiking import duties.
- Protectionism undermines opportunities to unbundle production of goods and get to be done in different countries, at a competitive cost. Fundamental flow in PLI is emphasis on protection.
- Indian courts performance in contract enforcement is worst in the world. NCLT is critical to bankruptcy and had 30 vaccines in July. Judicial system has huge backlogs and vacancies also. This dilutes efficiency of most reforms.
- India's economic change of status can happen by afore-said farm reform judicial reform and free trade.

**Relevant Thought:** Of course it is the same old story. Truth usually is the same old story. **Margaret Thatcher**

## China's Maritime Clout in Indian Ocean (Dt: 17.08.2022)

- Despite objections from India and US; China's research vessel "Yun Wong 5", a suspected spy ship could duck at Sri Lanka's Hambantota part, by its consent.
- Sri Lanka needs China's support to restructure its massive debt and quality for an IMF bailout. India's $4 billion emergency did count for less.
- Today China has the world's largest nave. Its activities in IOR will be security challenge to India. During last 8 years, China had restructured PLA to massively upgrade naval power. Therefore, it can now deploy a vast array of battleships and its fleet of maritime militia and research vessels like at Taiwan earlier in 2019, another Chinese research and survey ship, "Haiyang Dizhi8" tried to create trouble for oil and gas production in south China sea at Vietnamese off shore; an area that had ONGC.
- Sri Lanka had huge Chinese loan to finance major projects, for which it was forced to lease Hambantota port to the Chinese for 99 years. Protecting India's strategic interests in IOR won't be easy. Recently India has gifted Colombo a Dornier 228 maritime patrol aircraft, but it won't be enough. Taking on China in IOR India needs to work closely with Quad.

**Relevant Thought:** Relations with countries in the Indian Ocean Region and nurturing a climate of peace and stability are important corner stones of Indian foreign policy.

**-S Jaishankar**

## FIFA\s Suspension of AIFF (Dt: 18.08.2022)

- FIFA suspended AIFF was a terrible embarrassment Supreme Court asked the Centre on 17.08.2022 to ensure India does not lose to host U-17 Women's World Cup in October. Gokulam Kerala FC travelled to Uzbekistan for AFC women's club Championship is being grounded due to the suspension.

- Both Hockey India and Indian Olympic Association may face the similar fate. The common among the three (AIFF, Hockey India and India Olympic Assn.) is that their management has been taken over by court Appointed Committee of Administrations (COA) due to various violations of the Sports Code. COAs were supposed to restructure the management of three bodies and international bodies of sport federations see such top-down reform as 3rd party interference, which is against their charters.

- India lacks the ecosystem which produces administrators who love and respect the sport and sports code. Stakeholders including the sports ministry must work towards a system where federations voluntarily adopt the code, otherwise our sportspersons' participation in global event sis at risk.

**Relevant Thought:** One of the thrills of playing at eh top venues of the world is to see the India flag go up whenever I am participating.

**- Sania Mirza**

## The Trend in Inflation (Dt: 19.08.2022)

- Trend in Inflation appears to be cooling down. Sharp decline in food prices globally in July in comparison to June is the most positive development.

- For India falling crude prices are significant monthly average price so for in August is $ 97.2/barrel. India's consumer price index has declined to 6.7% in July. These indicate that the inflation challenge has not ended. It is still above RBI's tolerance threshold of 6%. But data shows the pace of increase in price level in slowing down.

- Since May, 2022, policy rate, repo has been increased by 1.4% points to current level of 5.4%. The sharp increase in interest rates were influenced by surge in energy and commodity prices after Russia's invasion of Ukraine.

- 40% bank loans are benchmarked to Repo, means tightening of money by borrowers. SBI Research estimated an increase in interest cost by about Rs 42,500 crore for retail and MSME borrowers. This will act as a drag on economic activity moderating inflation. Monetary Policy Committee (MPC) should recalibrate it.

- SBI's study shows more than 50% of inflation is being driven by supply factors. This indicates for should be nimble and agile in thinking

**Relevant Thought:** Inflation is taxation without legislation.

**- Milton Friedman**

## Electoral Rolls – A Controversy in J and K (Dt: 20.08.2022)

- There is recent controversy about outsiders being given voting rights in J and K following abrogation of Article 370 after spreading of a recent remark by Chief Electoral officer (CEO) that "there is likely 25 lakh additional voters including outsiders".
- EC's process should be widely perceived as credible in J and K as it has a troubled history. EC must explain the numbers and be open to corrections, if errors are found.
- J and K Government administration on 20.08.2022 clarified that likely addition of 25 lakhs voters after revision of electoral rolls is "misrepresentation of facts by vested interests". It said that the increase in voters is mainly due to the new voters attained the age of 18 years. There is no change in rules of buying property and getting jobs in J and K and have no link to the representation of voters or otherwise.
- All party meeting has been convened by Farooq Abdullah over the issue and formulate a common position. Congress said to oppose non-local voters in electoral rolls.
- CMIE data says unemployment in 20-29 ages in J and K is 55% about twice the national average. Rail and Air connectivity are well set. Economic opportunities are integral to its normalisation. Transparency and political buy in by stakeholders will be success of integration.

**Relevant Thought:** All the way through we have been willing to take risks, provided at the end of it, we can get a decent, lasting settlement in Northern Ireland.

**Tony Blair**

## Inadequate Patenting in India (Dt: 22.08.2022)

- Patenting is essential for startups and Innovation in India, which can create jobs PMEAC has published that manpower at patents office is inadequate leading to delayed issuing of patents and it needs attention of GOI.
- India's patent office had 858 examiners and controllers in 2020 against 13000 in China and 8000 in US-Patent applications of India have increased from 45,444 in 2016-17 to over 66000 in 2021-22, corresponding year 2020, numbers for China were 15 lakhs and US 6 lakhs. Obviously, R and D capabilities of Indian academia and industry are lagging hugely.
- Time disposes applications – 58 months in India against 15 in Japan, 20 in China, 21 in US require reduction. Slow disposal delays new technologies and sends serious innovators abroad. PMEAC paper states that hiring 2000 hands of patent office will help. WIPO data should India filed 1.2 lakh applications within the country and 1.07 lakh abroad, but only 13,670 patents were granted in India against 44000 abroad.
- Slow processing in major reason for half-baked applications which are raised for first- first-mover advantage.
- Well-staffed patent office can adhere to globally competitive timelines.

**Relevant Thought:** It is much easier to hire your twentieth person than your first.

**- Hank Green**

## Doctor-Pharma Relationships (Dt: 23.08.2022)

- FMRAI has initiated a PIL in the Supreme Court that Micro Labs distributed freebee to doctors for prescribing "Dolo 650" drug during Covid. Doctor's ignored side effects of overdose of paracetamol on liver, kidney. This is affecting the reputations of Micro Labs, Pharmaceuticals industry and doctors. The broader issue embodies a universal regulatory challenge.
- For Pharma firms there is voluntary code on marketing practices since Jan, 2015. The Indian Medical Council regulates the conduct of doctors. These are toothless due to reportedly misconduct within the fraternity. In India, the out-of-pocket medical expenditure is 55% of citizens' total spends as compared to the global average of 18%.
- GOI should neutralize doctor-pharma 'deals' by utilizing its existing bulk purchases and sales of generic drugs. Pharma Inc pushes branded drugs. Bulk buying provides 50-90% discount over branded medicines, but it is not very effective because GOI distribution is limited.
- Smartest solution is to use the network of private chemists. Awareness and availability of generics such as commonly prescribed drugs, analgesics can reduce the shady persuasion of doctors, and minimize the misuse.

**Relevant Thought:** If something is good, more is not necessarily better not always.

**Sidhartha Mukherjee**

## Creative Freedom (Dt: 24.08.2022)

- BJP legislator (MLA), T Raja Singh was suspended from the party due to his remarks alluding to the Prophet created protests by 1000 strong crowd and baying for his beheading.
- Today in India, creative freedom is often a matter of who are in power where and who are their political rivals. T Raja Singh claims to have been provoked by Munawar Farooqui's jokes in stand-up comedy at Hyderabad. Faruqui found his show cancelled in Bengaluru and

Mumbai, but supported by extraordinary police protection in Hyderabad.

- TRS Government of Hyderabad stood up against Singh's threat to beat up the performer and burn the venue.
- If the episode again exposed BJP's failure to moderate voices it labels fringe when under pressure, TRS righteousness cannot be taken at face value either.
- Standup comedy is political everywhere now in India. In the latest iteration of the permit system what show where to happened depends on which party runs the state government.
- Hence creative freedom now is who governs which state with what agenda, with police as enforces.

**Relevant Thought:** To do comedy, there are so many hurdles one has to cross.

**- Johny Lever**

## Rainfall – Now in India (Dt: 25.8.2022)

- India experienced a severe heat wave in March when several countries also faced the same. China's southwest regions, Europe's heat waves and wildfires and US government's water shortage on the Colorado River etc. are critical.
- At a regional level in India rainfall has been deficient across a vast swathe from UP to Bengal. While the gap has narrowed by recent southwest monsoon the dry spell in July-August is bound to adversely impact the national paddy output. There is strong link between paddy and water shortage as it is a water guzzling crops.
- India has 17% of world's population and 4% of its water resources. Irrigation takes up 90% of country's groundwater and Indian farmers use 2 to 4 times more water to produce a unit of grain compared to China and Brazil a great waste.
- Poor rainfall in east indicates conservation water and change of cropping patterns in India Punjab is unsuitable for paddy, but it yields paddy well above world average. Policies that incentivize farmers in

Punjab to move to less water intensive crops need to be complemented by higher yields in Eastern India. Free electricity incentivizes more borewells. Market prices reflect scarcity of resources.

**Relevant Thought:** It is not the quantity of water applied to a crop; it is the quantity applied which determines the result – there is more due to intelligence than water in every case.

**-Alfred Deakin**

## Incomprehensible Convoluted Language (Dt: 26.08.2022)

- Supreme Court recently set aside a judgment of Himanchal Pradesh High Court after finding that the verdict by the HC was utterly incomprehensible and incoherent. Language was deliberately made complex.
- Over last 2 decades, a movement to modernize and simplify the language of justice, law and administration began in some Western democracies. In the US, scholars of law-making regularly highlight opaque language and jargon in laws. But India has not even tried.
- It is high time India did the SC's call fox "Brevity, Simplicity and Clarity." From cops writing FIRs and preparing charge sheets to the executive drafting laws, to judges writing verdicts-it is almost impossible to find clarity, brevity, and simplicity.
- In the 75th year of independence, India is still following colonial time warp English which is widely used language of governance.
- Rule should be to ensure that laws and judgments are understood by the people, and they should not need experts to translate laws and court rulings that affect their lives.
- Politicians should be the catalysts for changes.

**Relevant Thought:** My goal is to simplify complexity. I just want to build stuff that really simplifies our base human interaction.

**Jack Dorsey**

## Warning for Grand Old Party (GOP) (Dt: 27.08.2022)

- Reputed Congress leaders such as Jyotiraditya Scindia, Aswini Kumar and Kapil Sibal have left congress. Now Gulam Nabi Azad has also resigned on 26th Aug. These are efficient warnings for GP to save itself from self- destruction. Azad its blame on Rahul Gandhi being dependent on inexperienced coterie group being feeble opposition to BJP.
- Next President Selection is the critical decision in Congress. As the party in last two decades stopped conducting elections; only nominees of Nehru-Gandhi have occupied top party positions hence there is possibility that a Gandhi proxy may become president when Sonia demits office.
- Free and fair elections encouraging several contenders to come forward and battle for the top post will be more credible. Nehru-Gandhi should welcome and fully back the winner a promise letting the new chief get on this job.
- Azad has said remote control destroys "institutional integrity."

**Relevant Thought:** My great concern is not whether you have failed but whether you are content with your failure.

**-Nesan Lancon**

## Demolition of Twin Towers (Dt: 29.08.2022)

- On 28.8.2022 Super tech Twin Towers of Noida was demolished by the orders of Supreme Court It was a brazen violation that happen when joint venture of graft a rule bending.
- Average Indian household have about 77% of total assets in real estate. The buyer pays a part of the project cast upfront, the bank covers the residual cost and the builder underwrites EMIs till possession is handed. In number of cases where builders default and banks chase the helpless buyer despite the agreement detailing the obligations of all sides; In rarest one such case Delhi HC this year ordered interim protection to buyers against coercive action by barks.

- RERA is the most promising reform for this. It brings about standardization of contracts, reduces the information asymmetry between buyers and after stakeholders by making relevant information public and minimizes misuse of upfront payment by buyers.

- RERA was enacted in 2016 and cannot address older problems like super-tech Towers. Neither can it resolve the corruption at the level of urban bodies. It also suffers in state capacity as each state needs to establish a regulatory body. It requires state Governments to invest in enhancing capacity. Buyers with be benefited.

**Relevant Thought:** A house is made with walls and beams; a home is built with love and dreams.

**-Ralph Walolo Emerson**

## Fed And Global Financial Markets (Dt: 30.08.2022)

- On 29.08.2022, Global Financial Markets experienced sharp volatility. US Fed (Federal Reserve) Chairman Jerom Powell said restoring price stability will take time and Fed would use its tools forcefully. It means; interest rate hikes may go on longer than expected which will undermine economic growth. The Rupee-Dollar exchange rate reached Rs 80 marks and BSE Sensex dipped by 1.5% to settle below 58000.

- Global economy, the US Europe and Japan are triggering recession and flashing red. India to 6.7 % in 2022-23. Since May RBI is MC has increased the Repo Rate by 1.4% points to 5.4% to check inflation.

- Oil price again rose to $99.6/barrel on 26 Aug, Also the rainfall may affect food grain prices. The acreages of paddy and pulses were lower by 65% and 5% respectively on 26 Aug.

- Financial market volatility will persist. Inflation in India is mainly driven by supply constraints. RBI and GOI will have to manage carefully deploying their monetary and fiscal instruments not only just interest rates.

**Relative Thought:** Restoring price stability will take some time and requirements using our tools forcefully to bring demand and supply into better balance.

**-Jerome Powell**

## India Offered Help to Pakistan (Dt: 31.08.2022)

- Prime Minister of India offered help to flood devastated Pakistan. Death toll in Pakistan is 1100 affected people are 33 million damages estimated to $ 10 billion. UN is to appeal for $ 160 million to help Pakistan.
- Annual inflation has hit 24.9% in July. On 29.08.2022 IMF approve $1.1 billion funds for Pakistan. Cotton crop of 45%, Key for textile sector which makes up 60% of its exports-has been washed away.
- Pakistan is considering import of vegetables from India through land routes. Although Pakistan had cut off all trade ties with India to protest the 2019 nullification of Article 370 J and K, that should not matter in this crisis period. Sending medicines food and shelters materials to the victims of natural calamities should be prioritized.
- For such need-based cooperation, and good generous move by India, Pakistan should response affirmatively. A genuine substantial help will be a good strategic move.

**Relevant Thought:** My vision is to work for the relationship between India and Pakistan which would be like the relation between Canada and the United States.

**Manmohan Singh**

## India's GDP Grew lower than expected (Dt: 01.09.2022)

- India's GDP grew 13.5% in April-Jun quarter to Rs 36.85 lakh crore, which is 2.7% point lower than what RBI had forecast. The growth rate was an upward revision compared to previous year. Despite lower growth rate, the economy recovered from the Covid shock. Both private consumption and investment have surpassed pre-pandemic levels.

- Contract-intensive sectors represented by trade hotels and transport have not recovered fully. Their output remains below the 2019 level. It is 16% in the April-Jun quarter of 2022 compared to 20% of 2019. This is important source of employment rate as per GOI data for April-Jun quarter was 7.6%, which is high. But the rate has trended downwards over four successive quarters.
- The hardening of interest rates by RBI will act as a drag on demand as 40% of bank advances are linked to RBI's report. Crude oil prices are rising Indian crude has risen by 10% over last few days to $ 102/barrel. Suicide of daily wagers increased to 25.6% of the total in 2021 from 23.4% in 2019.
- GOI has increased 25% in grass tax revenue in April-July period, which may have fiscal changes to support some sectors.

**Relevant Thought:** We will continue with 'whatever its takes' approach, give the new set of changes and very high uncertainties that we are confronted with.

**-Shaktikant Das**

## Defence Indigestion (Dt: 02.09.2022)

- Cabinet Committee on Security (CCS) has cleared the project of develop Tejas Mark-2 the indigenous light combat aircraft (which is ungraded Tejas Mark-1).
- Next few months the relevance of Rs 15000 plus crore project of build 5$^{th}$ generation advanced medium combat aircraft is expected. Tejas Mark-1 will replace Mig-21s and Tejas Mark-2 will substitute Mirage-2000s, Jaguars and MIG-29s. The fifth-generation fighter will catapult India to elite club which now comprises US, China and Russia.
- India's first home-built aircraft carrier, INS Vikrant is officially commissioned by the PM, Modi on 2.09.2022 more than 75% component have been procured domestically a shot in the arm of Indian Nay. For cost and vulnerability of depending on foreign manufactures, indigestion is the necessity.

- Made in India arms and defence systems will be a big fillip for Indian industry. Armed forces have projected to spend $130 billion in next 5 years.
- The domestic Kaveri engine project, failed. Big private sector companies should be invited for pint Rand D.

**Relevant Thought:** We do not want to be number one in importing defence equipment.

**Narendra Modi**

## STALKING A CRIMINAL OFFENCE IN RISE (Dt: 03.09.22)

- Since 2013, stalking has defined as a criminal offence. Stalkers are still not scared off and discouraged. In Jharkhand a schoolgirl was burnt to death by a young man and another and Delhi where a schoolgirl was short despite the complaint to the police. These show, stalkers do not fear the law or the law is not strong enough for deterrence.
- In 2014 such cases were 1091, in 2021 stalking reported cases of 9285, are in all probability a massive undercount. Cases acquitted compounded or compromised outnumbers convictions and 40000 were pending trial.
- More problematically 3540 is bailable from police station. This gives too much power to cops to settle cases offences like section 354(Criminal Force/Assault to Outrage Modesty) is not bailable, 80 is section is section 506(Criminal Intimidation to cause death or grievous hurt). Hence either stalking be made non-bailable or section 354 and 506 should be used against stalkers.
- Cops in India are immensely overworked. 17,000 police stations over 80,000 people in average. There are too few women cops just 12% and many of them face harassment at work. Cops should be trained to adopt zero tolerance against stalkers.

**Relevant Thought:** Male fantasies, make fantasies, is everything run by male fantasies.

**-Margarete Atwood**

## Make Million Indians Prosperous (Dt: 05.09.2022)

- India overtook UK to become the 5th largest economy. SBI research indicates that India could be 3rd largest economy before this decade ends. India could survive Covid pandemic and the Ukraine war, during inflation and energy crisis. GOI resolved to not run up a high fiscal deficit despite pressure to imitate West's generous stimulus packages.
- Law GDP per capita and continued covid relief of free food grains for 80 crore people are pointers to law individual productively. To take masses out of agriculture, manufacturing should be relied.
- India's GDP per capita of $2500 is dragged down by farm households; their average annual income is just $1500. For decades, India has not focused enough in education, skilling, and health care. UNESCO against its Education 2000 frame Work has appealed to countries to spend 4-6% of GDP on education India's Central and Sate combined budgeted expenditure on education in 2021-22 was just 3% of GDP.
- States should have transparent budgeting. Centre should devolve more tax revenues to states and avoid the cess route of resource mobilisation. Centre-state tangles reflect inadequate private sector job creation that increases reliance on governments. Economic reforms are needed.

**Relevant Thought:** You are only as good as the sum of your parts, and one person cannot be a team.

**- David Schwimmer**

## Economic Sanctions and Gas Disruptions (Dt: 06.09.2022)

- Russia has shut Nord Stream gas pipe last week indefinitely, ostensibly for maintenance Nord Stream is a 1200 KM pipeline under Baltic Sea that transports Russian gas to Germany. Gas price now surged 30% in Europe, an increase of 400% gas prices over the last year.

- Economic sanctions although repeatedly failed to achieve, US, UK and EU rushed into sanctioning Russia, commodity exporter and a dominant source of gas supply to Europe. The energy criticality has multiplied. For example, Germany just unveiled the year's 3rd energy crisis relief package. EU and UK will follow suit. Consequence will be spiraling debt and economic recession.
- US Government debt to GDP ratio was 103% in Jun 2019, became 136% a year later. EU's debt to GDP ratio was 92% in March 2021, rolled back to 88% a year later. The energy shock and looming recession is set to worsen once again. Britain's debt to GDP ratio is 99.6% in March, 2012 and there is for cast of economic contraction in coming months.
- In India the aggregate government debt to GDP ratio is in vicinity of 85% with GOI accounting for 60%. For stability and financial discipline in the country's economy, India may legislate FRBM Act which had emerged in 2003.

**Relevant Thought:** The fault, dear Brutus, is not in our stars, but in ourselves.

**-William Shakespeare**

## Waterlogged Silicon Valley of India (Dt: 07.09.2022)

- Torrential rain in India's IT capital (Silicon Valley) Bangalore threw life out of gear. Waterlogging, traffic jams, vehicle stuck up, flooding of streets, floating of house materials, refrigeration etc. and submerged houses lead to massive inundation. It had 114 mm rainfall in 12 hours.
- It was a city of lakes, tanks, and parks. Because of city's development, IT boom, Scarcity of land etc., it underwent a rapid change in ecosystem. Lakes and tanks have been filled up; channels choked. According to scientists and ecologists the natural canals along the valley have been blocked by rampant urbanization of the city.
- Lakes should be treated as flood mitigation centers and rain water harvesting points. All encroachments from the lakes and drains

should be removed. Storm water drains encroached, should be removed. Drains should be desisted and their connectivity with the lakes should be re-established.

- Decentralized governance of city with new planning and development should be ke to this India's tech capital, if it continues to be victim of had/corrupt planning and political machinations.

**Relevant Thought:** All water has a perfect memory and is fore-vex trying to get back to where it was.

**-Toni Morrison**

## Bharat Jodo Yatra (Dt: 08.09.2022)

- Congress started 3570 km Padayatra on Thursday 8/9/22 by the leadership of Rahul Gandhi, naming it as "Bharat Jodo Yatra". It is the mass contract attempt by congress. Earlier LK Advani, YSR Reddy, Mamata Banerji have also marched with their valuable to tell and sell but now Congress and Rahul has no such facts that will attract people.
- BJP became successful in social engineering with welfarist political activities and nationalism in the people pleasing way; whereas Congress has fast grounds in many states. It must do hard work of rebuilding in at least 4 or 5 major states.
- Leaders' attention to manage the organization discipline, party structure and corporation are missing in Congress. BJP lost 2 general elections and regional parties have bounded back. Congress amazingly has lacked enthusiasm and determination, carelessly acting without interest. It should strengthen local party structure and sort out the mass disaffection among long-standing supporters. Non-Congress regional parties have been prospering with more popularity.

**Relevant Thought:** It is no use walking anywhere to preach unless our walking is our preaching.

**-Francis Of Assisi**

## Clean Up Political Parties (Dt: 09.09.2022)

- This week the registered unrecognized political parties RUPPs were raided by income tax official across the country, for their murky financial transcriptions. These raids are needed in a large clean-up process initiated by Election Commission. Tax exemptions with funding anonymity and easy registration are the issues to be cleaned up.
- There were 2796 RUPPS a year ago, a 300% increase over 20 years. RUPPs are whose vote share is below a threshold needed for recognition. In 2019 Lok Sabha election, only 30% of RUPPs contested. In 2019 Lok Sabha election, only 30% of RUPPs contested. RUPPs are entitled to 100% income tax exemption provided they meet conditions to furnish tax returns. Trike all political parties, they can cloak the identity of donors who make cash contributions up to Rs. 2000.
- EC in June deleted 111 RUPPs from their list. Incentive of special privilege extended to the for-tax exemptions come from anonymity offered to donors contributing to parties. To tackle anonymity, it has been restricted to lowering the maximum permissible limit for cash contributions from earlier level of Rs 20,000.
- Electoral Bonds as promissory notes payable to the bearer on demand poses threat to integrity of electoral system as it allows anonymous contributions without a ceiling and opens door to sources of funding political parties.

**Relevant Thought:** How do anonymity and transparency go together? They are the antithesis of each other.

**-Jagdeep Chhokar.**

## Border Talks with China (Dt: 10.09.2022)

- Following the 16th round of commanders meeting on 8 September, India and China agreed to disengage troops in Gagra-Hot springs area in eastern Ladakh. It is the 4th point out of PLA's incursions at different points in eastern Ladakh. There has been no agreement on disengagement in critical Depsang Plateau. Practically, disengagement involves agreeing to buffer zones where the two countries will refrain from carrying out patrolling.

- Negotiations to reach agreements on disengagement at 4 points with China has been lasting for long time, longer than expected. It amounts to trying to move LAC westwards deploying its army. This has been supplemented by violation of mutually agreed no fly zones near the border using its Air Force. It is sign of revisionist power that in dispensation of President XI Jing Ping violated long standing agreements.
- India should need Japan as strategic ally and bilateral cooperation strengthening SQAD to counter China. Action against China should be through trade, having emphasis on economic integration by manufacturing supply chains seeking to exit China.

**Relevant Thought:** All warfare is based on deception.

**-Sun Tzu**

## Hospital Acquired Infection in ICU's (Dt: 12.09.2022)

- Rising cases of antimicrobial resistant infections and associated mortality have been revealed by year-long surveillance of hospital-acquired infections in ICUs across the country.
- As per **HAISI** (Healthcare Associated Infection Surveillance India) survey, drug-resistant microorganisms were found in 3080 blood samples and another 792 urine samples. Within 14 days 38.1% patients with bloodstream infections and 27.9% with urinary tract infections have died. These indicate misuse or overuse of antibiotics and poor measures of infections preventions in Indian ICU's.
- Indian ICUs are hotbeds of gram-negative pathogens. ICMR survey found: 87.5% samples of Acinetobacter Baumann, a gram-negative bacterium that causes infection in blood, urinary tracts and lungs were resistant to antibiotics like carbapenems. Mortality and cost of care will be high if such superbugs do multiply. WHO has declared rising antimicrobial resistance is among top 10 global public health challenges.

- In 2000s UK had widespread antibiotic resistant bacteria and a strain of MRSA posed a major threat. Government improved preventions measures, hygiene standards got 86% reduction in MRSA infection in 2012.
- India must now have guidelines of preventions in hospitals backed by regular audits, responsible stewardship of antibiotic use, mass awareness campaign on misuse of antibiotics. Otherwise, superbugs will make my entire antibiotic arsenal redundant

**Relevant Thought:** It is the end of the road for antibiotics unless we act urgently.

**-Tom Frieden**

**Low cutoffs for NEET and JEE Exam (Dt: 13.09.2022)**

- Both NEET (for medicals)and JEE(for engineers) examination have recorded low cutoff scores this year. Just 55 marks out of 360 is eligible for IIT seat and 50$^{th}$ percentile is eligible for medical seat this year. Such low scores have helped 9.9lakh to qualify for 92000 medical seats and 40712 for 16000 IIT seats without considering quality of the candidates.
- It allows rich candidates with low merit to buy their way(manipulate) to payment seat while more meritorious students are left out and even without scores for a government college seat or money for an overpriced payment seat. Many such students journey abroad to China and Eastern Europe for less expensive medical education.
- IIT seats are not available for payment. 10lakh students attended preliminary JEE-main which is qualifying exam for NITs and hundreds of engineering colleges. Of these, 1.5 lakh took JEE-advanced. Yet it has needed lowest cutoff to produce a pool of 40000 qualified candidates.
- National Achievement Surveys reveals that too many children are deprived of quality education and there are not enough quality seats to accumulate this pool. Hence, this year a record, 82000 Indians received US students visas for better opportunities. India needs strong universities and qualified admissions for quality higher education.

**Relevant Thought:** An investment in knowledge pays the best interest.

**-Benjamin Franklin**

## WFH and Moonlighting (Dt: 14.09.2022)

- Along with Work from Home (WFH), employees are doing 2nd job secretly in addition to their regular employment called "Moonlighting". This has evolved exponentially during pandemic, especially among techies. Employers have confronted the open secret of moonlighting. Infosys called it "Two timing" and Wipro chairman called it "cheating" but Swiggy and Cred are greenlighting moonlighting.
- Moonlighting gravitates to specific groups, where demand outstrips supply. Respondents agree that India faces shortage of skills sets. Some are worrying about side-hustles, lowering office productivity, and causing IP leagues and conflicts of interests.
- Other experts are open to the idea of working productively with such employees without having exclusive ownership of them. They argued moonlighting helps to do one's day job better. Academy of Management Journal of USA found that side hustles made employees feel empowered, and empower their mainline performance.
- Employee options will be decided by market forces. In booming sector, short of skilled people; employers will be hard pressed to oppose moonlighting.

**Relevant Thought:** I asked myself about the present; how wide it was, how much was mine to keep.

**-Kurt Vonnegut**

## States for industrial Development (Dt: 15.09.2022)

- All states should compete for industrial investment. Most projects have gone to a few states. Nearly, 87% of FDI goes to just 5 states.
- Maharashtra lost the Rs.1.54 lakh crore Vedanta-Foxconn Semiconductor project to Gujrat. Maharashtra lost it because it does not offer incentives which Gujrat did better. State governments

should court private investment aggressively and should not compete on promises of freebies, which was discussed in a national debate after PM's comment on it.

- Some states are trying to foreign investments by hard-selling their human capital resources, road and digital connectivity and multimodal infrastructure. Up have joined the battle on betting on improved road connectivity. Most states have electronic and manufacturing policies offering incentives like power, water tariff concessions, exemptions from stamp duty and property tax, capital subsidies etc. Due to completion of attracting projects; the gap has narrowed down between Maharashtra, Gujrat, and Karnataka.
- Apart from services computer and new investments in manufacturing is needed in India. UP, Odisha, Chhattisgarh, Andhra, Jharkhand, Rajasthan, Bengal, and MP have potential to attract manufacturing investments. Tamil Nadu has stable industrial policy irrespective of change of governments. Most projects go to a few states (84% of FPI inflows go to just 5 states) land acquisition differences must be sorted out in states e.g., Gujrat and Bengal.

**Relevant Thought:** No country is successful in the long term without a strong and vibrant manufacturing base.

**-Alan Mulally**

## Shanghai Cooperation Organisation (SCO) (Dt: 16.09.2022)

- PM Narendra Modi arrived in Samarkand Uzbekistan on 15/9/22 for the SCO summit. The agenda include SCOs progress ways to enhance cooperation in feature and bilateral talks. SCO is dominated by China, India, and Russia with 40% global population and 30% of its GDP.
- India's participation in SCO is important as it is and synchronism with approach of strategic autonomy. India did not import crude oil from either Russia or US in April to June 2021 quarter. In the aftermath of Ukraine war crude imports in April to June 2022 from Russia and 'US were \$6.2 billion \$2.6 billion respectively, propelling both into India's top five sources of crude imports.

- Modi and X2 have no meeting since PLA's aggression in eastern Ladakh in 2020. Likely gains from SCO may be limited on account of China. Pakistan's new P.M. Sharif is present there. Binaural meetings in summit may have meaningful progress.
- Given the backdrop of Japan and Australia, member of Quad, have higher economic in integration with China through RCEP, FTA, India's pursuit of strategic autonomy is wise course.

**Relevant Thought:** Part of diplomacy is to open different definition of self-interest.

**-Hillary Clinton**

## SC Reform in listing cases (Dt: 17.09.2022)

- Chief Justice of India (CJI), U.U. Lalit devised new case listing of Supreme Court (SC) is effective. It results in sharp reduction pendency. In 13 days, SC disposed of 5200 cases and admitted 1135 fresh matters. As of September 1, there were 70310 matters pending.
- This new listing system of CJI attempt to expedite hearing in after – notice matters which keep getting backlogged, listing move of them on Tuesday, Wednesday, and Thursday afternoon. Also, fresher at mission matters is being listed on Mondays and Fridays.
- Since beginning of new listing system, a bench of judge last week had critiqued a lower for seeking adjournment despite judges working longer hours preparing for cases. One -2 Judge Bench conference inabilities to hear to all afternoon matter listed. Promptly filling 4 vacancies in SC by November can reduce pressure on judges.
- Similar reforms must be pursued in HSC. Central and state Governments must upgrade judicial infrastructure promptly filling judicial vacancies and removing the frivolous litigation.

**Relevant Thought:** Time goes you say?

Ah, no! alas, time stays, we go.

**-Henry Austin Dobson**

## Today's Era Not of War (Dt: 19.09.2022)

- On the sidelines of SCO (Shanghai Corporation Organisation) submit on 16 September,2022 at Samarkand, Uzbekistan Pm Modi said to president Putin of Russia, "Today's era is not of war". It was buttressed by India twice voting to allow president Zelensky to address UN bodies. So, it is what Modi said and what India stands for can do.
- India has been asking for ending violence and hostilities from the beginning of Ukraine war. Delhi's approach has been driven by national interest. India did not rightly join the West in sanctions against Russia. European imports of Russian oil and gas were exempted from sanction.
- "Today's era is not war" became the global headlines that emphasized the necessity of peace. India is already the world's $5^{th}$ largest economy and as per current research, it would be $4^{th}$ largest economy by 2027 and $3^{rd}$ largest by 2029. It has excellent records of a non-aggressor. Peace is India's civilization ethos and it has Mahatma Gandhi as its $20^{th}$ century champion. India is $21^{st}$ century may emerge as an influential peace advocator.

**Relevant Thought:** The first bomb the first explosion burst in our hearts. We are cut off from activity, form striving from progress.

**– Erich Maria Remarque**

## Ways of Loon Recovery by Banks and NBFCs (Dt: 20.09.2022)

- On 15 Sep, 2022 (Thursday) a tragic incident in Jharkhand happened. A pregnant woman was crushed by a tractor. A third-party recovery agent representing the NBFC< Mahindra Finance, ran over her while taking possession of the tractor, for nonpayment of dues outstanding from a loan.
- A special investigation team headed by SP was formed to arrest those involved.
- The person Mehta took loan and was saying to repay 1.2 lakh out of balance amount. The company had threatened to take away the

tractor. The recovery agent refused to listen to Mehta and kept driving away the tractor. Her pregnant daughter, who had crushed the spot, ran after it, and was crushed to death under its wheels.

- The banks and NBFCs must face consequences for outrages by the recovery agents. But there is gap between what RBI's circulars mandate and approach of recovery agents. RBI, years ago had even requested Indian Bank Association (IBA) to formulate a training course for recovery agents.
- A healthy credit culture involving timely recoveries must be established within boundaries set by law. It is the RBI's job to crack the whip.

**Relevant Thought:** We deem it appropriate to remind banks and other financial intermediaries that we live in a civilized country and are governed by the rule of law.

– **Supreme Court**

## Courts On Death Penalty (Dt: 21.09.2022)

- A constitution bench is now entrusted to evolve uniform norms for hearing on cases of death penalty. A code of procedures will help the lower courts to correctly judge the mitigating circumstances, traumatic past, and mental health before pronouncing a death sentence. They will be helped by authoritative Supreme Court (SC) guidelines.
- Death penalty is seldom executed, reserving to rarest of rare case in the country-26/11 terrorist attacks in Mumbai, 2001 attempt of Parliament attack, Nirbhaya gangrape murder.
- Poorer convicts do not get quality legal assistance. Innocents getting capital punishment is miscarriage of justice.
- Supreme Court's guidelines for hearing arguments on sentencing in highly relevant. Trial courts also ignore SC's guidelines many times. Constitution bench must ensure lower courts follow its rules.

**Relevant Thought:** I think perfect objectivity is an unrealistic goal; fairness, however, is not.

- **Michael Pollan**

## Live streaming of Constitution Bench Hearing (Dt: 22.09.2022)

- Supreme Court of India decided that the constitution bench hearings will be live-streamed. On can watch it although not being a lawyer nor a court official, not court attend
- It may not be even at Delhi. It will create awareness in crucial matters, India's governance and accountability for judges and lawyers.
- In 2018, Supreme Court had allowed live-streaming, but could not happen due to the intervening pandemic. Last year SC released model rule for live-streaming court proceeding. Subsequently, Odisha, Gujarat Karnataka and some other HCs have court proceedings to a great effect. It becomes a great enabler for litigants unable to attend courts. This will also spare the witnesses and litigants form personal appearance being available through video-conferencing apps and will minimize the adjournments.
- Concerns raised by some retired judges are: It makes judges frequent target of public ire or a target of social media trolls. But these are not valid argument against live streaming globally, the top courts e.g. International Criminal Court, the UK Supreme Court has long allowed live streaming. SC's constitution bench hearings may have to borrow a term form TV industry, high TRPs. It is good for India.

**Relevant Thought:** I must learn there is a virtuous cycle to transparency and a very vicious cycle of obfuscation.

**- Jeff Weiner**

## Draft Indian Communication Bill (Dt: 23.09.2022)

- A draft Indian Telecommunication Bill has been put out by Government of India inviting comments. Telcom Companies (Telcos) for years have wanted some regulations to apply to them and as well to Apps providing communication services.

- OTT services should not be asked to obtain licenses just as Telcos have to. Otherwise, the tempo for domestic innovation, creative interfaces with global ecosystem and India's attraction as global digital hub all these will suffer. Telcos services are based on spectrum, a national resource that is auctioned whereas Apps ride on internet, so not exactly equivalent. Licensing is undesirable, because an internet ecosystem flourish is India's economic interest.
- The universal service obligation fund has been proposed to be used to spur investment in R and D is a progressive idea. By this Government of India can choose talent wisely and fund the incubation period generously, so that India Apps can effectively compete with American Apps.
- The draft says state agencies will have wide powers to intercept messages for national security and other reasons. How will be that differing from other laws and what happens to privacy protections etc., are the critical questions. Communication law should be smart. Promoting innovation should to a key objective.

**Relevant Thought:** Competition is a tough weed, not a delicate flower.

**-George Stigler**

## Financial Markets Global Storm (Dt: 24.09.2022)

- On 23.09.2022, Sensex was down by 1021 points with banking and financial stocks. The Rupee breached the Rs 81/ Dollar a record low level for the first time in line with major global markets. The BSE Sensex closed lower by 1.7% at 98,098.92 overseas risk is main policy challenge. Uncertainly and volatility are high.
- Sources of risk are: i) Unclear measures of central banks against inflation and ii) the fluid geopolitics. Recently most major central banks had increased interest rates and may repeat the same. Most currencies have weakened against dollar. Hardening of interest rates will affect economic progress.
- Because of ongoing energy supply readjustments, the inflation will not quickly trend down even as demand falls. Gas and electricity in

Europe have risen 105% is rapidly slowing down, and price levels are high. UK's inflation is at 9.9%, almost 5 times its target.

- It is good that Government of India has fiscal space-gross tax revenue increased f25% to Rs 8.69 lakh crore in April – July 2022.

**Relevant Thought**: Inflation is being caused by a series of unprecedented shocks, which have led to turning points in the global economy.

**Christine Lagarde**

## Old Pension System Vs National Pension (Dt: 26.09.2022)

- Punjab Government is studying the modality of reverting the old Pension System (OPS). Feature of OPS is guaranteed monthly payout that gets adjusted for inflation. Now the trends of many governments around the world are moving away from guaranteed pension payouts to the one linked to market returns on retirement savings of employees like private employee's Employees Provident Fund Organization (EPFO).
- Government of India faced rise of pension payments from0.6% of GDP in 1993 – 94 to 1.7% in 2002-03. In 2001-02 union budget faced this challenge and the solution was to move government employees from OPS to National Pension System (NPS), like EPFO.
- Government employees who joined in 2004 were moved to NPS Many states with Punjab Rajasthan, Chhattisgarh did the same. Now both Rajasthan and Chhattisgarh have announced revers in to OPS. Punjab may join Rajasthan and Chhattisgarh.
- OPS commitments can eat into spending on genuine welfare schemes for the larger population. The huge challenges faced by Indian armed forces are a warning. Defence think tank Institute for Defence studies and Analysis IDSA's study showed in 2011-12; 49% of defence budget went to salaries and pension and 27% to arm's purchases. A decade later, salaries and pension ate up 61% of the budget and 19% went towards buying weapons. State governments should take this as a warning. Reversion to OPS is fiscally ruinous and politically ineffective.

**Relevant Thought:** Reckless action is worse than wise restraint.

**– Danielle Trussoni**

## Rupee Depreciates against Dollar (Dt: 28.09.2022)

- On 27 Sept, 2022, Rupee closed at Rs 81.58 against the dollar. Sin beginning of 2022, it has lost 10% value against dollar, because of developed country's inflation and geopolitical concerns. Ukraine war triggered mast server inflation in last 4 decades.
- India's macroeconomic metrics are relatively sound. It is a symptom of global economic environment. RBI has been prudent in its intervention. Exchange rate stability and capital account openness cannot be realized simultaneously.
- Checking depreciation in rupees will impact India's inflation. RBI has approach of intervening to curb volatility, which Government of India has sensibly avoided comment on exchange rates. India's foreign reserves stood at $ 545.6 billion on September 16, adequate to cushion the economy form external shocks.
- RBI has successfully managed the global financial crisis. Country's currency value is outcome of complex interplay of global factors that are beyond the influence of emerging markets. Fighting inflation is the priority.

**Relevant Thought:** They lose the day in expectation of the right and the right in fear of the down.

**Seneca**

## Landmark For Women's Rights (Dt: 30.09.2022)

- On 22.09.2022 the Supreme Court (SC) Bench gave historic judgment that unmarried women in a consensual relationship are also entitled to safe and legal abortion; upto 24 weeks of their pregnancy, legal abortion; upto 24 weeks of their pregnancy, thus bringing them in par with married women.
- Under the Medical termination of Pregnancy Act, (MTP Act) first enacted in 1971 and amended in 2021 all women can undergo

abortion upto 20 weeks, but single women were barred between 20 and 24 weeks on account of complications of health, mental and rape.

- The court ruled that under MTP Act, rape must include marital rape. The decision of carry pregnancy to full term or terminate it is firmly rooted under right to bodily autonomy and decisional autonomy of the pregnant woman.

- The landmark verdict came on a petition by a 25-year-old unmarried woman. She appealed against Delhi High Court order that she is not entitled to abortions under the Act as she was unmarried and the pregnancy followed a consensual relationship. She submitted that she was having 23 weeks pregnancy and the partner had refused to marry her. She is the eldest of 5 sidings and parents are farmers, stressing that she does not have the means to bring up a child. On July 21 the court had allowed to abort provided a medical board concluded that it will not harm her.

- The bench had said the MTP Act, 2021 now include the word "Partner" instead of "Husband".

**Relevant Thought:** If the misery of the poor be caused not by the laws of nature, but by our institutions, great is our sin.

**- Chaples Darwin**

## RBI Hiked Repo Rate (Dt: 01.10.2022)

- On 30.09.2022, RBI hiked Repo Rate by 0.5% upto 5.9%. It is the 4th increase since May. Since April 1, the rupee dropped 6.8% against dollar while major currencies in world depreciated 16%. Also 60% dip in foreign exchange reserves is due to their valuation following rate hikes by US Federal he serves. But depreciation is rupee against dollar and dip in forex reserves are not alarming.

- RBI retained current financial year's inflation projection at 6.7%. Economic growth was marked down to 7% from earlier 7.2%. The main aim of rate hikes is to head off inflation. Government of India and states simultaneously have embarked on fiscal consolidation which is prudent to hold back in an uncertain situation.

- Increase of inflation in April-September was mainly on account of supply shocks. Cut in fuel taxes in May knocked off 0.4% points from core inflation.
- In near future, global recession will dampen demand. Hence it would be the time for a slower pace of rate hikes.

**Relevant Thought:** The global economic outlook continues to be bleak. Financial conditions are tightening and recession fears are mounting.

**-Shaktikant Das**

## Launch of 5G In India (Dt: 03.10.2022)

- Ushering in a new technological era, Prime Minister Shri Narendra Modi launched 5G services in Pragati Maidan New Delhi on 01 October, 2022. Reliance Jio connected a teacher form a school in Mumbai with students in Maharashtra, Gujrat and Odisha. Demonstrated Augmented Reality (AR).
- Vodafone-Idea demonstrated safety of workers in construction Airtel demonstrated immersive education to learn about solar system with Virtual Reality (VP) and Augmented Reality (AR). PM Modi also launched C-DOT designed 5G No standalone Core.
- Airtel has launched non-standalone 5G network (5G on 4G) in 8 cities while Jio's standalone 5G is coming this Diwali in 4 metros. Vodafone-Idea has not revealed a timeline.
- 5G has fast download speeds, low network delay (latency), big data live autonomous devices, robots, VR, AR and cloud-based healthcare.
- Three frequency bands are being deployed: a) Lower Band (600 MHz-1GHZ) spectrum with speed closer to 4G requires fewer cell towers b) Mid Band (3300 MHz) offering 100-500 Mbps speed, needs cell towers every 100 meters. c) Private networks for enterprise use.
- Jio's strategy is large quantities of low band spectrum and Airtel must catch up with Jio in 5G cheaper non-standalone 5G.

**Relevant Thought:** We are all now connected by the Internet, like neurons in a giant brain.

**- Stephen Hawking**

## India's light Combat Helicopters (LCHs) (Dt: 04.10.2022)

- India has made Light Combat Helicopters indigenously. They have 45% indigenous content which will gradually increase to 55% and are with HAL's Shakti engine, developed collaborating with French engine-maker, saffron. LCH can operate at 20,000 feet and can perform combat, search, and rescue operations. It will boost our defence along LAC with China.
- India has urgent need to replace obsolete choppers live Chetak and Cheetah of 1960s-70s vintage. Also, the dependency on Russian hardware puts India in a tough spot both in terms of maintenance and wording off US sanctions. India being the largest importer of arms in the world should reduce the import bill now.
- India inducted American helicopters to replace its Russian Mi-25 and Mi-35 choppers was a good step. But indigenous LCH is the real gain as it will play as India's combat helicopters like as the Tejas LCA for fighter jets.
- HAL is tasked with developing light utility helicopter in short period a Russian Lavrov, KA-31 was suspended by India this year. After failure of indigenous Kaveri jet engine project, we still lack deep expertise in engine development. LCHs now shows the capability of India in defence manufacturing, and how much more to be done.

**Relevant Thought:** Helicopters make everything better.

**- Gage Munroe**

## Leveling of Male / Female IMR (Dt: 05.10.2022)

- Infant Mortality Rate (IMR) is the number of infant deaths for every 1000 live births. UN data for 2020 shows that among countries where the IMR was above 20, India was the only one where male and female

IMR were the same at 28. Earlier India had bad reputation that a larger proportion of girls below age of 1 ear died than boys.

- In 16 states of India, female IMR is still higher than male IMR. India's IMR has fallen slowly from 44 per 1000 live births in 2011 to 33 in 2017 and 28 in 2020.
- To meet UN Sustainable Development Goals (SDG), to 25 (per 1000), neonatal (new born) mortality to 12 (per 1000) and Maternal Mortality Rate (MMR) to 70 (per lakh live births) by 2030. India's latest corresponding figures are 32, 20 and 103.
- MP, Chhattisgarh, UP and Assam have MMR over 150 while Kerala and Maharashtra have fallen below 50.
- Live births in hospitals shot up from 35% in 2006 to 67% in 2011 to 82% in 2020. Deaths with medical attention at hospitals has risen form 28% in 2006 to 34% in 2011 and 49% in 2020.
- Government expenditure on health had increased form Rs 2.73 lakh crore in 2019-20 to Rs 4.72 lakh crore in 2021-22 a 73% increase. MMR of Jharkhand is now 61 against 304 in 2004-06. Thus, are great results achieved.

**Relevant Thought:** You do not need to invade a place or install a new government to help bring about a positive change.

**- Nicholas Kristof**

## Regional Parties in National Image (Dt: 06.10.2022)

- Regional political parties of provincial identity have efforts to shine for a national one. TRS party of Telangana has been renamed as BRS (Bharat Rashtra Samithi) by KCR, the CM of Telangana.
- Strong regional parties TMC, BJD and AAP are better placed in their core area to fight BJP in poll. Some of them tried their luck in other states TMC's foray into Goa and Tripura has not worked. JD (U) legislators in Manipur and Arunachal have defected and the results have been poor.

- Only AAP won Punjab, as Punjab was utterly fed up with all other parties – BJP, Congress and Akalis. AAP does not have that advantage in other states. Its attempt in Uttarakhand and Goa failed.
- Family run parties are with self-interest cloaked in federalist rhetoric. Nitish Kumar's ambitions contrast with reality of JD (U)'s footprint even within Bihar.
- Both Udhav Thackeray and Sharad Powar are on the back foot in Maharashtra. Mamata Banerjee is not in combative self for few months now. KCR appears shaky in Telangana after defeat in by polls to BJP. KCR will fight BJP in Telangana as BRS.

**Relevant Thought:** Do not confuse visibility with credibility.

**Harvey Mackay**

## Global Economy Challenges (Dt: 07.10.2022)

- Oil prices are likely to remain elevated, because of the supply cartel of Optec-plus which includes Saudi Arabia and Russia, decided to trim production with a view of keeping the price high.
- The group producing more than 50% of world's crude, plans to reduce output by 2 million barrels / day beginning from November by using August's production as a benchmark. It is about 2% of production which may set a floor to any price decline.
- WTO has forecast that growth in trade will be slow by 1% lower than 3.4% forecasted a few months ago. Trade growth is being dragged down by economic slowdown of 3 majors US Europe and China. Monetary tightening in US, and energy shock of 350% in gas price year on year in Europe will lead to reduced consumer spending. In case of China, the zero-covid strategy has been a toll on its growth.
- Energy shock is due to economic sanction by US and Europe on Russia and Europe's dependence on Russian gas. The world fell impacts through oil price surge and price hike of food items.
- India has dual challenges: Supply pressure of commodities for high inflation and global slowdown dragging on the growth. Crude price

($116/barrel) in June declined ($91/barrel) in September. Petrol and diesel remain unchanged since May 2022, ring fencing the economy.

**Relevant Thought:** When you impose sanctions against an economy like Russia, this will have dramatic spillover effects.

**-Nicholas Mulder**

## Gambia Tragedy by Indian Cough Syrup (Dt: 08.10.2022)

- Death of 66 children in Gambia after consumption of 4 cough syrups made by Haryana based Maiden Pharmaceuticals and a WHO alert calls for an overhaul of drug regulation in India.
- India's pharma industry is the pharmacy of the world with 1/3rd of the global share in drugs by volume. Indian pharma's global reputation is once again at risk (after Ranbaxy).
- State drug controllers tasked with licensing and monitoring of manufacturing units and quality control need to have stringent and stricter policing with criminal and financial liability on perpetrators and industries.
- The central regulator CDSCO (Central Drugs Standard Control Organisation) under Directorate General of Health Services, Ministry of Health, and Family Welfare, Government of India, the National Regulatory Authority (NRA) of India is now answerable to WHO for the failure.
- With 3000 companies and 10,500 manufacturing units in India the drug regulator faces massive challenge in effective policing due to shortage of personnel. Reports of adverse events, labs safety checks and surprise random checks by regulatory officials are imperative.

**Relevant Thought:** Democracy is not a state of perfection. It must be improved, and that means constant vigilance.

**-Antonio Taguchi**

## Central Bank Digital Currency (CBDC) (Dt: 10.10.2022)

- A CBDC is the existence of currency in digital form. RBI has issued a concept note on this and added that a pilot project will soon be launched for specific use cases. Private crypto currencies lack stability in value; hence they can never be a threat to currency issued by central bank.
- RBI takes caution in not having hasty transition to CBDC. It aims to complement and not replace currency.
- India's rapid evolution to digital payments system is an achievement that has evoked global interest. About 10 countries beginning with Bahamas in 2020 have launched CBDC. Among major economies, China and South Korea have launched. In India CBDC will work best if it is interoperable with the existing payment system.
- CBDC will serve for real time cross-border payments. If major economics adopt digital currencies that are stable and that flow through a global payments system; there is less need for everyone to accept one national currency as reserve currency.

**Relevant Thought:** At its core, trust in the currency holds the monetary system together. Like the legal system, this trust is a public good.

**- Agustin Carstens**

## Appointment of Judges (Dt: 11.10.2022)

- A clarification was issued by 5-member Supreme Court (SC) collegium after the reported differences over appointment of 4 SC vacancies.
- A very important public disclosure was made in the 26 September, 2022 collegium meeting. SC's statement revealed "procedure of circulating the judgment of prospective candidates and making an objective assessment of their relative merit was introduced for the first time."
- Different yardsticks have been formalized beyond 2nd and 3rd Judges Cases (1993 and 1998) and Justice Departs Memorandum of Procedure (MOP) for appointment of judges (1999).

- There are disagreements among collegium members, over what constitutes proper procedures in a good thing. The main problem is that too little of the process is codified.
- Since 3rd Judge case and 1999 MOP that shaped the present collegium, the system is unable to cope up controversies over judicial appointments.
- Following SC's constitution bench striking down National Judicial Appointments Commission (NJAC) and reinstalling collegium in 2015, SC had tasked GOI to finalize new MOP for transparency and improve selection of judges by collegium. This process was stalled. But SC collegium can fine tune, publicize and intuitional internal criteria to find judges. The collegium must lay down parameters.

**Relevant Thought:** What is it that makes us trust our judges? Their independence in office and manner of appointment.

**John Marshall**

## Allow Citizens to Choose (Dt: 12.10.2022)

- Lieutenant Governor (LG) of Delhi has decided to allow 300 establishments to work round the clock in their business such as hotels and delivery services etc. A modern economy never sleeps.
- There are encouraging changes coming from the public. In a small town, Muvattupucha in Kerala, local authorities organized 4-night package of activities, including live music performance and a woman's, marathon. The effort was named 'Girl's Night Out' to encourage women to go out after sunset and nudge the town creating nightlife. The response was overwhelming.
- India aspiring to be a developed nation require governments to trust people more. Imposing unreasonable curbs and laws on where and when women can work must be stopped. The rule should be that women know what is in their best interest. Let them choose.
- Police need personnel for ensuring peaceful co-existence and governments have a role to ensure no-labour exploitation. Enabling a fairer environment will remain undiminished.

- GOI did well by opening theatres in J and K again and mode liberalized policy of stocking beer in departmental stores. Journey to a developed country status will have to allow citizen choice what they wish to consume. Authorities of Delhi, J and K and Muvattupucha are praised worthy.

**Relevant Thought:** The only purpose for which power can be rightfully exercised over any member of a civilized community, against his will, it to prevent harm to others.

**- JS Mill**

## Indian Economy Better and In Tight Spot (Dt: 13.10.2022)

From the data of 11 and 12 October, 2022, it indicates that Indian economy is better off than most major economies, but is in a tight spot. Inflation continued to rise and industrial growth shrank. IMF estimated India's growth in 2022-23 will be 6.8% which is 1.4% reduction in April forecast. This happens due to upward pressure by supply shocks on the price level, while demand remains fragile.

- Consumer Price Index (CPI) in September was 7.4% (from 7% in August) overshooting RBI's upper threshold tolerance of 6%. Most worrisome is food inflation 8.6% driven mainly by cereal inflation of 11.5%. This is by supply shock, come from abnormal weather pattern during the harvest phases.

- RBI must struggle with impact of currency depreciation on oil imports and pressure on domestic inflation. It is an uncertain situation linked with Ukraine war.

- Government of India and state governments can mitigate matters through fiscal measures. Populist giveaways like freebies phases must stop. There should be no cutbacks on budgeted capital expenditure (capes) which is a growth driver especially when private sector is wary of investing amidst uncertainties.

- Government of India has led with 47% increase in capital expenditure (capes) in April-August to Rs. 2.52 lakh crore. States must follow up enhancing their capex.

**Relevant Thought:** In short, the worst is yet to come and, for many people, 2023 will feel like a recession.

**– Pierre-Olivier Gourinchas**

## NAAC Assessment and Accreditations (Dt: 14.10.2022)

- NIRF (National Institutional Ranking Framework) and NAAC (National Assessment and Accreditation Council) are the two institutions for ranking and assessment accreditation of Higher educational Institutions (HEI) such as colleges and universities.
- Indian Institute of Science is again the top Indian entry in this year's (2022) 'The World University Rankings' and has topped the Indian government's NIRF ranking.
- But in the NAAC scores a different result has been established this year. SOA (Siksha 'O' Anusandhan), a deemed university in Bhubaneswar has secured the highest ever NAAC score 3.88 out of 4.00 and has been awarded A++, the highest grade. The accreditation will be valid for 7 years with effect from 10 May, 2022. SOA had been placed 20th in the country by NIRF.
- Close on its heels is an engineering college in Bengaluru which NIRF puts in the 175-200 band. Another deemed university in Coimbatore has jumped 5 grades in 5 yrs between 2 NAAC assessments. A record number of institutes have scored A++ this year. Such range of anomalies need audit to find out.
- Higher NAAC grades bring increased autonomy, UGC funds, foreign collaborations, distance educations and online courses. High caliber team of national and international experts must have to be the process reforms.
- Ensuring transparency, accountability and honesty of NAAC scores is and urgent task.

**Relevant Thought:** We all want progress, but if you are on the wrong road, progress means doing an about turn and walking back to the right road.

**– CS Lewis**

## UAPA's Safeguard by Prosecution Sanction (Dt: 15.10.2022)

- GN Saibaba, ex-Delhi University professor and five others given life terms on charges of membership of banned CPI (M) aiding and abetting its activities were acquitted by Bombay High Court.
- UAPA (Unlawful Activities Prevention Act) has 2 safeguards to prevent wrongful implication of innocents. UAPA trial court had framed charges against Saibaba before prosecution sanction was arrived. UAPA judges must wait prosecution sanction before taking cognizance of charge sheets. This prosecution sanction in turn must be considered and granted by government only after an independent authority conducts a review of the evidence by investigation and makes a recommendation.
- The conviction was struck down citing a constitution bench ruling that a trial proceeding without valid sanction would stand vitiated.
- Bombay High Court sent a strong message on sanctity of due process and procedural safeguards by acquitting Saibaba. The judges warned that "empirical evidence suggests departures form the due process of law foster an ecosystem in which terrorism burgeons."

**Relevant Thought:** Peace and justice are two sides of the same coin.

**- Dwight D Eisenhower**

## Cybercrime In Digital Transaction (Dt: 17.10.2022)

- There are increased number of cybercrimes through smartphones and online banking's due to lake of awareness of their risks. Many are impelled to respond What's App and SMS messages and phone calls when these are threatened to disconnect key services or promise attractive rewards. Governments, Cops, Banks Telcos, Payment, and Messaging services should keep educating citizens about safe practices.
- Scam messages threatening users for failure of paying bills or being swayed away by sharing OTP or PIN are devastating experiences of wiping out bank accounts in the blink of an eye.

- NCRB (National Crime Record Bureau) revealed that cybercrime of 9,622 cases in 2014 have shot up 450% to 52m974 in 2021. Polices charge sheeting rate in cybercrimes is just 33% against 90% n murder or rape cases, suggesting a real difficulty in investigating many have complained lackluster bank assistance in helping recover the funds.
- RBI is reportedly planning a fraud registry to monitor dubious transactions using AI and big data Telcom and messaging companies should also closely track the caller and senders.

**Relevant Thought:** The number one rule of thieves is that nothing is too small to steal.

**Jimmy Breslin**

## National Highway Are Potholed (Dt: 18.10.2022)

- Bountiful monsoon this year (2022) has become misery for road travelers. The national Highways are the arterial network of country's entire road system. Although their qualities are marked and reported against international standards, those are dilapidated, broken having many pots hole.
- For example, NH-8 from Gurgaon to Jaipur had hiked toll from 1 September, 2022, but it remains incomplete and heavily potholed.
- Supreme Court had ruled out that tolls cannot be collected form commuters if roads are in bad shape. Annual budgetary outlay for maintenance and repairs is only about 40% for NHs directly under GOI's supervision. Budgetary allocation of maintenance is less than 4% of overall budget. This allocation is lopsided with expansion of HSs getting disproportionate share. Niti Aayog wants to raise allocation to at least 10%.
- Road quality, road building and maintenance needs and up gradation, synchronizing with the overall integrated logistic policy. Although the NH expansions over few years are impressive, it does not drive quality.

**Relevant Thought:** It is the quality of our work which will please God and not the quantity.

**- MK Gandhi**

## A New CJI with Admirable Record (Dt: 19.10.2022)

- The new Chief Justice of India (CJI) Justice DY Chandrachud is now for 2-year plus term carries his stint on important constitution benches. He chairs Supreme court's e-committee that looks the digital initiatives like virtual hearing and live court proceedings
- Current CJI, Mr. UU Lalit's efforts to reform the listing of regular and admission matters in SC by having more hearings daily and disposed of and setting up constitution benches are widely appreciated.
- New CJI must continue these reforms, and attempt to speed up justice delivery at HC and Subordinate courts.
- There are 5 vacancies of judges in SC presently and 336 in HCs (High Courts). HC judges retire at 62 years should stay till 65 like SC judges.
- Centre's NJAC was quashed, but has not dissipated and the task of collegium has become harder. Other aspects of justice delivery are outdated and poorly drafted laws. Sexual assault laws distinguishing rape and false promise of marriage, divorce laws for breakdown of marriage, prohibition, and sedition laws etc.
- Bail is casually denied. Under investigation and under trial has become the punishment. Cases, are pending for long periods. Judiciary and government together must make the system better.

**Relevant Thought:** We have it in our power to begin the world over again.

**-Thomas Paine**

## Short-lived Government in Britain (Dt: 21.10.2022)

Marry Elizabeth Truss (Liz Truss), Prime Minister of UK has served the country for a short period of 45 days from 6 September, 2022 to 20 October, 2022. She resigned admitting she could not deliver the mandate on which she had been elected. Backed by Truss, Finance Minister, Kwasi Kwarteng unveiled $45 bn of tax cuts on 23 September sending markets into turmoil. Truss sacked Kwarteng and his replacement,

Jeremy Hunt scraped all of Truss's taxes cuts and no public spending cuts Hom Secretary, Suella Braveman also stepped down.

- With economy heading into recession and inflation running at 40-year high, millions of Britons are struggling with a cost-of-living crisis.
- Markets and the country needed prudence; some plans to cut spending and smart policies for growth. Policy mistakes, unfunded tax cuts and discredited growth modals were the mistakes.
- Britain is the warning to the Western Countries those are merrily borrowing and cutting rates for years. It also serves as a lesson for India where economic populism has gained traction. Economic crisis always engulfs the political system and widen social faults. Growth needs an environment of macroeconomic stability. It is our reminder to our politicians to give up fiscal populism.

**Relevant Thought:** We know what we are, but know not what we may be.

**-William Shakespeare**

## CCI's Provisional Penalty on Google (Dt: 22.10.2022)

- Competition Commission of India has passed order on 20.10.2022 levying a provisional penalty of Rs 1,337.7 crore on Google, for imposing dominant position of its Android mobile phone operating system.
- CCI asked Google to implement 10 remedial measures that will open the mobile phone eco system measures that will open the mobile phone eco system. It is remarkable in curbing monopolistic behavior in the digital economy. Android has 96% market share in India among mobile phones as popular access to internet.
- The business model creates economies of scope that lock consumers into complementary services provided by Google. The abuse of market power is through agreements that the mobile phone makers sign with Google to pre-install its applications such; that

discriminates against standalone application developers. Hence competing service providers are out.

- CCI gives Google 3 months to modify agreements and have changes to break the company's strangled hold on the market through are-installation route.
- This order is an important precedent in preventing market abuse in India's economy and the work underlying it helps build the regulator's capabilities.

**Relevant Thought**: Those types of markets where you have deep asymmetries of power, sometimes on multiple sides, can lead to all sorts of business practices that are harmful.

**- Lina Khan**

## Total Factor Productivity (TFP) Growth (Dt: 27.10.2022)

- Productivity is the measure of the output extracted form combination of inputs. Increasing this is the source of economic growth. In West and China, productivity is falling, threatening the growth. China's economy transformed through 4 decades double digit growth had run out of steam, the return in investment had collapsed. It is world's most serious threat of economic stagnation and social turmoil.
- Western economies declined in TFP in 1990, and getting acute after 2008 financial crisis. India in 2010s recorded higher TDP growth of 2.2%, but its performance over last decade shows, we too are in danger of losing steam. Between 2014 and 2017, TFP growth received boost form non-market services like public administration, which is not a durable source of growth. By 2018-19 TFP growth began losing. Productivity enhancement is pathway to prosperity. India's agricultural sector presents the biggest challenge.
- Agriculture contributes 18% of economy's annual value addition but employs about 41% of workforce. Substantial workers are unproductive. India's economic advancement depends on getting them out of agriculture to more productive sectors.

- Reluctance to carry out deep economic reforms and luring to protectionism are the biggest obstacles to TFP growth today.

**Relevant Thought:** Productivity is not everything, but in the long run it is almost everything.

**-Paul Knegman**

## Elon Musk Bought Twitter (Dt: 29.10.2022)

- Finally, Elon Musk bought Twitter, with large debt. The business model heavily reliant on advertisement will be facing regulatory constraints.
- Five leading technology companies, Facebook, Amazon, Apple, Netflix, and Google have lost $2.5 trillion in market value over last year. The reason is the incompatibility of advertising driven business model with refusal to take responsibility for content hasted by the platforms.
- It has led conflict with regulators such as in India when Twitter took GOI to court over orders to take down some tweets.
- GOI on 28.10.22 correctly brought in new rules of high responsibility on companies for contents. New IT rules are to put more obligations on social media platforms. Government will set up 3 members Grievance Appellate Committee (GAC) to redress grievances of users against social media (like Twitter and Facebook). It is to ensure that no unlawful content or misinformation is posted.
- The days of ignoring the social consequence of lousiness model are over. Elon Mulslus challenge is GOI and other governments are getting tough.

**Relevant Thought:** By "free speech," I simply mean that which matches the law.

**-Elon Musk**

## Morbi Bridge Tragedy

- On 30 October, 2022, (Sunday) the suspension footbridge at Morbi, Gujrat on Macchu river collapsed, causing death of 134 persons including 48 children.
- M/s Oreva Group recently renovated the 143-year-old British built footbridge. It was thrown open to pedestrians without a formal fitness clearance, after being closed for months to carry out repairs.
- India's 55% population lives in urban like governance which is in poor state. State government agencies headed by bureaucrats who report to the political executive. It leads to lack of accountability and corruption.
- Morbi Bridge was designed for 125 visitors at a time, but 450 visitors were allowed.
- Ajanta Manufacturing, Flagship of Oreva without having expertise in bridge maintenance was given a contract to maintain and manage 143 years old bridge.
- In 2018, India's rail track of 67368 km including 1.47 bridges many of which are existing over a century. Government was inattentive in maintaining them. It was only recently GOI announced the Indian bridge management to collect information on bridges, which will be prerequisite to improve the quality of maintenance.

**Relevant Thought:** Science is about knowing; engineering is about doing.

**-Henry Petroski**

## Middle Class Expands Rapidly (Dt: 03.11.2022)

- On 1.11.22 Think tank Price concluded by a quality survey that the middle class doubled to over 30% of Indian household. Price has categorized households with annual income of Rs 5lakh to Rs 30lakh at 2020-21 prices as middle class.
- Price forecasts India with political and economic reforms the middle class will expand to 63% of households to 2041.

- Nearly 55% of Indian population is expected to the rank of middle class. India's middle class could be the largest in the world, by 2025, by joining almost a billion people in rank of middle class.

- Empirical evidence based on households' surveys, changing demographics and favourable trends in urbanization show that a massive shift towards a middle-class society is already in the marking.

- There are 4 key contributions that middle class makes to economic growth and social progress.

  a) It is the source of entrepreneurship

  b) Major contributor to savings and human capital

  c) They link with democracy, free press, education and fair election

  d) Special to high consumption of consumer durables.

- The middle class is claimed to be the Bird of Gold, an engine of growth.

**Relevant Thought:** Upper classes are nations past; the middle class is its future.

**-Ayn Rand**

## SC okays EWS for Quotas (Dt: 08.11.2022)

- SC (the apex court) held on 7.11.2022 that 10% quota will be reserved in government jobs and seats in educational institutions for Economically Weaker Sections (EWS).

- The 3-2 SC verdict is the disagreement between majority and minority judgments on the question of 50% cap on reservations may stage for future controversies, SC for first time allowed breach of the 50% cap.

- It saw the exclusion of already reserved groups from a narrow 10% band as a compromise making to address to upper caste angst.

- Indra Sawhney verdict in 1992 upheld quotas for OBCs –seems to have agreed with government's point that social and political realities demand expanding ambit of quotas to include OBCs- and now EWS.
- Whether Rs 8lakh income ceiling makes sense in helping the truly deprived since the annual per capita income for a 5-member household in Rs 6.5 lakh as per available data.
- To truly benefit the poor, it needs quantification via extensive government surveys.

**Relevant Thought:** Man is the plural and collective unity in which the unity of destination and the differences of destinies are to be understood through each other.

**-Paul Ricoeur**

## Acquittals by Higher Courts (Dt: 09.11.2022)

- SC's acquittal of three death –row prisoners in 2012 chowla gangrape murder case due to procedural failing during investigation and trial is a terrible situation. This crime happened in Delhi months before Nirbhaya case that to change the laws .
- SC noted 10 out of 49 witnesses were not cross-examined by defence council and many were not adequately cross examined, and trial judges were passive umpires.
- There were big lapses in investigation. Test identification parade of accused was not conducted. The trial court and Delhi HC accepted police version without corroborative evidence. Collecting samples and dispatching for forensic analysis violated procedures.
- Last December 2021 Bombay HC acquitted a death row prisoner convicted for raping 2 and murdering 1 victim. In May, 2022 Bombay HC acquitted a man on death-row for double murder case, noting fabrication of evidence. NLU (National Law University) Delhi's project 39A reveals 33 prisoners on death row were acquitted nationwide in 202. Such cases often take a decade for final disposal. This is injustice to both the accused and victims and their families.

- Police, Lawyers, and Judges have huge responsibilities in discharging their duties, as they raise troubles in citizens.

**Relevant Thought:** You are guilty until proven innocent. Perception is reality, that is the way that it is in this world.

**-Chris Webber**

## The Threat Across LAC (Dt: 11.11.2022)

- LAC stands for line of Actual Central between India and China in a bilateral agreement in1993. Armed forces maintaining operational readiness across LAC during Severe Himalayan winter is a big event in security dynamics. India and China are keeping their troops for 3rd consecutive winter in Eastern Ladakh is a real two-front challenge.
- XI Jinping recently instructed PLA to be ready to fight and win wars. XI has aggressive posture by promoting "Action Men" to the new Chinese Central Military Commission. One of those Action Men is He Weidong, now CMC Vice Chairman who led PLA's command during Doklam standoff in India in
- We saw some signs of Chinese overtures, initiating move towards negotiations, informal proposal or offers by visit of Chinese foreign Minister, Wang Yi to New-Delhi, this year (2022). India should stick to stance that it cannot be business as usual unless Beijing drops aggressive steps and restore status quo at LAC.
- After Doklam we had Wuhan summit between Modi and Xi. After Mamallapuram summit, we had Galwan. Thus we should remain wary of Chinese moves and enhance coordination with QUAD and keep ongoing Malabar naval exercise off the coast of Japan. India must keep guard up against Chinese challenge.

**Relevant Thought:** We continue to strive for a relationship with China, but one that is built on mutual sensitivity, mutual respect, and mutual interest.

**- S. Jaishankar**

## Judges Appointment by Collegium and GOI (Dt: 12.11.2022)

- Supreme Court issued notice to Union Law secretary over delay in greenlighting collegium cleared collegium-cleared judge appointments.
- Justices said it was unacceptable that Centre was neither appointing or nor communicating its reservation on 11 names recommended by the collegium. The bench said delays makes the judiciary lose the services of talented candidates.
- Union Law Minister has criticized the collegium system.
- Chief Justice of India said the collegium ensures judicial independence but the system could do with more transparency and diversity in appointments.
- Neither GOI attempted to revive NJAC since 2015, nor has SC taken steps towards fostering transparency or diversity.
- Now as it stands, it authorizes the collegium to propose judicial appointments. GOI should object only in rare cases quickly until centre is to enact an NJAC both the collegium and GOI must adhere to set timelines.
- Bombay HC Chief Justice was recommended by collegium for elevation to SC, has not yet been appointed. There are 7 vacancies in SC and 335 in HCs.
- GOI and SC must think of ordinary litigants who suffer.

**Relevant Thought:** Some of the most impressive judicial nominees are grossly mistreated.

**-Neil Gorsch**

## Transition From Coal Reliance (Dt: 14.11.2022)

- Phase down of coal was called for in the COP-26 in Glasgow held from 31 Oct to o13 Nov 2021. But it is now pronounced phase-up this year large disruption of conventional energy supplies by Ukraine war has sent Germany reviving coal fired plants and China mining record volumes.

- In COP-27 in Sharm El-Sheikh, Egypt (6 Nov-18 Nov, 2022) India has proposed hazing down all fossil fuels rather than making a villain out of only coal.
- This follows from 2 factors (i) Natural Gas and Oil contribute to GHG (Green House Gas) emissions as well, so do not whitewash them (ii) India does keep heavy goal reliance for its energy needs.
- Rich countries have fallen short of their commitments. US energy use per capita is 6,804 kg of oil equivalent compared to India's 637 kg. India has 85% of coal production in poor eastern and central states while 60% of renewable energy potential and 80% of current capacity in wealthy southern and western states. It must transition millions of livelihoods and are unaffordable.
- It is also everyone's interest for smog hovering and global carbon emissions for fossil fuels, to use cleaner technologies and put hard times to such transitions, India until at least 2040.

**Relevant Thought:** A good beginning makes a good end.

**-Louis Lamour**

## G20 Summit in Bali on 15 and 16 Nov, 2022 (Dt: 15.11.2022)

- G20 is a global body comprising 19 countries and the EU. It represents 85% of global GDP and 66% of the world's population. Formed in 1999 during Asian financial crisis, it got its heft in 2008 when G20 leaders' summit was added by the global financial crisis.
- The core goal of improving the economic policy environment has expanded to tackling climate change and terrorism among other things.
- Indonesian President handed over G20 presidency to India on 16$^{th}$ Nov, 2022 at Bali, summit of G20 which was held on 15$^{th}$ and 16th November. India will host G20 meetings in 2023 and will set agenda for next annual leaders' summit.
- Strategic rivalry between the US and China and the events since 2020 have cast shadow on global trade. In 3 decades before covid, more than 1 billion people globally escaped extreme poverty dismantling

the protectionism. India's G20 presidency can contribute to preserving these gains and finding ways to build on it. Enabling environment for world trade with success require painstaking negotiations over years.

**Relevant Thought**: The problem we have is not globalization. The problem is a lack of global governance.

**-Klaus Schwab**

## World Population Trends (Dt: 16.11.2022)

- World's population now is 8 billion, which has doubled over the last 60 years. Curbing population expansion was a priority in most developing countries. Now we are in a demographic downturn. Collapse in fertility rates and greying population will be dominant demographic trend in this century.
- India will be most populous nation in next year surpassing China. Also, in GOI's sample registration survey, 2020; India has a marked drop in fertility, following a decline in both mortality and fertility, there is change in the age structure which would cause an economic growth spurt. The economic growth spurt comes from the large share of working age population (15-64 yrs).
- Globally, the working age population is as at 66% in 2012. India with SRS 2020 estimates the working age population is at 70%. Research indicates that in India, the economic benefit from demographic transition has been lower than the Asian peers.
- The working age population in labour force is poorly 46% in 2021, when the global average is 59%. In case of women labour force, it is mere 19% against global average of 46%. It is a challenge for Ind

**Relevant Thought:** Demographic are not, however, set in stone. Nor are their implications for individual and collective wellbeing.

**-David E Bloom**

## Economic Indicators: Inflation and Exports (Dt: 17.11.2022)

- Retail inflation and exports are two keenly tracked monthly economic indicators. The consumer price index (CPI) in October was 6.8% above RBI's threshold of tolerance, but sequentially lower. Reeducation in CPI after a rise in 2 months was food price level cooling. This should ease RBI's increase in rates to combat inflation.
- In October, exports declined by 16.7% to $29.8 billion. Merchandise exports have contracted for 3 straight months with stripped of petroleum products. Non-petroleum merchandise exports in April-October were %206 billion higher by 3%. The April-October trade surplus in services was $ 75 billion higher by 24.5%.
- Data suggests, RBI should temper the increase in rate, repo which has hardened by 1.9% points in last 6 months. Price including core inflation is influenced mostly by supply side challenges. Crisil showed that 43% of MSMEs by value won't touch pre-covid profit margin this fin-year as demand is not enough.
- Feature of Indian export is the dominance of petroleum products. It comprises 22% of merchandise exports. Fiscal and industrial policies should have emphasis on labour intensive exports e.g. readymade cotton garments that contribute less than 5% to the export basket India. However, though India is not badly placed, we should focus on competitiveness.

**Relevant Thought:** Extremes are always dangerous; 100% frontloading can easily overshoot.

**Ashima Goyal**

## Heinous Crimes and our Legal System (Dt: 18.11.2022)

- Supreme Court ruled that juvenile committed brutal Kathua gang-rape murderer (Sangra) should be tried as adult Juvenile Justice Act changes in 2016 had made allowance for trial of 16–18-year-olds as adults in heinous offences. Birth certificate issued purportedly in 2004 showed his birth as Oct 2002, but birth certificates issued for his elder brother and sister revealed an impossible 2 months gap between their births.

- There are huge delays and procedural loopholes after J and K HC ruled in Sangra's favour in Oct, 2019, it took 3 years for SC's ruling.
- Indians being document-poor and influential persons can falsify documents modern techniques for medical determination of age-the "Epigenetic Clock" technique suggested by SC, must be adopted.
- Gurgaon's 16-year boy murdered a class 11 student in Sep, 2017 revealed serious flows in Juvenile Justice System Local Juvenile Justice Board cleared for trial as an adult but HC wanted the assessment repeated. An appeal in SC took until July 2022 for disposal.
- Five years elapsed, Gurgaon JJB reassessed now 21-year old and ruled him fit to be tried as adult in 2021 for rape. Many heinous offences require a robust system, more psychology experts and faster hearing of appeals.

**Relevant Thought:** The dead cannot cry out of justice. It is a duty of the living to do so for them.

**Lois MC Master Bujold**

## Negotiations at COP 27 (Dt: 21.11.2022)

- Important breakthrough in COP 27 held at Sharm-El-Sheikh, Egypt on 6 November to 18 November 2022 was the climate compensation fund i.e. a loss and damage fund. It has two hurdles: (i) the largest emitters had to accept responsibility for irretrievable damage as warning above pre-industrial levels is having an effect. (ii) COP 27 works on consensus; everybody had to come on board.
- A bigger challenge is to clear these 2 hurdles. A transitional committee to operationalize the compensation fund will have to come up with an acceptable solution. So far promises on financing have not been kept, notably $100 billion per year developed countries agreed to jointly mobilize in 2010. Financing it represents biggest challenge.
- COP27 agreed to transition out of fossil fuels. Three aspects: (i) a 'phase down' of coal (ii) a 'phase out' of inefficient fossil fuel subsidies (iii) providing support for economically vulnerable.

According to COP27 statement, if investments of $ 4-6 trillion a year, ten this global transformation to a low carbon economy is doable.

- COP 27 showed that there is a greater sense of urgency now. India has set a target of reducing emission intensity by 45% in 2030 while using 2005 as baseline. India must now plan of pirating to green hydrogen and use of nuclear power.

**Relevant Thought:** Our planet is still in the emergency room.

**-Antonio Guterres**

## District Judges Hesitant Granting Bail (Dt: 22.11.2022)

- Chief Justice of India, D.Y. Chandrachud observed a critical issue that district judges are hesitant about granting bails in heinous offences for fear of being targeted. They function under great fear of High Court judges who perform administrative superintendence. While HC and Supreme Court judges are protected by the Constitution, district judges do not have such protections.
- Conviction rates are just 42% for murder, 28% for rape and 29% in economic offences. Denying bail in such dismal figures is injustice. SC observed in July when suggesting Parliament frame a Bail Act, low conviction rates have spurred undertrial imprisonment, reversing the "innocent until proven guilty" dictum.
- Most UTPs (undertrial prisoners) are poor to afford legal assistant from HC. About 3000 boil pleas are pending in SC and 1 lakh in HCs. Over 75% of prison inmates are undertrials. In most crime cases, courts are disposing of less than 10% of total pending cases annually.
- CJI has also spoken of the need for bringing to the district judiciary "a sense for dignity, sense of self-worth, sense of confidence". They should apply the bail rule properly.

**Relevant Thought:** If you have a hierarchy, you are repeating the strengths and weaknesses of one person without allowing for the accumulative strength of a group.

**-Gloria Steinem**

## Appointment of Election Commissioners (Dt: 24.11.2022)

- Currant selection process of Election Commissioners has been challenged by SC bench. The bench suggested that CJI should have presence in the appointment committee and that despite 6 years term provided to CEC, they are getting very brief tenures.
- Centre countered by questioning the wisdom of judicial intervention and by citing the separation of power doctrine. Demands for bipartisan appointments to EC have not been agreed by governments. Present constitutional challenge is an interesting development.
- A bipartisan, consultative appointment process should be desirable as it has been trend of India's legislative and democratic evolution. CBC act 2003 empowers a committee comprising the PM, CJI and leader of opposition recommend (a) Central Vigilance Commissioner (b) Lokpal body and (c) CBI – Director cinder Lokpal Act 2013.
- The quashed NJAC Act 2014 has asked the trio to select 2 eminent persons to be part of the 6-member judges appointment commission.
- Whether SC should intervene in appointments to a coordinate institution since no abuse of power has happened is the pricklier question.
- Political parties should have consensus in Parliament and work out the EC appointment process.

**Relevant Thought:** When the collective works the individuals will show themselves.

**- Gabriel Jesus**

## Processed Food Regulation is lenient (Dt: 25.11.2022)

- FSSAI (Food Safety and Standards Authority of India) has given the snack industry a long 4-year period before front of packet labeling (FOPL) becomes mandatory. Its limits for permissible sugar, salt and fat content in processed foods are very high. Process food is not healthy.

- Good practices should start without waiting 4 years. Citizens have rights to know what they are eating and its consequences. Such consumer awareness will force the industry to adhere to safer level of sugar, salt, and fat content.
- FSSAI is opting for 5 stars for healthiest food and half a star for unhealthiest. But it the sugar, salt or fat content are high in 5 star rated foods of vegetables, fruits, nuts, millets, fibers etc., it will be farcical.
- Consumers will be only helped by knowing % of recommended dietary allowance (RDA) for a day what they consume.
- FSSAI's reference value for food risk factors at 21 high considering WHO's recommendation of keeping daily sugar intake to below 25 grams, in 2015.
- Products high in sugar, salt and fat can be taxed higher while those are low in these parameters get taxed lower.

**Relevant Thought:** You find that the cheapest calories are the ones that are going to make you the fattest the added sugars and fats in processed foods.

**-Michael Pollan**

## Promises of Freebies in Gujarat Election (Dt: 28.11.2022)

- BJP election manifesto of Gujarat plays to Hindutva by promising to implement Uniform Civil Code, a law for seizing assets of rioters, a deradicalization cell in the police and strict curbs on religious conversion.
- Competition to promise welfare and freebies has become common in Indian welfare and a freebie has become common in Indian politics. Congress/ AAP promises to offer free power free education, free healthcare, subsidized cylinders, old pension scheme, farm debt waiver.
- Matching to this, BJP promises free education, free healthcare, two free cylinders, subsidized Chana and cooking oil, free electric scooters for college-going girls.

- Quality education not just free access can up lift students. Similarly, 99% shortage of specialists in Government Hospitals does not inspire like free medical treatment and diagnostic services.
- Making Gujarat a $1 trillion economy and bringing Olympics to Ahmedabad in 2036 typifies BJP. Three parties promise to generate 10 lakhs and 20 lakh jobs between them, as a Job full growth.

**Relevant Thought:** Everyone is a millionaire where promises are concerned.

**- Ovid**

## Chinese Protests Against Pandemic Policies (Dt: 29.11.2022)

- Multiple protests zero covid pandemic policies broke out across China. It is the biggest political challenge to Chinese leadership in decades. Some are demanding step down of President XI Jinping and Chinese Communist Party (CCP).
- XI has reimposed the authority of the party over all units of the Chinese state. China has just 6 covid deaths in last 6 months from tens of thousands of symptomatic cases-more than acceptable condition to ease restrictions. But it continues with snap lockdowns mass testing and real time tracking of citizens health status through smartphone apps, the restrictions are being blamed for non-covid deaths.
- Other countries e.g. Vietnam, New Zealand followed Zero-Covid strategy at the beginning of pandemic have long abandoned zero-covid. But China is unable to follow. With wide scale protests now, the party is more adamant to bend and susceptible to public pressure.
- Chinese economy and markets fell and the yuan tumbled against the dollar, signaling cooling of investors. There are 2 lessons: (i) Authoritarian regimes do not have flexibility to deal with pandemic (ii) They cannot handle the sophisticated economics and choose primacy of regime over growth.

**Relevant Thought:** Why did the Soviet Union disintegrate? Why did the Soviet Communist Party collapse? An important reason was that their ideals and beliefs had been shaken.

**-Xi Jinping**

## Record Levels of Shores by Domestic Investors (Dt: 30.11.2022)

- On 29.11.2022 Sensex closed at 62681 points, a record high. Indian equities are unaffected by flow of negative global economic and geopolitical news.
- Foreign portfolio investors (FPIs) had influence on equity indices here. Over the last 20 months, $22 billion of FPI investment has flown out of equities BSE Sensex during the same period has risen 25%. This is most important change as domestic inflows into equities have more than offset FPIs.
- The main source of savings, the 'Households' in India have driven the change. RBI data shows that 3 years preceding 2020-21 household net financial savings as a % of gross national disposable income was 7.5% and 7.9%. In pandemic year, this surged to 11.5%. A part of surge was in shares and in equity-oriented mutual funds, which saw an increase in assets under management by more than 50% to over Rs 15 lakh crore between April 2021 and October 2022.
- Other household saving such as life Insurance and EPFO have a tilt in favour of equities. EPFO now invests 15% of annual inflow linked to equities.
- RBI estimates that half of dataflow of bank credit accounts is in commercial sector. India's entrepreneurs are delighted.

**Relevant Thought:** The most important quality for an investor is temperament not intellect.

**ffett**

## RBI's Rate Hikes Approach (Dt: 01.12.2022)

- India's GDP in July-Sep quarter was Rs 38.16 lakh crore, higher by 6.3% of previous year.

- Manufacturing output in 2nd quarter of 2022-23 was Rs. 5.98 lakh crore lower by 4.3%.
- Another sign of drag is the economies gross value addition in 2nd quarter was Rs. 35.05 lakh crore higher by just 5.6%.
- Cabined effect of these factors was 9.7% expansion in private consumption in 2nd quarter to Rs. 22.29 lakh crore. New investment or gross fixed capital formation increased 10.4% to Rs 13.21 lakh crore.
- Contact-intensive segments of trade, transport hotels etc. grew 14.7% to Rs 6.49 lakh crore. This segment is source of employment for low-skilled labour force; hence its recovery from pandemic is the highlights o 2nd quarter GDP data. Government. capital expenditure has been frontloaded in keeping economic momentum going. It expanded 49.5% to Rs 3.42 lakh crore.
- Gross tax revenue between April and September was Rs 13.9 lakh crore, higher by 18%. This rate of growth is slower than nominal GDP growth of 21.2% indicates on-going recovery is not quite robust. RBI should revisit its approach of frontloading interest rate increases.

**Relevant Thought:** If we were to continue to tighten without a reality check we would run the risk of overshooting the repo rate needed to achieve price stability.

**-Jayanth Varma**

## Economic Gap is growing (Dt: 02.12.2022)

- National income survey by think-tank PRICE shows that the gap between southern and western India and many of North, central and east is wide. It is also further diverging.
- Karnataka's per capita income at Rs. 2055 a year was 2 times that of Bihar. In 2019-20 the pre-pandemic year, the gap had widened over 5 times with Bihar's annual per capita income Rs. 29794 and of Karnataka Rs 1,55869. This trend holds with west and south of India

pulling away from eastern and central Indian states such as UP and MP.

- Fiscal institutions such as finance commission are designed to mitigate the gap by allocating taxes in a manner that brings equity between states.
- Government of India has projected a national population increase of 311 million between 2011 and 2036. Of this increase, only 9% will come from the 5 southern states which the survey by PRICE shows currently contributes 30% of national income with 20% population.
- These trends are playing out of impending delimitation of political constituencies that widens fault lines. India's economic divergence deserves more study and policy attention. Convergence is the only answer to it.

**Relevant Thought:** One possible hypothesis is that convergence fails to occur due to governance or institutional traps.

**-Arvind Subramaniam, G Gayathri N Sharma**

## Price Ceiling on Russia's Oil Export (Dt: 05.12.2022)

- G7 Plus Australia have imposed price cap of $60 a barrel on sea-exports of Russian Crude oil. to squeeze the revenue and war capabilities. The price cap is with support of EU by using clout with shipping insurance companies.
- Eight months sanctions on Russia since it invaded Ukraine in February have no impact. Sanctions are blunt tools those end up hurting countries unrelated to the problem.
- Examples of US sanctions initiated by US on Iran since 1979 had no impact on Iranian foreign policy. None of the sanctions have prevented Iran from developing its armaments; while India is hurt as it sourced crude oil from there. Russia is now India's 3rd largest crude oil supplier.
- Squeezing Russian oil supplies by dominance of West will hurt Bangladesh which finds tough balance of payments because of energy shock.

- Current price cap will not achieve the aim of deterring Russia India should act in its national interest.

**Relevant Thought:** Sanctions are a bad idea.

**Mohamed ElBaradei**

## Women Tubectomy Without Anesthesia (Dt: 07.12.2022)

- Two government hospitals in Bihar executed Tubectomy of 24 women without applying anesthesia. It is the incidents of callous disregard of poor patients by public healthcare system.
- Wounds are yet to heal and memory of unbearable pain is still vivid; for which women choose not to be bringing any more children into poverty and joblessness. Women now feel that they must pay for it with torture. 24 women had remained conscious crying in pain on the operating table.
- Bihar has highest family planning closely followed by Uttar Pradesh. It is utter apathy in public health services upon which 68% of women use modern contraceptive methods; hence the stale government should make the public health system less indifferent to women suffering.
- Male sterilization is at only 0.3%. NFHs find that 1/3$^{rd}$ men believe that contraception is women's business. Female sterilization remains most popular contraceptive used by 38% of married women aged 15-49.
- Choice of when to have children or to stop having more children should not be hard-won for women. It needs long-term social re-education. Government must ensure on war footing that women's access to family planning is smooth and safe.

**Relevant Thought:** Sometimes the best thing a mother can do for her children is not to have another.

**- Melinda Gates**

## Poor Turnout in MCD Election (Dt: 08.12.2022)

- Fierce contests among political parties in India's advanced urban MCDs like Delhi, Hyderabad, and Mumbai have resulted in poor turnout of voters.
- Turnout for MCD was just above 50%. It reflects the dysfunctional state of India's urban bodies.
- This is best captured by RBI's descriptions that Indian cities are "emaciated financially." The core problem is that state governments are unwilling to functions as constitutions $74^{th}$ amendments recommended 30 years ago.
- Urban bodies are underfunded. In India the average municipal revenue is around 1% of GDP. The comparable figures in Brazil and South Africa are 7.4% and 6% respectively.
- Municipalities largely depend upon property tax for revenue RBI's data shows that MCD's own tax revenue as a proportion of total revenue not only trails the national average, it is even lower than a relatively poor urban Assam. Voters are losing interest. MCD poll results are politically significant but unlikely are to change urban life.

**Relevant Thought:** The first basic truth is that the operational control of urban planning and management is with the state governments.

**-Isher Judge Ahluwalia**

## Power of Women's Votes (Dt: 10.12.2022)

- Voter tarn out in 2022 Gujarat election was 61.8% for women and 66.7% for men. In 2017, women's vote was 66.1% and in 2012, it was 69.5%.
- In Maharashtra 2019 recorded women's turnout at 59.3% and men's at 62.8%. These are some exceptions, but female turnout has trended upward in general. In Himachal Pradesh 2022 recorded women's vote at all-time high of 76.8% compared to male of 72.45%. In UP 2017 women were at 62.2% Where men at 59.5%. In Bihar and West Bengal too women have left the men behind.

- In 2019 LS polls, women's turnout was 67.18% compared to men at 67.01%. But in terms of representation and authority, women are few in no.
- Women's reservation bill has lapsed in 2010 Rajya Sabha. While a third of local body seats are reserved for women roughly 1.4 million female panchayats leaders have no ladders to enter legislative assemblies and Parliament. Women get fewer tickets and often from tougher seats, even though they are no less 'winnable' than men. This is a systematic denial of women's talents effort and ambition and most of all, their equal right to representation.

**Relevant Thought:** The right is ours. Have it we must. Use it we will.

**– Elizabeth Cady Stanton**

## Poor Air Quality: A countrywide problem (Dt: 12.12.2022)

- Air pollution in India is often a challenge confined to the Indo-Gangetic Plan (IGP) airshed the 7 states from Punjab in northwest to West Bengal. Recently, the coastal metros, Mumbai and Chennai recorded air quality index worse than Delhi. World Air Quality Report this year showed that of 50 global cities with toxic air, 35 are in India.
- Global Burden of Disease Study in 2019 estimated that 18% of deaths that year in India were attributable to air pollution. The economic cost came to 1.36% of GDP
- World Bank's cross-country data for 25 years (1990-2015) shows that China and Vietnam recorded a higher average GDP per capita growth with a smaller change in mean annual PM 2.5.
- PM 2.5 is the most damaging with a diameter of $1/30^{th}$ the width of human hair; it arises from many sources including dust/ Therefore air pollution in India can no longer be about localized solution. So far Indians policy of city-centric will not work as the source of problem is an airshed, which represents a common geographic area of pollutants.

- GOI must play proactive role of coordination as airshed span clusters of states. A solution must be in common interest, given the health and economic cost of toxic air.

**Relevant Thought:** Breath is the eking of mind.

**-BKS Iyengar**

## Covid Outbreak in US and China (Dt: 13.12.2022)

- Covid related hospitalization in US and China has risen, with elderly hit the most. Who has sounded alert. Genome sequencing consortium InaCom has discovered a new Omicron variant with a Delta Mutation.
- Nearly 1 crore people in India have not taken 2$^{nd}$ dose and across 95crore fully vaccinated individuals, just 22crore have availed the booster dose. Just over 40% of eligible senior citizens have availed the booster dose and only 25% of those in 45-49 age groups.
- Most Indian vaccine companies have stopped production of covid vaccine. SII stopped producing Covishield last December after lakhs of doses expired.
- Bharat Biotech's new intranasal wax has been approved as a heterogeneous booster after passing safety and immunogenicity trials. BB had demanded its inclusion in CoWin.
- Government of India should provide monetary incentive to domestic SII, BB Biological E to update their wax for the latest variants.
- Alternatively, famous international companies updating their wax like Pfizer and Moderna should be invited to produce in India.
- Our citizens should continue use of marks and complete their wax cou5rse.

**Relevant Thought:** Money will not buy happiness, but it will pay the salaries of a large research staff to study the problem.

**-Bill Vaughan**

## Taiwan Clashes with China (Dt: 14.12.2022)

- On 1 December, 2022 Chinese troops tried to unilaterally change the status quo of LAC in Yangtse in Taiwan sector of Arunachal Pradesh. It was near replay of Galwan clashed happened in June 2020. The Chinese were firmly resisted by the Indian troops resulting physical scuffles and injuries to both sides.
- This shows that China will not give up slicing Indian Territory along LAC westward and not interested in dialogue to resolve border issue.
- It is not coincidence that Taiwan clashes happened just days after India and US held military exercises close to LAC. China has aggressive tactics Suila as with Japan in dispute in East China see over Japan's Senkaku islands. Japan remains firm on its territorial maritime position. India similarly should act firm and do more to buttress infrastructure along the entire LAC.

**Relevant Thought:** A bully is a bully and it is important that you stand up to them.

**-David Hugg**

## Bihar Prohibition and Hooch Tragedy (Dt: 16.12.2022)

- Bihar imposed complete prohibition in the state in April, 2016. But the state continues to witness liquor sales on the black market and deaths owing to consumption of locally mode spurious liquor. Chhapra hooch tragedy in which 70 people have lost their lives is the cost of prohibition policy.
- Ironically because of Bihar's prohibition, neighbours like Bengal and Jharkhand have reported excise fillips after 2016, suggesting how liquor is flowing into the state. Even the hospital in industry has lost out.
- Unlike the middle class who get IMFL (Indian Mode Foreign Liquor) from neighbouring states, the poor can access only unsafely produced country liquor.

- Patna High Court has also suffered collateral damage. Thousands of bail applications filed by those arrested under prohibition law swamped the HC.

- Due to improvement in numbers of women vote, Bihar Chief Minister continues this policy. But prohibition does not stop people from drinking. It is economically and socially damaging.

**Relevant Thought:** Food is not rational. Food is culture, habit, craving and identity.

**Jonathan Saran Foer**

## Left-Wing Extremism (LWE) (Dt: 19.12.2022)

- On 17.12.2022 a meeting in Kolkata of the Chief Ministers representing states in the East Zone Council was chaired by Union Home Minister.

- LWE related incidents and fatalities across India are declining. From 833 incidents resulting in 240 deaths in 2018 reduced to 509 incidents and 147 deaths in 2021. The cutting-edge combating LWE is state police backed by central paramilitary forces and funds.

- Surrender-cum-rehabilitation policies for LWE initiated by states backed by GOI's funding produced results. Between 2018 and 2021;2295 LWE cadres have surrendered.

- Real gamechangers have been India's economic progress India's economic migration is mostly temporary or circular migration, according to GOI's survey. About 17% to 29% of workforce of 100 million people are migrating for short duration of work.

- Survey made 3 observation is in the context of LWE.

  a) Language is not a barrier to economic migration.

  b) There is significant share of youth in circular migration.

  c) There are an increasing proportion of women.

- Economic opportunities in Western, Southern and NCR states are the dimensions to deprive LWE foot soldiers. States such as Jharkhand,

Odisha Bihar, West Bengal, and Chhattisgarh have economic out-migration. Economic growth of India should be future strategy.

**Relevant Though:** An ideal society should be mobile, should be full of channels for conveying a change taking place in one part to other parts.

**-BR Ambedkar**

## Global Biodiversity Framework (GBF) (Dt: 21.12.2022)

- On 19 Dec 2022 a landmark Global Biodiversity Framework (GBF) took place under the umbrella of the UN Convention on Bio logical Diversity. To limit environmental damages Biodiversity will be accorded. There are realistic measures among the 4 goals and 23 targets for achievement by 2030.
- Most importantly, the level of biodiversity protection which today is limited to 17% of world's terrestrial and 10% of world marine areas will now be enhanced to 30%.
- Biodiversity represents the collection of all living things on earth. Scientists have identified about 1.6 million different species, only part of it exist. This biodiversity is the result of at least 4 billion years evolution.
- The 3 direct causes for biodiversity loss are (i) land use change (30%), (ii) Over-exploitation (20%) and (iii) climate change and pollution (14%)
- Due to technological advancement, biodiversity protection is not against economic development. GBF calls for reform of subsidies that undermine biodiversity. GBFs target is to raise annual International flows to poorer countries to at least $ 25 billion by 2025 and $ 30 billion by 2030.

**Relevant Thought:** Only about 1% of the species that have existed during the history of species that have existed during the history of life on earth live in the ecosystems into which humans evolved and live now.

**Partha Dasgupta**

# Editorial

## FIFA World Cup Qatar 2022 (Dt: 21.12.2022)

- It was the football match truly worthy of occasion. It was a classical contest as when one team takes lead, then the other comes back. Penalties are a cruel way to sort out winners, but are the only quick and pragmatic way.
- Argentina has owned the FIFA world cup 2022 by defeating France in the penalty shootout by 4-2 after the match was drawn at 3-3 in the regular time and extra time.
- Argentina suffering from decades of despondency induced by an economy, staggering inflation and almost 40% of the country are below poverty link. It needed the cup perhaps more than France. Argentina found another hero, goalkeeper Emiliano Martinez who played magnificently and saved the goals.
- Qatar tournament saw the best-ever performance by non-European and Non-South American teams Morocco, the first African nation made a fairytale run to the semi-final.
- This world cup surely proved that football is no monopoly of a select few. It is a lesson for India-currently ranked 106 by FIFA-would do well to take to heart.
- Argentina footballer Leo Messi, French footballer Kylian Mbappe, Morocco and Qatar delivered a great world cup. India a nation of 1.4 billon and large fast-growing economy should shine high in such sport endeavor.

## Doubtful Integrity (Dt: 26.12.2022)

- Forced retirement of 10 senior officials of telecom department with doubtful integrity is a high-visibility action by Government of India. Government has retired ground 400 officers for, lock of integrity or non-performance.
- Telecom and Railway minister had approved disciplinary action on 40 Railway officers. With 90,000 Group A and 2.9 lakh Group B

employees in position in central services such episodic disciplinary action will not solve systemic problem.

- Too many senior officers have deficits in integrity and performance. Government must identity and offload them following recruitment of meritorious replacements.
- Assured promotions without performance, many departments without significant functions and corrupt nexus being close to Netas and moneyed interests are the issues need administrative change and systemic reforms.
- Mid-career appraisals should be established to weed out inept officers along with greater public service recruitment concurrently.
- Only 4% of Indian workforce emprise work public servants compared to 22.5% in U.K>, 13.5% in US and 28% in China.
- State bureaucracy's interface with ordinary citizen is much larger. State and the Centre with their 444 control PSUs and 1136 state PSUs should pursue disinvestment vigorously and proceed to reform administration.

## Ransomware Attacks (Dt: 31.12.2022)

- Ransom ware is a malware designed to deny a user or organization access to files on their computer. Cyber-attackers place organizations to pay ransom to regain accuse to their, files.
- In November, 2022 CDSL had detected Malware in some machines and disconnected itself from the capital market. Later AIIMS, New Delhi found its services compromised. Government of India told parliament that 5 servers were affected.
- CERT In's India Ransomware Report said there has been a 51% year-on-year increase in ransom wave incidents. Most attacks are on datacenters.
- This is a global problem. Ireland was forced to shut down its public healthcare service for a while following ransom ware attack.
- Most serious problems come from organized cyberattacks on large data depositories and critical public infrastructures.

- India's forthcoming personal data protection bill needs to emphasize on this aspect.
- Purpose limitation in collecting data to be strictly enforced.
- Collcction of biometric data, highly sensitive data needs to be limited.

**Relevant Thought:** There are only 2 types of companies: those that have been hacked and those that will be.

**Robert Mueller**